# THE KAISER'S MEMOIRS

## ILLUSTRATED ENLARGED

## SPECIAL EDITION

**The Kaiser's Memoirs**
**Illustrated Enlarged Special Edition**

**by Wilhelm II**



**Cover Design by**
**Mark Bussler**

Kaiser Wilhelm II. im Felde

# The Kaiser's Memoirs

WILHELM II
Emperor of Germany 1888-1918

English Translation by
THOMAS R. YBARRA

1922

# CONTENTS

WILHELM II

# CHAPTER I

## Bismarck

PRINCE BISMARCK'S greatness as a statesman and his imperishable services to Prussia and Germany are historical facts of such tremendous significance that there is doubtless no man in existence, whatever his party affiliations, who would dare to place them in question. For this very reason alone it is stupid to accuse me of not having recognized the greatness of Prince Bismarck. The opposite is the truth. I revered and idolized him. Nor could it be otherwise. It should be borne in mind with what generation I grew up—the generation of the devotees of Bismarck. He was the creator of the German Empire, the paladin of my grandfather, and all of us considered him the greatest statesman of his day and were proud that he was a German. Bismarck was the idol in my temple, whom I worshiped.

But monarchs also are human beings of flesh and blood, hence they, too, are exposed to the influences emanating from the conduct of others; therefore, looking at the matter from a human point of view, one will understand how Prince

Bismarck, by his fight against me, himself destroyed, with heavy blows, the idol of which I have spoken. But my reverence for Bismarck, the great statesman, remained unaltered.

While I was still Prince of Prussia I often thought to myself: "I hope that the great Chancellor will live for many years yet, since I should be safe if I could govern with him." But my reverence for the great statesman was not such as to make me take upon my own shoulders, when I became Emperor, political plans or actions of the Prince which I considered mistakes. Even the Congress of Berlin in 1878 was, to my way of thinking, a mistake, likewise the "Kulturkampf." Moreover, the constitution of the Empire was drawn up so as to fit in with Bismarck's extraordinary preponderance as a statesman; the big cuirassier boots did not fit every man.

Then came the labor-protective legislation. I most deeply deplored the dispute which grew out of this, but, at that time, it was necessary for me *to take the road to compromise, which has generally been my road both on domestic and foreign politics.* For this reason I could not wage the open warfare against the Social Democrats which the Prince desired. Nevertheless, this quarrel about political measures cannot lessen my admiration for the greatness of Bismarck as a statesman; he remains the creator of the German Empire, and surely no *one* man need have done more for his country than that.

Owing to the fact that the great matter of unifying the Empire was always before my eyes, I did not allow myself to be influenced by the agitations which were the commonplaces of those days. In like manner, the fact that Bismarck was called the majordomo of the Hohenzollerns could not shake my trust in the Prince, although he, perhaps, had thoughts of a political tradition for his family. As evidence of this, he felt unhappy, for instance, that his son Bill felt no interest in politics and wished to pass on his power to Herbert.

### HIS GRANDFATHER'S SUCCESSOR

The tragic element for me, in the Bismarck case, lay in the fact that I became the successor of my grandfather—in other words, that I skipped one generation, to a certain extent. And that is a serious thing. In such a case one is forced to deal constantly with old deserving men, who live more in the past than in the present, and cannot grow into the future. When the grandson succeeds his grandfather and finds a revered but old statesman of the stature of Bismarck, it is not a piece of good luck for him, as one might suppose, and I, in fact, supposed. Bismarck himself points that out in the third volume of his memoirs (p. 40), when he speaks, in the chapter about Bötticher, of the oldish caution of the Chancellor, and of the young Emperor.

And when Ballin had the Prince cast a glance over the new harbor of Hamburg, Bismarck himself felt that a new era had begun which he no longer thoroughly understood. On that occasion the Prince remarked, in astonishment, "Another world, a new world!"

This point of view also showed itself on the occasion of the visit of Admiral von Tirpitz at Friedrichsruh, at the time when he wished to win the old Imperial Chancellor over to favoring the first Navy bill.

As for me personally, I have the satisfaction of recalling that Bismarck intrusted to me in 1886 the very delicate Brest mission, and said of me: "Some day that man will be his own Chancellor." This shows that Bismarck must have had some belief in me.

I feel no grudge against him for the third volume of his reminiscences. I released this volume after I had sought and obtained my rights. To withhold the volume any longer would have been pointless, since the main contents had become known already through indiscretions; were this not true, there might have been varying opinions as to the advisability in the choice of the time for publication. Bismarck would turn over in his grave if he could know at what time the third volume appeared, and what consequences it had. I should be honestly grieved if the third volume had damaged the memory of the great Chancellor, because Bismarck is one of the heroic figures whom the German people need for their regeneration. My gratitude and reverence for the great Chancellor cannot be impaired or extinguished by the third volume nor by anything else whatever.

## BISMARCK

In the first half of the 'eighties I had been summoned to the Foreign Office at the behest of Prince Bismarck; it was then presided over by Count Herbert Bismarck. Upon reporting myself to the Prince he gave me a short sketch of the personages employed at the Foreign Office, and when he named Herr von Holstein, who was then one of the most prominent collaborators of the Prince, it seemed to me that a slight warning against this man ran through the Prince's words.

I got a room all to myself, and all the documents concerning the preliminary history, origin, and conclusion of the alliance with Austria (Andrassy) were laid before me in order that I might study them. I went often to the home of the Prince and to that of Count Herbert.

### THE MAN WITH THE HYENA'S EYES

When I had thus become more intimate in the Bismarck circle I heard more open talk about Herr von Holstein. I heard that he was very clever, a good worker, inordinately proud, an odd sort of man, who never showed himself anywhere and had no social relations, full of distrust, much influenced by whims, and, besides all this, a good hater, and, therefore, dangerous. Prince Bismarck called him "The Man with the Hyena's Eyes," and told me that it would be well for me to keep away from him. It was quite apparent that the bitter attitude which the Prince showed later toward Holstein, his former collaborator, was forming even at that time.

The Foreign Office was conducted with the strictest discipline by Count Herbert, whose rudeness toward his employees particularly struck me. The gentlemen there simply flew when they were summoned or dismissed by the Count, so much so that a joking saying arose at the time that "their coat tails stood straight out behind them." The foreign policy was conducted and dictated by Prince Bismarck alone, after consultation with Count Herbert, who passed on the commands of the Chancellor and had them transformed into instructions. Hence *the Foreign Office was nothing but an office of the great Chancellor,* where work was done according to his directions. Able men, with independent ideas, were not schooled and trained there.

This was in contrast to the General Staff under Moltke. There new officers were carefully developed and trained to independent thinking and action, in accordance with approved principles, and by dint of preserving old traditions and taking into account all that modern times had taught. At the Foreign Office there were only executive instruments of a will, who were not informed as to the important interrelationship of the questions turned over to them for treatment, and could not, therefore, collaborate independently. The Prince loomed up like a huge block of granite in a meadow; were he to be dragged away, what would be found beneath would be mostly worms and dead roots.

I won the confidence of the Prince, who consulted me about many things. For instance, when the Prince brought about the first German colonial acquisitions (Gross and Klein Popo, Togo, etc.), I informed him, at his wish, concerning the state of mind created in the public and the navy by this move, and described to him the enthusiasm with which the German people had hailed the new road. The Prince remarked that the matter hardly deserved this.

Later on I spoke often with the Prince about the colonial question and always found in him the intention to utilize the colonies as commercial objects, or objects for swapping purposes, other than to make them useful to the fatherland or utilize them as sources of raw materials. As was my duty, I called the Prince's attention to the fact that merchants and capitalists were beginning energetically to develop the colonies and that, therefore—as I had learned from Hanseatic circles—they counted upon protection from a navy. For this reason, I pointed out that steps must be taken for *getting a fleet constructed* in time, in order that German assets in foreign lands should not be without protection; that, since the Prince had unfurled the German flag in foreign parts, and the people stood behind it, there must also be a navy behind it.

### BISMARCK'S CONTINENTAL PREPOSSESSIONS

But the Prince turned a deaf ear to my statements and made use of his pet motto: "If the English should land on our soil I should have them arrested." His idea was that the colonies would be defended by us at home. The Prince attached no importance to the fact that the very assumption that the English could land without opposition in Germany—since Heligoland was English—was unbearable for Germany, and that we, in order to make a landing impossible from the start, needed a sufficiently strong navy, and, likewise, Heligoland.

The political interest of the Prince was, in fact, concentrated essentially upon continental Europe; England lay somewhat to one side among the cares that burdened him daily, all the more so since Salisbury stood well with him and had, in the name of England, hailed with satisfaction the Double (*i. e.,* Triple) Alliance, at the time of its formation. The Prince worked primarily with Russia, Austria, Italy, and Rumania, whose relations toward Germany and one another he constantly watched over. As to the prudence and skill with which he acted, Emperor William the Great once made a pointed remark to von Albedyll, his chief of Cabinet.

The General found His Majesty much excited after a talk with Bismarck, to such an extent that he feared for the health of the old Emperor. He remarked, therefore, that His Majesty should avoid similar worry in future; that, if Bismarck was unwilling to do as His Majesty wished, His Majesty should dismiss him. Whereupon the Emperor replied that, despite his admiration and gratitude toward the great Chancellor, he had already thought of dismissing him, since the self-conscious attitude of the Prince became at times too oppressive. But both he and the country needed Bismarck too badly. Bismarck was the one man who could juggle five balls of which at least two were always in the air. That trick, added the Emperor, was beyond his own powers.

Prince Bismarck did not realize that, through the acquisition of colonies for Germany, he would be obliged to look beyond Europe and be automatically forced to act, politically, on a large scale—with England especially. England, to be sure, was one of the five balls in his diplomatic-statesmanly game, but she was merely one of the five, and he did not grant her the special importance which was her due.

For this reason it was that the Foreign Office likewise was involved entirely in the continental interplay of politics, had not the requisite interest in colonies, navy, or England, and possessed no experience in world politics. The English psychology and mentality, as shown in the pursuit—constant, though concealed by all sorts of little cloaks—of world hegemony, was to the German Foreign Office a book sealed with seven seals.

### SOURCE OF RUSSIAN ENMITY

Once Prince Bismarck remarked to me that his main object was to not let Russia and England come to an understanding. I took the liberty of observing that the opportunity to postpone such an understanding for a long time lay ready to hand in 1877-78, when the Russians might have been allowed to occupy Constantinople—had this been done, the English fleet would have sailed in without further ado to defend Constantinople and the Russo-English conflict would have been on. Instead, I continued, the Treaty of San Stefano was forced upon the Russians and they were compelled to turn about at the very gates of the city which they had reached and saw before them, after frightful battles and hardships.

This, I went on, had created an inextinguishable hatred in the Russian army against us (as had been reported by Prussian officers who had accompanied the Russian army on the Turkish campaign, especially Count Pfeil); moreover, the above-mentioned treaty had been cast aside and the Berlin Treaty substituted for it, which had burdened us even more with the hostility of the Russians, who looked upon us as the enemy of their "just interests in the East." Thus the conflict between Russia and England, which the Prince desired, had been relegated far into the future.

Prince Bismarck did not agree with this judgment of "his" Congress, concerning the results of which he, as the "honest broker," was so proud; he remarked earnestly that he had wished to prevent a general conflagration and had been compelled to offer his services as a mediator. When I, later on, told a gentleman at the Foreign Office about this conversation, he replied that he had been present when the Prince, after signing the Berlin Treaty, came into the Foreign Office and received the congratulations of the officials assembled there. After he had listened to them the Prince stood up and replied: "Now I am driving Europe four-in-hand!" In the opinion of the said gentleman the Prince was mistaken in this, since, even at that time, there was the threat of a Russo-French friendship in place of the Russo-Prussian —in other words, two horses were already to be counted out of the four-in-hand. As Russia saw it, Disraeli's statecraft had turned Bismarck's work as "honest broker" into the negotiation of an Anglo-Austrian victory over Russia.

Despite considerable differences in our opinions, Prince Bismarck remained friendly and kindly disposed to me, and, despite the great difference in our ages, a pleasant relationship grew up between us, since I, in common with all those of my generation, was an ardent admirer of the Prince and had won his trust by my zeal and frankness—nor have I ever betrayed that trust.

During the time of my assignment at the Foreign Office, Privy Councilor Raschdau, among others, discoursed with me on commercial policy, colonies, etc. In these matters, even at that early date, my attention was called to our dependence upon England, due to the fact that we had no navy and that Heligoland was in English hands. To be sure, there was a project to extend our colonial possessions under the pressure of necessity, but all this could happen only with England's permission.

This was a serious matter, and certainly an unworthy position for Germany.

### INTERCOURT POLITICS

My assignment at the Foreign Office brought a very unpleasant happening in its wake. My parents were not very friendly toward Prince Bismarck and looked with disfavor upon the fact that their son had entered into the Prince's circle. There was fear of my becoming influenced against my parents, of superconservatism, of all sorts of perils, which all sorts of tale bearers from England and "liberal circles," who rallied around my father, imputed against me. I never bothered my head with all this nonsense, but my position in the house of my parents was rendered much more difficult for me and, at times, painful. Through my work under Prince Bismarck and the confidence reposed in me—often subjected to the severest tests—I have had to suffer much in silence for the sake of the Chancellor; he, however, apparently took this quite as a matter of course.

I was on good terms with Count Herbert Bismarck. He could be a very gay companion and knew how to assemble interesting men around his table, partly from the Foreign Office, partly from other circles. However, true friendship never ripened between us two. This was shown particularly when the Count asked to go at the same time that his father retired. My request that he stay by me and help me to maintain tradition in our political policy elicited the sharp reply that he had become accustomed to report to his father and serve him, wherefore it was out of the question to demand that he come, with his dispatch case under his arm, to report to anybody else than his father.

When Tsar Nicholas II, he who has been murdered, came of age, I was assigned at the instigation of Prince Bismarck to confer upon the heir-apparent at St. Petersburg the Order of the Black Eagle. Both the Emperor and Prince Bismarck instructed me concerning the relationship of the two countries and the two reigning dynasties with each other, as well as concerning customs, personages, etc. The Emperor remarked in conclusion that he would give his grandson the same piece of advice that was given him, on the occasion of his first visit as a young man to Russia, by Count Adlerberg, *viz.,* "In general, there as well as elsewhere, people prefer praise to criticism." Prince Bismarck closed his remarks with these words: "In the East, all those who wear their shirts outside their trousers are decent people, but as soon as they tuck their shirts inside their trousers and hang a medal around their necks, they become pig-dogs."

From St. Petersburg I repeatedly reported to my grandfather and to Prince Bismarck. Naturally, I described, to the best of my knowledge, the impressions which I got. I noticed especially that the old Russo-Prussian relations and sentiments had cooled to a marked extent and were no longer such as the Emperor and Prince Bismarck in their talks with me had assumed. After my return, both my grandfather and the Prince praised me for my plain, clear report, which was all the pleasanter for me since I was oppressed by the feeling that, in a number of things, I had been forced to disillusion these high personages.

### TO OFFER DARDANELLES TO RUSSIA

In 1886, at the end of August and beginning of September, after the last meeting at Gastein of Emperor William the Great and Prince Bismarck with Emperor Franz Josef, where I also was present at the command of my grandfather, I was commissioned to report personally to Tsar Alexander II concerning the decisions made there and to take up with him the questions relating to the Mediterranean and Turkey. Prince Bismarck gave me his instructions, sanctioned by Emperor William; they dealt most especially with Russia's desire to reach Constantinople, to which the Prince meant to raise no obstacles. On the contrary, I received direct instructions to offer Russia Constantinople and the Dardanelles (in other words, San Stefano and the Berlin Treaty had been dropped!). There was a plan to persuade Turkey in a friendly way that an understanding with Russia was desirable for her also.

The Tsar received me cordially at Brest-Litovsk and I was present there at reviews of troops and fortress and defensive maneuvers, which, even then, unquestionably bore an anti-German look.

To sum up my conversations with the Tsar, the following remark by him is of importance: "If

I wish to have Constantinople, I shall take it whenever I feel like it, without need of permission or approval from Prince Bismarck." After this rude refusal of the Bismarck offer of Constantinople, I looked upon my mission as a failure and made my report to the Prince accordingly.

When the Prince decided to make his offer to the Tsar, he must have altered his political conceptions which had led to San Stefano and the Congress of Berlin; or else, on account of the development of the general political situation in Europe, he considered that the moment had come for shuffling the political cards in another way or, as my grandfather had put it, to "juggle" differently. Only a man of the world importance and diplomatic ability of Prince Bismarck could embark on such a course. Whether the Prince had planned his big political game with Russia in such a way that he might, first, by means of the Congress of Berlin, prevent a general war and cajole England, and then, after having thus hindered Russia's Eastern aspirations, cater to these aspirations later, by a stroke of genius, in an even more striking manner, it is impossible for me to say—Prince Bismarck never told anyone about his great political projects.

If the above is true, Bismarck, trusting absolutely to his statesmanlike skill, must have reckoned upon bringing Germany all the more into Russian favor because Russian aspirations were brought to fulfillment by Germany alone—and that at a moment when the general European political situation was less strained than in 1877-78. In this case, nobody except Prince Bismarck could have played the tremendous game to a successful end. And therein lies the weakness in the superiority of great men. Had he also informed England of his offer to the Tsar? England must have been opposed to it, as in 1878.

In any event, the Prince now adopted the policy which I had already noted when I realized the disillusion of the Russians at having stood before the gates of Constantinople without being allowed to enter.

### PROPHECY OF RUSSIAN DOWNFALL

At Brest-Litovsk, in the course of the constant military preparations of all kinds, I could easily see that the conduct of the Russian officers toward me was essentially cooler and haughtier than on the occasion of my first visit to St. Petersburg. Only the small group of old generals, especially those at the Russian court, who dated from the days of Alexander II, and who knew and esteemed Emperor William the Great, still showed their reverence for him and their friendly feeling toward Germany. In the course of a talk with one of them concerning the relations between the two courts, armies, and countries, which I had found undergoing a change in comparison with former times, the old General said: "C'est ce vilain congrès de Berlin. Une grave faute du Chancelier. Il a détruit l'ancienne amitié entre nous, planté la méfiance dans les cœurs de la Cour et du Gouvernement, et fourni le sentiment d'un grave tort fait à l'armée russe après sa campagne sanglante de 1877, pour lequel elle vout sa revanche. Et nous voilà ensemble avec cette maudite République Française, pleins de haine contre vous et rempli d'idées subversives, qui en cas de guerre avec vous, nous coûteront notre dynastie."[1]

A prophetic foreshadowing of the downfall of the reigning Russian dynasty!

From Brest I went to Strassburg, where my grandfather was attending the Imperial maneuvers. In spite of the failure of my mission I found calm judgments of the political situation. My grandfather was pleased at the cordial greetings from the Tsar, which, in so far as the personal relationship of the two rulers was concerned, showed no change of heart. Also, to my surprise, I received a letter from Prince Bismarck wherein he expressed gratitude and appreciation to me for my actions and my report. This meant all the more since my statements could not have been agreeable to my grandfather and the Chancellor. The Congress of Berlin had, especially in Russian military circles, done away with the remnants of the brotherhood in arms still fostered among us and had engendered a hatred against everything Prussian and German, stirred up by association

[1] "It is that confounded Congress of Berlin. A serious mistake on the part of the Chancellor. He has destroyed the old friendship between us, sown distrust in the hearts of the Court and the Government, and engendered the idea of a great injustice done the Russian army after its bloody 1877 campaign, for which it wishes revenge. And here we are by the side of that damned French Republic, full of hate for you and of subversive ideas, which, in case of a war against you, will cost us our dynasty."

with French officers, which was increased by the French until it developed into the desire of vengeance by means of arms. That was the soil in which, later, the World War ambitions of our foes found nourishment. "Revanche pour Sedan," combined with "Revanche pour San Stefano." The words of the old General at Brest have remained unforgettably engraved upon my memory; they induced me to bring about my many meetings with Alexander III and Nicholas II, at which my grandfather's wish, impressed upon me on his deathbed, that I watch over our relations with Russia, has always been my guiding motive.

### RELIEF AT CHANCELLOR'S DISMISSAL

In 1890, at the Narva maneuvers, I was obliged to describe minutely to the Tsar the retirement of Prince Bismarck. The Tsar listened very attentively. When I had finished, the usually very cool and reserved sovereign, who seldom spoke about politics, spontaneously seized my hand, thanked me for this token of my confidence, regretted that I had been brought into such a situation and added, in exactly these words: "Je comprends parfaitement ta ligne d'action; le Prince avec toute sa grandeur n'était après tout rien d'autre que ton employé ou fonctionnaire. Le moment ou il réfusait d'agir selon tes ordres, il fallait le renvoyer. Moi pour ma part je me suis toujours méfié de lui, at je ne lui ai jamais cru un mot de ce qu'il faisait savoir ou me disait lui-même, car j'étais sur et savais qu'il me blaguait tout le temps. Pour les rapports entre nous deux, mon cher Guillaume [this was the first time that the Tsar so addressed me], la chute du Prince aura les meilleures conséquences, la méfiance disparaîtra. J'ai confidance en toi. Tu peux te fier à moi." [1]

I immediately wrote down this important talk at the time it occurred. I am objective enough to ask myself to what extent the courtesy of one ruler to another and possibly, in addition, the satisfaction at the elimination of a statesman of Bismarck's importance, can have influenced the Tsar, consciously or unconsciously, in making the abovementioned statement. Prince Bismarck's belief in the Tsar's trust in him was, subjectively, undoubtedly genuine; and, moreover, there can be no doubt as to the esteem in which Alexander III held Bismarck's ability as a statesman.

In any even, the Tsar remained true to his word up to the day of his death. This, to be sure, did little to change Russia's general policy, but Germany, at least, was safe from an attack from that quarter. The straightforward character of Alexander III guaranteed this—it became otherwise under his weak son.

Whatever one's attitude may be toward Bis-

[1] "I understand perfectly your line of action; the Prince, with all his greatness, was, after all, merely your employee or official. As soon as he refused to follow your orders, it was necessary to dismiss him. As for me, I always distrusted him, and I never believed a word of what he had told me or said to me himself, for I was sure and knew that he was hoaxing me all the time. As to the relations between us two, my dear William, the downfall of the Prince will have the best of results; distrust will disappear. I have confidence in you. You can trust me."

marck's Russian policy, one thing must be acknowledged: the Prince, despite the Congress of Berlin and the rapprochement of France to Russia, was able to avoid serious friction. That is equivalent to saying that, reckoning from the time of the Berlin Congress, he played a superior diplomatic and statesmanlike game for twelve years (1878-90).

### GERMANY AS PEACEMAKER

One must also lay stress upon the fact that it was a German statesman who, in 1878, prevented a general war, even at the cost of weakening the relations of Germany to Russia, in the justified belief that he would succeed, being a statesman of genius who knew exactly what he was aiming at, in strengthening these relations once more, or, at least, in avoiding conflicts after he had overcome the crisis threatening all Europe.

He succeeded in doing that for twelve years and his successors at the helm of the ship of state succeeded in doing likewise for twenty-four more years.

When I was a Prince I purposely held aloof from party politics, concentrating my entire attention upon my duties in the different army branches to which I was assigned. This afforded me satisfaction and filled up my whole life. For this reason I avoided, while I was Prince of Prussia, all attempts to drag me into party activities. Often enough endeavors were made, under the cloak of harmless functions, teas and the like, to ensnare me into political circles or for electioneering purposes. But I always held aloof.

The outcome of the treacherous malady which killed Emperor Frederick III was frankly told me in advance by German physicians called into consultation as experts by the English physician, Sir Morell Mackenzie. My deep grief and sorrow were all the greater because it was almost impossible for me to speak alone with my beloved father. He was guarded like a prisoner by the English physicians and, though reporters from all countries could look upon the poor sick man from the physicians' room, every kind of obstacle was placed in my path to keep me from my father's side and even to prevent me from keeping in constant touch with him by writing; my letters were often intercepted and not delivered. Moreover, from among the group of watchers, an infamous, organized compaign of slander was conducted in the newspapers against me. Two journalists were especially active in this: one Herr Schnidrowitz and M. Jacques St. Cère, of the *Figaro*—a German Jew—who slandered him who was later Emperor in the most poisonous way in France, until the "Petit Sucrier" trial put an end to his activities.

I gave the dying Emperor his last joy on earth when I had the Second Infantry Brigade march past him, led by me in person. These were the first and last troops seen by Frederick III as Emperor. He delighted his son by writing on this occasion, on a little card, that he was grateful for having had the pleasure of seeing these troops and proud to call them his own. This event was a ray of light during the gloomy ninety-nine days, which brought upon me also, as Crown Prince, much grief, humiliation, and suspicion. In fulfillment of my duty during this crisis, I kept a watchful eye upon all happenings in military, official, and social circles, and was inwardly outraged at the signs of slackness which I noted everywhere, most especially at the hostility against my mother, which was becoming more and more noticeable. Moreover, I was naturally deeply hurt at the constant campaign of slander directed against me which depicted me as living in discord with my father.

### HE BECOMES EMPEROR

After Emperor Frederick III had closed his eyes forever, the heavy burden of governing the Empire fell upon my youthful shoulders. First of all I was confronted with the necessity of making changes in the government personnel in various quarters. The military entourage of the two emperors, as well as the body of officialdom, had grown too old. The so-called "maison militaire" (military household of Emperor William the Great) had been retained in its entirety by Emperor Frederick III, without being required to discharge military duties. In addition, there was the entourage of Emperor Frederick III. I proceeded to dismiss, in the friendliest way, all those gentlemen who wished to go into retirement; some of them received positions in the army, a few of the younger remained in my service for the transition period.

During the ninety-nine days, while I was still Crown Prince, I had silently concerned myself with those personages to whom I proposed later to give appointments, since the physicians had left me no doubt that my father had only a short time to live. I ignored court or external considerations; nothing but previous achievements and character moved me to my choice. I did away with the term "maison militaire" and transformed it into "Main Headquarters of His Majesty." In choosing my entourage I took the advice of only one man in whom I reposed special confidence, my former chief and brigade commander, General—afterward Adjutant General—von Versen, a man of straightforward, knightly, rather harsh character, an officer of the old Prussian school, a typical chip of the old block. During his military service in line and guard regiments he had noted with an observing eye the court influences and tendencies which had often worked to the disadvantage of the officer corps in the old "maison militaire." In this direction the circle of ladies of high position, jokingly known among the officers as "trente et quarante" on account of their age, also played a certain part. I wished to eliminate such influences.

I appointed General von Wittich my First Adjutant General and General von Hahnke, commander of the Second Infantry Guard Division, chief of my Military Cabinet. The latter was a friend of Emperor Frederick III and, while I was still serving with the First Infantry Guard Regiment, he was my brigade commander. These two were men of military experience and iron principles, who shared absolutely the sentiments of their master, and remained bound to me to the end of their lives by the most exemplary fidelity.

As the head of my court I appointed a man known to me from his youth, the former Court Marshal of my father, Count August Eulenburg, who remained at the head of the Ministry of the Royal House until his death in June, 1921, at the age of eighty-two years. He was a man of fine tact, uncommon ability, clear insight in court as well as political matters, sincere character, and golden fidelity to his King and his King's family. His manifold abilities would have enabled him, to the same degree that they had made him known as Court Marshal throughout Europe, to act with equal success as ambassador or as Imperial Chancellor. Working with unswerving zeal, endowed with winning politeness, he stood by me with helpful counsel in many matters—dynastic, family, court, public life. He had to do with many men, in all social strata and all walks of life, by all of whom he was revered and esteemed, and he was treated by me likewise with friendship and gratitude.

### VICTORIA'S HAND IS FELT

After consultation with Prince Bismarck, Herr von Lucanus from the Ministry of Public Worship and Instruction, was appointed chief of the Civil Cabinet. Prince Bismarck observed jokingly that he was pleased with this choice, since Herr von Lucanus was known to him as an able and enthusiastic huntsman, which was always a good recommendation for a civilian official; he added that a good huntsman was a regular good fellow. Herr von Lucanus took over his post from His Excellency von Wilmowski. He discharged his duties admirably and, being well endowed in all pertaining to art, technical matters, science, and politics, he was to me a counselor, untiring collaborator, and friend. He combined with a healthy knowledge of men a strong dash of refined humor, which is so often lacking in men of the Germanic race.

With Prince Bismarck I had stood on very good and trustful terms ever since my assignment at the Foreign Office. Then, as well as before, I revered the powerful Chancellor with all the ardor of my youth and was proud to have served under him and to have the opportunity now to work with him as my Chancellor.

The Prince, who was present during the last hours of the old Emperor and had listened with me to the latter's political testament to his grandson—*i. e.,* his wish as to the special care to be lavished upon relations with Russia—brought about my summer trip to St. Petersburg as my first political act before the eyes of the world, in order to emphasize our relationship to Russia in accordance with the last wish of my dying grandfather. He also had "travel arrangements" drawn up for me.

An obstacle was placed in the way of carrying out this plan by a letter from Queen Victoria of England, who, upon hearing of the projected visit to St. Petersburg, expressed to her eldest grandson, in a good-humored but authoritative tone, her disapproval of the contemplated journey. She said that a year of mourning must first elapse, after which my first visit was due to her, since she was my grandmother, and to England, it being the native country of my mother, before other lands should be considered. When I placed this letter before the Prince, he gave way to a violent fit of anger. He spoke about "family dictation in England," of interference from that quarter which must cease; the tone of the letter showed, he said, how the Crown Prince and Emperor Frederick had been ordered about and influenced by his mother-in-law, wife, etc. Thereupon the Prince wished to draw up the text of a reply to the Queen. I remarked that I would prepare the appropriate answer, steering the proper middle course between the grandson and the Emperor, and that I would show it to the Prince before dispatching it.

The answer paid heed in its outward form to the close relationship between a grandson and his grandmother, who had carried him in her arms when he was a baby and, in view of her age alone, commanded great respect—but, in its essentials, it laid stress upon the position and duty of the German Emperor, compelled to carry out unconditionally a command of his dying father affecting Germany's most vital interests. It stated that the grandson was obliged to respect this command of his grandfather in the interest of the country, the representation of which interests had now devolved upon him by the will of God, and that his royal grandmother must leave to him the question of deciding in what manner this was to be done. I added that, otherwise, I was her loving grandson, who would always be grateful for any advice from his grandmother, who had derived so much experience from her long reign; but that I was, nevertheless, in matters affecting Germany, compelled to retain my freedom of action; the visit to St. Petersburg, I said, was politically necessary, and the command of my Imperial grandfather was consonant with the close family relations between me and the Russian Imperial house; therefore it would be carried out.

The Prince approved of the letter. The answer, which arrived after a while, was surprising. The Queen agreed that her grandson was in the right; he must act in accordance with the interests of his country; she would be glad to see him, even if it were later on, at her own home. From that day onward my relations with the Queen, who was feared even by her own children, were of the best imaginable; from that day onward she never treated her grandson except as a sovereign of equal rank with herself!

On my first journeys I was accompanied by Count Herbert, as the representative of the Foreign Office. He drew up the speeches and conducted the political conferences, in so far as they were of an official nature, in accordance with the instructions of his father.

### CONFLICT ON TURKISH POLICY

Upon my return from Constantinople in 1889 I described to the Prince at his request my impressions of Greece, where my sister Sophie was married to the heir-apparent, Crown Prince Constantine, and also my Constantinople impressions. In doing this, it struck me that Prince Bismarck spoke quite disdainfully of Turkey, of the men in high position there, and of conditions in that land. I thought I might inspire him in part with essentially more favorable opinions, but my efforts were of little avail. Upon asking the Prince the reason why he held such an unfavorable opinion, he answered that Count Herbert had reported very disapprovingly on Turkey. Prince Bismarck and Count Herbert were never favorably inclined toward Turkey and they never agreed with me in my Turkish policy—the old policy of Frederick the Great.

During the last period of his tenure of office as Chancellor, Bismarck declared that the maintenance of friendly relations with Russia, whose Tsar reposed special trust in him, was the most important reason for his remaining at his post. In this connection it was that he gave me the first hints concerning the secret reinsurance treaty with Russia. Up to then I had heard nothing about it, either from the Prince or the Foreign Office, although it happened that I had concerned myself especially with Russian matters.

When I assumed the reins of government owing to the early death of my father, the generation of the grandson, as I have already remarked, followed upon the generation of the grandfather, which meant that the entire generation of Emperor Frederick was overleaped. This generation, through its dealings with Crown Prince Frederick William, was imbued with many liberal ideas and projects of reform which were to be carried out under the direction of the Emperor Frederick. Upon his death, this entire generation, especially the politicians, found itself deceived in its hopes of exerting influence, and felt itself, to a certain extent, in the position of an orphan. Those belonging to it, despite the fact that they did not know my inner thoughts and aims, adopted a distrustful and reserved attitude toward me, instead of transferring their interest from the father to the son, for the purpose of furthering the welfare of the fatherland.

There was one exception to this—a representative of the National Liberals, Herr von Benda—a man still in the full bloom of youth. While I was still Prince I had made his acquaintance at the great hare hunts got up by Councilor Dietze at Barby. There Herr von Benda had won my affection and confidence when I, surrounded by older men, had listened to discussions on political, agricultural, and national-economic questions. In the course of these, Herr von Benda held my attention by means of his independent, interesting judgment. I accepted with pleasure an invitation to Benda's country seat, Rudow, near Berlin, and from this arose the custom of a regular yearly visit.

The hours spent in the family circle at Rudow stand out pleasantly in my memory. His talented daughters used to regale us with music. The political conversations there proved Herr von Benda to be a man of great foresight, which, free from partisan considerations, gave him an open mind as to the general needs of the state to an extent seldom found among members of political parties. He gave me many a helpful piece of advice for the future, drawn from the depths of his faithful, genuinely Prussian heart, by which he was attached firmly to the family of his sovereign; yet he was able to feel broad tolerance for other parties.

### HIS ATTITUDE TOWARD PARTIES

The later periods of my reign proved that I was not hostile to any party, with the exception of the Ultra-Socialists; also, that I was not anti-Liberal. My most important Finance Minister was the Liberal, Miquel; my Minister of Commerce was the Liberal, Moeller; the leader of the Liberals, Herr von Bennigsen, was Chief President of Hanover. I stood very close, especially in the second half of my reign, to an elderly Liberal deputy, whose acquaintance I made through Herr von Miquel. This man was Herr Seydel (Celchen), owner of an estate in eastern Germany—a man with two clever eyes, which gazed forth from a clean-shaven face. He worked with Miquel in railway and canal questions, and was a thoroughly able, simple, practical man—a Liberal with a streak of conservatism.

Naturally, I had numerous dealings and points of contact with the Conservative party, since the gentlemen of the country nobility often met me at court hunts and other hunts, or else came to court and served in court positions. Through them I could become thoroughly informed on all agrarian questions and learn where the farmer's shoe pinched him.

The Free Thinkers, under the "unswerving" leader, entered into no relations with me; they limited themselves to opposition.

In my conversations with Benda and Bennigsen we often spoke of the future of Liberalism, and, on one occasion, Benda made this interesting observation: "It is not necessary and also not advisable to have the Prussian heir-apparent dabble in Liberalism—we have no use for that sort of thing. He must be essentially conservative, though he must, at the same time, combine this with breadth, and avoid narrowness and prejudice against other parties."

Bennigsen agreed with me when I spoke to him of the necessity of having the National Liberals revise their program, which—originally bearing the motto: "Maintenance of the German Empire and Freedom of the Press"—had long since rallied the members around the Liberal banner—in order that, by such revision, the proselytizing power of the old brand of Prussian Liberalism should not be lost among the people. Both the Prussian Liberals and the Conservatives, I continued, made the mistake of remembering too well the old period of conflict of 1861-66; and, at elections and other political fights, they were prone to fall back into the habits of those days. That period, I said, had already passed into history and come to an end so far as our generation was concerned; the present had begun for us with the year 1870 and the new Empire; our generation had drawn a line under the year 1866; we must build anew upon the foundations of the Empire; political parties must shape their course also in this direction and not take over from the past stuff that was outworn and, moreover, calculated to create discord. Unfortunately, all this has not come to pass. Bennigsen made a very telling point when he said: "Woe to the North German Liberals if they come under the leadership of the South German Democrats, for that will mean the end of real, genuine Liberalism! Then we shall get the masked democracy arising from below, for which we have no use hereabout."

The Conservative party, honorable and faithful to its King, unfortunately has not always produced leaders of superior endowments who were at the same time skillful, tactically trained politicians. The agrarian wing was at times too strongly marked and was a burden to the party. Moreover, memories of the period of conflict were still too lively. I counseled union with the Liberals, but found little support. I often pointed out that the National Liberals in the Empire were true to the Empire and to the Emperor, for which reason they should be thoroughly welcome to the Conservatives as allies; that I could not and did not wish to govern without them in the Empire, and was absolutely unwilling to govern against them; that North German conservatism was misunderstood in some parts of the Empire because of differences in historical development; and that, therefore, the National Liberals were the natural allies. It was owing to these views of mine, for instance, that I removed Court Preacher Stocker, a man of brilliant achievement as a social missionary, from his post, since he made a demagogical provocative speech in South Germany, aimed against the Liberals there.

The Center party was welded together by the "Kulturkampf" and was strongly anti-Protestant and hostile to the Empire. Notwithstanding this, I had dealings with many important men of the party and managed to interest them in practical collaboration for the good of all. In this Schorlemer (the father) was especially helpful to me. He never made a secret of his Prussian loyalty to his King. His son, the well-known Minister of Agriculture, even joined the Conservative party. In many matters the Center co-operated; at one period it possessed in its old leader, Windthorst, the keenest politician in the legislature. Nevertheless, in spite of all this, one could not help being aware of the underlying Centerist conviction that the interests of the Roman Church must always be maintained and never relegated to a secondary place.

### THE BREAK WITH BISMARCK

When I was Prince William I was placed for a long time under the Chief President of the Province of Brandenburg, von Achenbach, in order that I might learn about home administration, get experience in economic questions, and, moreover, take an active part in the work. Spurred on by the captivating discourses of Achenbach, I derived from this period of my life a special interest in the economic side of the inner development of the country, whereas the purely judicial side of the administration interested me to a lesser degree. Improvements, canal construction, highway building, forestry, improvement in all kinds of transportation facilities, betterment of dwellings, introduction of machines into agriculture and their co-operative development—all of these were matters with which I busied myself later on; this being especially true of hydraulic work and the development of the network of railways, particularly in the badly neglected territory of Eastern Germany.

I discussed all these matters with the Ministers of State after I had ascended the throne. In order to spur them on, I allowed them free rein in their various domains. But it turned out that this was hardly possible so long as Prince Bismarck remained in office, since he reserved for himself the main deciding voice in everything, thereby impairing the independence of those working with him. I soon saw that the Ministers, being entirely under Bismarck's thumb, could not come out in favor of "innovations" or ideas of the "young master" of which Bismarck disapproved.

The Ministry, in short, was nothing but a tool in the hands of Bismarck, acting solely in accordance with his wishes. This state of things was, in itself, natural enough, since a Premier of such overwhelming importance, who had won for Prussia and Germany such great political victories, naturally dominated his Ministers completely and led them despotically. Nevertheless, I found myself in a difficult position; the typical answer with which my suggestions were met was: "Prince Bismarck does not want that done; we cannot get him to consent to that; Emperor William I would not have asked such a thing; that is not in accordance with tradition, etc." I understood more and more that, in reality, I had no Ministry of State at my disposal; that the gentlemen composing it, from long force of habit, considered themselves officials of Prince Bismarck.

Here is an example to show the attitude of the Cabinet toward me in those Bismarck days: The question came up of renewing the Socialist law, a political measure devised by Prince Bismarck for fighting socialism. A certain paragraph therein was to be toned down, in order to save the law.

Bismarck opposed the change. There were sharp differences of opinion. I summoned a Crown Council. Bismarck spoke in the antechamber with my adjutant; he declared that His Majesty completely forgot that he was an officer and wore a sword belt; that he must fall back upon the army and lead it against the Socialists, in case the Socialists should resort to revolutionary measures; that the Emperor should leave him a free hand, which would restore quiet once for all. At the Crown Council Bismarck stuck to his opinion. The individual Ministers, when asked to express their views, were lukewarm. A vote was taken—the entire Ministry voted against me.

This vote showed me once more the absolute domination exerted by the Chancellor over his Ministers. Deeply dissatisfied, I talked over the matter with His Excellency Lucanus, who was as much struck as I was by the situation. Lucanus looked up some of the gentlemen and took them to task for their attitude, whereupon they made it clear that they were "not in a position" to oppose the Prince and declared that it was quite impossible for anybody to expect them to vote against the wishes of the Prince.

### HANDLING A COAL STRIKE

The great Westphalian coal workers' strike in the spring of 1889 took the civil administration by surprise, causing great confusion and bewilderment, especially among members of the Westphalian provincial administration. From all sides came calls for troops; every mine owner wanted, if possible, to have sentries posted outside his room. The commanders of the troops which were summoned immediately made reports on the situation as they had found it.

Among these was one of my former barrack comrades, belonging to the Hussar Guard Regiment, von Michaelis by name, who was famous as a wit. He rode, alone and unarmed, among the striking crowds of workers, who—the early spring being remarkably warm—were camped upon the hillsides, and soon managed, by his confidence-inspiring, jovial ways, to set up a harmless intercourse with the strikers. By questioning them he obtained much valuable information about the grievances—real and imaginary—of the workers, as well as about their plans, hopes, and wishes for the future. He soon won for himself general appreciation and affection among the workers and handled them so well that complete quiet reigned in his territory. When I, on account of nervous and worried telegrams from the big industrial leaders and officials received at the office of the Imperial Chancellor, inquired of Michaelis how the situation stood, the following telegraphed answer came from him: "Everything quiet excepting the Government officials."

A mass of material was collected, during the spring and summer, from the announcements and reports received which showed clearly that all was not well in industrial circles; that many a wish of the workers was justified and, to say the least, entitled to sympathetic investigation on the part both of the employers and of the officials. The realization of this, which was confirmed in me when I questioned my former private teacher, Privy Councilor Dr. Hinzpeter—a man particularly well informed on social phenomena, especially those in his own province—caused the resolve to ripen in me to summon the State Council, include employers and employees in its deliberations, and bring about, under my personal direction, a thorough investigation of the labor question. I decided that in so doing guiding principles and material were to be acquired which would serve the Chancellor and the Prussian Government as a basis for working out appropriate projects for new laws.

Inspired by such thought I went to His Excellency von Bötticher, who at once prophesied opposition on the part of the Chancellor to such action, and advised strongly against it. I stuck to my ideas, adducing in support of them the maxim of Frederick the Great: "Je veux être un Roi des gueux" ("I wish to be King of the rabble"). I said that it was my duty to take care of those Germans who were used up by industry, to protect their strength and better their chances of existence.

### FURTHER CONFLICT WITH CHANCELLOR

The predicted opposition from Prince Bismarck was not long in coming. There was much trouble and fighting before I put through what I wanted, owing to the fact that some of the big industrial interests ranged themselves on the side of the Chancellor. The State Council met, presided over by me. At the opening session the Chancellor unexpectedly appeared. He made a speech in which he ironically criticized and disapproved the whole undertaking set in motion by me, and refused his co-operation. Thereupon he walked out of the room.

After his departure the strange scene had its effect on the assemblage. The fury and ruthlessness which the great Chancellor brought to the support of his own policy and against mine, based upon his absolute belief in the correctness of his own judgment, made a tremendous impression upon me and all those present. Neverthless, it stood to reason that I was deeply hurt by what had occurred. The assemblage proceeded to take up its work again and turned out a wealth of material for the extension of that social legislation called into being by Emperor William the Great, which is the pride of Germany, evincing, as it does, a protective attitude toward the laboring classes such as is not to be found in any other land on earth.

Thereupon I decided to summon a general social congress. Prince Bismarck opposed this also. Switzerland was contemplating something similar, and had thought of convening a congress at Berne. Roth, the Swiss ambassador, hearing of my scheme, advised canceling the invitations to Berne and accepting an invitation to Berlin. What he wished occurred. Thanks to the generosity of Herr Roth, it was possible to convene the congress at Berlin.

The material collected as a result of it was worked out and applied in the form of laws—only in Germany, however.

Later on I talked with Bismarck concerning his project of fighting the socialists, in case they resorted to revolutionary acts, with cannon and bayonets. I sought to convince him that it was out of the question for me, almost immediately after William the Great had closed his eyes after a blessed reign, to stain the first years of my Government with the blood of my own people. Bismarck was unmoved; he declared that he would assume responsibility for his actions; that all I need do was to leave the thing to him. I answered that I could not square such a course with my conscience and my responsibility before God, particularly as I knew perfectly well that conditions among the laboring classes were bad and must be bettered at all costs.

The conflict between the views of the Emperor and the Chancellor relative to the social question—*i. e.,* the furtherance of the welfare of the laboring classes of the population, with participation therein by the state—was the real cause of the break between us, and caused a hostility toward me, lasting for years, on the part of Bismarck and a large part of the German nation that was devoted to him, especially of the official class.

This conflict between the Chancellor and me arose because of his belief that the social problem could be solved by severe measures and, if the worst came to the worst, by means of soldiers;

not by following principles of general love for mankind or humanitarian nonsense which, he believed, he would have to adopt in conformity to my views.

### BISMARCK'S LABOR VIEWS

Bismarck was not a foe to the laboring classes—on that I wish to lay stress, in view of what I have previously said. On the contrary! He was far too great a statesman to mistake the importance of the labor question to the state. But he considered the whole matter from the standpoint of pure expediency for the state. The state, he believed, should care for the laborer, as much and in whatever manner it deemed proper; he would not admit of any co-operation of the workers in this. Agitation and rebellion, he believed, should be severely suppressed; by force of arms, if necessary. Government protection on the one hand, the mailed fist on the other—that was Bismarck's social policy.

I, however, wished to win over the soul of the German workingman, and I fought zealously to attain this goal. I was filled with the consciousness of a plain duty and responsibility toward my entire people—also, therefore, toward the laboring classes. What was theirs by right and justice should become theirs, I thought; moreover, I believed that this should be brought about, wherever the will or power of the employers ceased, by the lord of the land and his Government, in so far as justice or necessity demanded. As soon as I had recognized the necessity for reforms, to some of which the industrial elements would not consent, I took up the cudgels for the laboring classes, impelled by a sense of justice.

I had studied history sufficiently to guard myself against the delusion of believing in the possibility of making an entire people happy. I realized clearly that it was impossible for one human being to make a nation happy. The truth is that the only nation which is happy is the one that is contented, or at least is willing to be contented; a willingness which implies a certain degree of realization of what is possible—a sense of the practical, in short. Unfortunately, there is often a lack of this.

I was well aware that, in the unbounded demands of the Socialist leaders, unjustified greed would be constantly developed anew. But, for the very reason that I wished to be able to combat unjustified aspirations with a clear conscience and in a convincing way, it behooved me not to deny recognition and aid to justified aspirations.

### GERMAN SOCIAL PROBLEMS

The policy that kept in view the welfare of the workers unquestionably imposed a heavy burden upon all the industrial elements of Germany in the matter of competition in the world market, through the well-known laws for the protection of workingmen. This was especially true in relation to an industrial system like the Belgian, which could, without hindrance, squeeze the last drop out of the human reserves of Belgium and pay low wages, without feeling any pangs of conscience or compassion for the sinking morale of the exhausted, unprotected people. By means of my social legislation I made such conditions impossible in Germany, and I caused it to be introduced also in Belgium, during the war, by General von Bissing, in order to promote the welfare of the Belgian workers. First of all, however, this legislation is—to use a sporting term—a handicap upon German industry in the battle of world competition: it alienated many big leaders of industry, which, from their point of view, was quite natural. But the lord of the land must always bear in mind the welfare of the whole nation; therefore, I went my way unswervingly.

Those workers, on the other hand, who blindly followed the Socialist leaders, gave me no word of thanks for the protection created for them nor for the work I had done. Between them and me lies the motto of the Hohenzollerns, "Suum cuique." That means, "To each his own"—not, as the Social Democrats would have it, "To everyone the same!"

I also harbored the idea of preventing to some extent competitive warfare, at least in the industrial world of the European continent, by bringing about a sort of quota-fixing in foreign lands, thereby facilitating production and making possible a healthier mode of life among the working classes.

There is great significance in the impression which foreign workers get in studying Germany's social legislation. A few years before the war people in England, under the pressure of labor troubles, awoke to the conviction that better care must be taken of the workers. As a result of this, commissions visited Germany, some of them composed of workingmen. Guided by representative Germans, among them Socialists, they visited the industrial regions, factories, benevolent institutions, sanatoria of insurance companies, etc., and were astonished at all the things they saw. At the farewell dinner given them the English leader of the workingmen's deputation turned to Bebel and made this concluding remark:

"After all we have seen of what is done in Germany for the workers, I ask you: Are you people still Socialists?" And the Englishmen remarked to a German that they would be quite satisfied if they could succeed, after long fights in Parliament, in putting through one tenth of what had already been accomplished years before in Germany toward bettering the condition of the laboring classes.

I had observed with interest these visits of the English deputations and marveled at their ignorance of German conditions. But I marveled even more at a question asked by the English Government, through the channel of the English Embassy, on the same subject, which betrayed an absolutely amazing lack of knowledge of the progress made in Germany in the province of social reform. I questioned the English ambassador, remarking that England, having been represented in 1890 at the Berlin Social Congress, must certainly have been informed, at least through the Embassy, of the Reichstag debates, which had dealt in a detailed way with the various social measures. The ambassador replied that the same thing had also occurred to him and caused him to have the earlier records of the Embassy investigated, whereupon it had transpired that the Embassy had sent the fullest reports on the subject to London and that thorough reports had been forwarded home concerning every important stage in the progress of social reform; but, "because they came from Germany, nobody ever read them; they were simply pigeonholed and remained there ever since; it is a downright shame; Germany does not interest people at home."

Thus the Briton, with a shrug of his shoulders. Neither the British King nor Parliament had enough conscience or time or desire to work for the betterment of the working class. The "policy of encirclement" for the annihilation of Germany, especially of its industry, and, thereby, of its working population, was, in their eyes, far more important and rewarding. On the 9th of November (1918) the German Radical Socialist leaders, with their like-minded followers, joined forces with this British policy of annihilation.

### "WELFARE WORK" AT THE COURT

In a small way, in places where I had influence, as, for instance, in the administration of my court and in the Imperial Automobile Club, I laid stress upon the social point of view. For instance, I caused a fund to be established, out of the tips paid for visiting palaces, which was destined solely to the benefit of the domestic staff, and which, in the course of time, reached a magnificent total. From this fund the domestics and their families received money for trips to bathing resorts, cost of taking cures, burial expenses, dowries for their children, confirmation expenses, and similar payments.

When I, at the request of the newly founded Imperial Automobile Club, took it under my protection, I accepted an invitation to a luncheon in the beautiful rooms of the clubhouse, built by Ihne. In addition to magnates like the Duke of Ratibor, the Duke of Ujest, etc., I found there a number of gentlemen from Berlin's high financial circles, some of whom behaved rather wildly. When the conversation turned to the subject of drivers, I suggested establishing a fund which, in case of accident, illness, or death befalling these men, should provide means of livelihood for those whom they left behind. The suggestion met with unanimous approval, and the fund has had most excellent results. Later on I brought about the establishment of something similar for the skippers and pilots attached to the Imperial Yacht Club at Kiel.

Special pleasure was afforded me by the Kaiser Wilhelm Children's Home, founded by me at Ahlbeck, at which, in peace times, between May and the end of September in each year, a large number of children from the most poverty-stricken working people's districts in Berlin were accommodated in successive detachments, each lot staying four weeks. This home is still under the tried direction of the admirable superintendent, Miss Kirschner, daughter of the former Chief Burgomaster of Berlin, and it has achieved most brilliant results, both in the physical and the psychical domain. Weakened, pale, needy children were transformed there into fresh, blooming, happy little beings, concerning whose welfare I often joyfully convinced myself by personal visits.

For the very reason that I have spoken of my quarrel with Bismarck as a result of labor questions, I wish to add to what I have already said about his basic position in the matter—an example showing how brilliantly the Prince behaved in something that concerned the workers. In this, to be sure, he was impelled by nationalistic motives, but he also realized at once that it was necessary to protect a large element against unemployment, which caused him to intervene with the full weight of his authority.

Sometime around 1886, while I was still Prince Wilhelm, I had learned that the great Vulcan shipping concern at Stettin was confronted, owing to lack of orders, with bankruptcy, and its entire force of workmen, numbering many thousands, with starvation, which would mean a catastrophe for the city of Stettin. Only by an order for the building of a big ship could the Vulcan shipyards be saved.

Spurred on some time before by Admiral von Stosch, who wished to free us once and for all from the English shipbuilders, the Vulcan people had set to work courageously to build the first German armored ship, christened by my mother in 1874 on her birthday, on which occasion I was present. Ever since that time the warships built at the Vulcan yards had always satisfied naval experts—the concern, however, seldom built warships.

### THE CHANCELLOR IN ACTION

The German merchant marine, on the other hand, had not dared to follow the path courageously blazed by Admiral von Stosch. And now the brave German shipyard company was faced with ruin, since the North German Lloyd had refused its offer to build a passenger steamer, alleging that the English, because of their years of shipbuilding traditions, could build it better. It was a serious emergency. I hastened to Prince Bismarck and laid before him the matter as I have described it above.

The Chancellor was furious; his eyes flashed, his fist came crashing down on the table.

"What! Do you mean to say that these shopkeepers would rather have their boats built in England than in Germany? Why, that is unheard of! And is a good German shipyard to fail for such a reason? The devil take this gang of traders!"

He rang the bell and a servant entered.

"Have Privy Councilor X come here immediately from the Foreign Office!"

In a few minutes—during which the Prince

stamped up and down the room—the man summoned appeared.

"Telegram to Hamburg, to our envoy—the Lloyd in Bremen is to have its new ship built by the Vulcan Company in Stettin!"

The Privy Councilor vanished in hot haste, "with his coat tails sticking straight out behind him." The Prince turned to me and said: "I am greatly obliged to you. You have done the fatherland, and also myself, an important service. Henceforth ships will be built only in our yards—I'll take care to make this clear to the Hanseatic crowd. You may telegraph to the Vulcan people that the Chancellor will guarantee that the ship will be built in the Vulcan yards. May this be the first of a whole lot of such ships! As for the workers whom you have thus saved from unemployment, I hope that they will express their thanks to you!"

I passed on the news to Privy Councilor Schlutow at Stettin and great was the joy caused thereby. This was the first step upon the road destined to lead to the construction of the magnificent German express steamers.

When I went, after I had ascended the throne in 1888, to Stettin, in order to place honorary insignia on the flags of my Pomeranian Grenadiers, I also visited the Vulcan shipyards, at the invitation of the directors. After my reception by the directors outside the yards, the great doors were flung open and I walked inside. But, instead of work and pounding hammers, I found deep silence.

The entire body of workmen was standing in a half circle, with bared heads; in the middle stood the oldest workman of all, a man with a snow-white beard, bearing a laurel wreath in his hand.

I was deeply moved. Schlutow whispered to me: "A little pleasure for you, which the workmen themselves have thought up." The old workman stepped forward and, in pithy, plain words, expressed to me the gratitude of the workmen to me for having saved them, and, above all, their wives and children, from hardship and hunger, by my appeal to Bismarck about the building of the ship. As a token of their gratitude, he asked my permission to hand over the laurel wreath. Most deeply moved, I took the wreath and expressed my pleasure at receiving my first laurels, without the shedding of a drop of blood, from the hands of honest German workmen.

That was in the year 1888! In those days, the German laboring classes knew how to appreciate the blessing of labor.

German Postcard from World War 1

## CHAPTER II

### Caprivi

WHEN I began my reign, General von Caprivi was Chief of the Admiralty. He was the last general to hold this post. I at once took energetically in hand the development and reform—in fact, one may say the foundation anew—of the Imperial German Navy, based on my preliminary studies in England and at home. That was not to the liking of the General, who was able, but rather self-willed, and not entirely devoid of pride.

Unquestionably he had rendered valuable services in mobilization, improvement of the officer corps, and the improvement and development of the torpedo-boat organization. On the other hand, the building of ships and the replacement of worn-out material were in a deplorable state, to the detriment of the fleet and to the dissatisfaction of the shipbuilding industry, which was growing and looking about for employment.

Being an old Prussian general, Caprivi's way of thinking was that of his day—that of his comrades of 1864, 1865, 1870, 1871—in his eyes, the army had always done everything and would continue to do so in the future; therefore, no great demands for money to be devoted to the navy should be imposed upon the country, since, should this be done, there was danger that the sums destined to the army might be decreased and its development thereby hampered. This idea, from which he was not to be dissuaded, is false. The amounts granted did not flow into a reservoir from which they might be directed, by the mere turning of a valve, now into army, now into navy, channels. Whenever Caprivi was unwilling to demand anything for naval construction, in order, by so doing, to turn more money toward the army, things did not happen as he foresaw. By his action the army received not one penny more, but merely whatever the Minister of War asked for and received in accordance with his budget.

There was need of creating a Secretaryship of State for the Navy which, entirely independent of the Ministry of War, should have as its duty to demand and obtain for the navy as much as was required for the protection of our commerce and colonies. And that is what came to pass later on.

Caprivi soon came to me with the request that I relieve him from his post. He stated that he was not satisfied with it in itself; that, moreover, I had all sorts of plans for the future affecting the navy which he considered impossible of realization, in the first place, because there existed no means of replacement for the officer corps—at that time the yearly influx of cadets was between sixty and eighty—and a large navy without a large officer corps was unthinkable. In addition to this, he informed me, he had soon seen in the course of the inspection tours of His Majesty that the Emperor knew more about naval matters than he, the General, which placed him in an impossible situation in relation to his subordinates.

In view of these circumstances, I parted with him, placing him in command of an army corps. Following the motto, "The navy for the seamen!" I chose, for the first time, an admiral as its chief, a step which was received in maritime circles with great joy. The man chosen was Admiral Count Monts.

### BISMARCK'S SUCCESSOR

When I was soon afterward confronted with the rather unexpected retirement of Prince Bismarck, I found the choice of his successor a difficult one. Whoever it might be was sure to have a hard task, without any prospect of appreciation for what he might achieve; he would be looked upon as the usurper of a post to which he was not entitled, and which he was not qualified to fill. Criticism, criticism, nothing but criticism—that was sure to be the daily bread upon which the new Chancellor must reckon; and he was also certain of becoming the target for the hostility of all those who favored Prince Bismarck as well as with that of the many who previously could not do enough in opposition to him. There was bound to be a strong current of enmity toward the new

Chancellor, in which the old Prince himself would not be the least serious factor.

After taking all this into consideration, it was decided to choose a man belonging to Prince Bismarck's generation, who had held a leading position in the wars and had already filled a Government position under him. Hence Caprivi was chosen. His age was a guarantee that he would be a careful and calm adviser for the "orphaned" young Emperor.

Very soon the question arose of the extension of the reinsurance treaty with Russia. Caprivi declared that, out of consideration for Austria, he was unable to renew it, since the threat against Austria contained therein, when it became known in Vienna—as it almost unavoidably would—was such as to lead to very disagreeable consequences. For this reason the treaty lapsed. To my way of thinking, it had already lost its main value from the fact that the Russians no longer stood wholeheartedly behind it. I was confirmed in this view by a memorial written by Count Berchem, Under Secretary of State, who had worked with Prince Bismarck.

The Agrarian Conservatives opposed Caprivi as a man without landed property and a violent fight raged around the commercial treaties. These difficulties were greatly enhanced because Prince Bismarck, ignoring his former maxims, took part in the fight against his successor with all his characteristic energy. Thus arose the opposition of the Conservatives against the Government and the

Crown, and the Prince in person sowed the seed from which later grew the "misunderstood Bismarck" and that "Reichsverdrossenheit" (unfriendliness to the Empire) so often taken up in the newspapers. The "misunderstood Bismarck" created permanent opposition throughout my reign against my suggestions and aims by means of quotations, speeches, and writings, as well as by passive resistance and thoughtless criticism. Everything that was done was painted in black colors, made ridiculous, and criticized from top to bottom, by a press that placed itself quite willingly at the disposal of the Prince and often out-Bismarcked Bismarck in its behavior.

This phenomenon became most apparent at the time of the acquisition of Heligoland. This island, lying close in front of the great waterways leading to the principal Hanseatic commercial ports, was, in the hands of the British, a constant menace to Hamburg and Bremen and rendered impossible any project for building up a navy. Owing to this, I had firmly resolved to win back this formerly German island to its fatherland.

### THE DEAL FOR HELIGOLAND

The way to cause England to give up the red rock of Heligoland was found in the colonial domain. Lord Salisbury proved inclined to exchange the "barren rock" for Zanzibar and Witu in East Africa. From commercial sources and the reports of the commanders of German cruisers and gunboats which were stationed there and cruised along the coast of the recently acquired German East African colonies, I knew that, as soon as Togo, Dar-es-Salaam, etc., rose to prosperity, the importance of Zanzibar on the coast of Africa as the principal port of transshipment would be a thing of the past, since, as soon as the above-mentioned harbors were made deep enough and provided with sufficient cargo-loading equipment for trading steamers, there would no longer be any need of ferrying goods coming from the interior in dhows to Zanzibar, in order to have them again loaded on vessels there, since they could be loaded direct at the new harbors along the coast.

Therefore, I was convinced that we had, first, an acceptable asset for swapping purposes, and, secondly, a good opportunity to avoid colonial friction with England and come to a friendly understanding with her. Caprivi agreed, the negotiations were concluded, and one evening, shortly before dinner, I was able to tell the Empress and a few intimates the exceedingly joyful tidings that Heligoland had become German.

A first and very important extension of the Empire had been achieved—without bloodshed—the first condition for the upbuilding of the fleet was fulfilled, something which the natives of the Hanseatic towns and the rest of the North Germans had wished for centuries had come to pass. In silence, an important event had occurred.

Had Heligoland been acquired in the Chancellorship of Prince Bismarck, it would probably have been valued very highly. Having happened under Caprivi, it loosed a lot of criticism. It was merely Caprivi, the usurper, who had had the audacity to sit in the Prince's chair, and the "irresponsible," "ungrateful," "impulsive" young master who had done such a thing! Had Bismarck only wished, he could have had the old rock any day, but he never would have been so unskillful as to give up to the English for it the very promising African possessions, and he never would have allowed himself to be thus worsted. That was the sort of thing heard almost everywhere. The newspapers of the Prince joined loudly in this sort of criticism, to the great grief of the people of the Hanseatic cities.

Curious indeed were the criticisms occasioned by the swapping of Zanzibar and Witu, which appeared in the Bismarckian press, although previously, when I worked under him, these newspapers had always explained that he had not much belief in the value of colonies in themselves and looked upon them merely as objects to be exchanged, possibly, for something else, in deals with the British. His successor acted according to these ideas in the Heligoland question, and was most violently criticized and attacked. Not until the World War was on did I see articles in the German press which unreservedly admitted the acquisition of Heligoland to be an act of far-sighted politics and added reflections as to what would doubtless have happened if Heligoland had not become German.

The German nation has every reason to be thankful to Count Caprivi for this achievement, since thereby the building of its navy and its victory at the Skagerrak were made possible. As for the German navy, it long ago acknowledged this.

The school law of Count Zedlitz aroused violent new conflicts. When they led to Zedlitz's retirement, the cry arose among his adherents: "If the Count goes, so must the Chancellor."

Caprivi left his post, in a calm, dignified manner. He tried honestly, within the measure of his powers and abilities, to continue the traditions of Prince Bismarck. In this he found little support among the political parties, and, for this reason, all the more criticism and hostility in the public and among those who, had they acted for the right and the interests of the state, should have stood by him. Without one word of apology, Caprivi, in noble silence, lived all the rest of his life in almost solitary retirement.

German Postcard from World War 1

# CHAPTER III

## Hohenlohe

AGAIN I was confronted with the difficult task of choosing a Chancellor. His position and activities were to be under somewhat about the same auspices and subject to the same conditions as in the case of his predecessor. But now there was more of a desire that he should be a statesman, an older man, of course, qualified to inspire Prince Bismarck with more confidence than a mere general could do.

It was assumed that a statesman would know better how to walk in the footsteps of the Prince, politically speaking, and provide Bismarck with less opportunity for criticism and attacks. These latter had tended to create gradually among all Government officials, who dated mostly from the period of Bismarck, an unmistakable nervousness and dissatisfaction, by which the work of the entire governmental system was impaired to an extent by no means inconsiderable. Moreover, it lent to the opposition in the Reichstag a constantly renewed strength drawn from elements previously faithful to the Government, and made itself felt in a detrimental manner. Especially in the Foreign Office, the spirit of Holstein, the supposed representative of the "old, tried Bismarckian traditions," began to assert itself, so that the unwillingness to collaborate with the Emperor became particularly strong and the belief grew up that it was necessary to carry on, independently, the policy of Bismarck.

After mature deliberation, I decided to intrust the post of Chancellor to Prince Hohenlohe, who was then Governor of Alsace-Lorraine. At the outbreak of the War of 1870 he had succeeded, as Bavarian Minister, in getting Bavaria to enter the war on the side of Prussia. Ever since he had been highly esteemed by Prince Bismarck on account of his fidelity to the Empire. It was natural to expect that Bismarck's opposition would cool off when confronted with such a successor. Thus, the choice of Hohenlohe as Chancellor was strongly influenced by consideration for Prince Bismarck and for the public opinion inspired by him.

Prince Hohenlohe was the typical old-style grand seigneur. He was thoroughly urbane by nature and in his dealings with others: a man of refined mind, with a slight touch of playful irony sometimes glinting through, keen on account of his years, a level-headed observer and judge of men. Despite the great difference in age between him and me he got along very well with me, which was shown on the surface by the fact that he was treated both by the Empress and by myself as our uncle, and addressed as such, which brought about a certain atmosphere of intimate confidence in our intercourse. In his talks with me, especially in giving his opinion as to appointments of officials, he offered very characteristic descriptions of the gentlemen being discussed, often combined with philosophical observations which proved that he had reflected deeply on life and humanity, and which were evidence of a maturity and wisdom grounded on experience.

Something happened during the first period of Hohenlohe's régime as Chancellor which throws an interesting light upon the relations between France and Russia. Having, at the time of the fraternization between Russia and France, received reliable information from the General Staff as well as from our Embassy at Paris to the effect that France contemplated withdrawing a portion of her troops from Algeria, in order to shift them to southern France either against Italy or against Alsace, I apprised Tsar Nicholas II of this news, adding the remark that I should be obliged to adopt counter-measures unless the Tsar could dissuade his ally from so provocative a step.

### SOME DIPLOMATIC FENCING

At that time the Russian Minister of Foreign Affairs was Prince Lobanoff, formerly ambassador at Vienna, well known for his pro-French proclivities. During the summer of 1895 he had visited France and been very cordially entertained. During the autumn, just as I was staying for the hunting at Hubertusstock on the Schorfheide near Eberswalde, Prince Lobanoff, on his return journey from Paris, requested to be received in audience, at the behest of the Tsar. Upon being received by me he described the calm and sensible frame of mind which he had found in Paris and sought to quiet me, too, with regard to the abovementioned troop movements, which, according to him, were mere empty rumor and chatter without any real basis. He added that he was bringing to me the most quieting assurances, that there was no reason for my feeling the slightest alarm. I thanked him heartily for his report, remarking that the word "alarm" was not to be found in the dictionary of a German officer; and I added that, if France and Russia wished to make war, I could not prevent it.

Whereupon the Prince, piously casting up his eyes toward heaven, made the sign of the cross and said: "Oh, la guerre! quelle idée; qui y pense?—cela ne doit pas être" ("Oh, war! what an idea; who thinks of such a thing? it must not be"). To that I replied that I, in any event, was not thinking about it, but that an observer—and he need not be very keen eyed—must assuredly consider the constant celebrations and speeches, as well as the official and unofficial visits exchanged between Paris and St. Petersburg, as significant symptoms which could not be ignored, and which were calculated to arouse great dissatisfaction in Germany; that, should it come to war, against my own will and that of my people, I felt that, trusting in God and in my army and people, it would be possible for Germany to get the better of both opponents.

To this I added still another statement, reported to me from Paris, which had been made by a Russian officer who was in France as a member of an officers' deputation. Having been asked by a French comrade whether the Russians believed that they could beat the Germans, the gallant Slav replied: "Non, mon ami, nous serons battus à plate couture, mais qu'est-ce que ça fait? Nous aurons la République" ("No, my friend, we shall be thoroughly beaten, but what does that matter? We shall get a republic").

At first the Prince eyed me, speechless, then, shrugging his shoulders, he remarked: "Oh, la guerre, il ne faut pas même y penser" ("Oh, war, one must not even think about it"). The officer had merely expressed the general opinion of the Russian intelligentsia and social circles. As far back as my first visit to St. Petersburg, in the early 'eighties, a grand duchess said to me at dinner, quite calmly: "Here we sit all the time on a volcano. We expect the revolution any day! The Slavs are not faithful, they are not at all monarchical, all of them are republicans at heart; they disguise their sentiments, and they lie, every one of them, all the time."

Three important events, related to foreign politics, came within the period of Prince Hohenlohe's incumbency of the Chancellorship: the opening, in 1895, of the Emperor William Canal (North Sea-Baltic Canal), begun under Emperor William the Great, to which squadrons or individual ships representing countries all over the world were invited; the annexation, in 1897, of Tsing-tao; and, third, the much-discussed Kruger dispatch.

### THE SEIZURE OF TSING-TAO

Prince Hohenlohe played an especially important rôle in the annexation of Tsing-tao. He, too, was of the opinion that Germany needed some coaling stations for her ships, and that the demands of commercial elements that the opportunity for opening up China to international trade be not allowed to pass were justified. It was resolved that, under unimpaired Chinese sovereignty and after payment of the likin (octroi, or internal revenue tax), a trading port, with a marine coaling station as protection, was to be founded, wherein it was contemplated to allow China to co-operate to the utmost possible extent.

The station was to serve the ends of commerce, before all else, the military measures being limited solely to the protection of the trading center as it developed; they did not constitute an end in themselves or a basis for further military enterprises.

Already several places had been considered, but these had proved, upon more careful investigation, to be unfitted, mostly because they had either bad connections or none at all with the interior regions, were not promising from a commercial-political standpoint, or were encumbered by privileges already granted to other foreign countries. Finally it was agreed—because of the reports of Admiral

Tirpitz, who was, at that time, chief of the East Asiatic cruiser squadron, and because of the opinion of the geographical expert, Freiherr von Richthofen, who, having been questioned on the subject, had drawn a most promising picture of the possibilities of development in Shantung—to found a settlement on the bay of Kiao-Chau.

The Chancellor proceeded to collect data on the political questions which arose as a result of this and which must be taken into consideration. It was particularly necessary not to interfere with Russia's designs, nor to disturb her. Further information was obtained, some of it from our East Asiatic division; from this source favorable reports came in as to anchorages and the ice-free nature of the bay of Kiao-Chau, and as to the prospects, if a port were to be founded there. From conversations among the officers of the Russian China division, which had come to our ears in our intercourse with them, it was learned that the Russian Admiral, in accordance with orders from his Government, had anchored one winter in the bay, but had found it so desolate and so atrociously lonesome—there were no tea houses with Japanese geisha girls, which the Russians deemed absolutely indispensable to winter quarters—that the Russian squadron would never go back there any more.

It was also reported that the Russian Admiral had advised his Government most earnestly against prosecuting any further its intention of founding a settlement on this bay, since there was absolutely no advantage to be derived from it. Hence, the Russians had no intention of gaining a foothold there.

This last piece of news arrived at about the same time as the answer from the Russian Foreign Minister, Count Muravieff, sent through the German ambassador, relative to the sounding of Russian opinion, which had been made pursuant to instructions from the Chancellor. Muravieff set forth that Russia, to be sure, had no direct claims, based on treaty with China, to the bay, but that she, nevertheless, laid claim to it on the basis of the "droit du premier mouillage" ("right of first anchorage"), since the Russian ships had anchored there before those of any other fleet. This answer, it will be seen, ran counter to the report of our East Asiatic division relative to the statements made by the Russian Admiral.

When I, with Hollmann, met the Chancellor, in order to discuss the Russian claim to Kiao-Chau, the Prince listened to the reading of it with his little ironical smile, and remarked that he had been unable to find any jurist at the Foreign Office who could tell him anything about this wonderful claim. Was the navy in a position to do so? Admiral Hollmann declared that he, in all his experience on foreign service, had never heard of it; that it was nonsense and an invention of Muravieff, whose only motive was unwillingness to have some other nation settle on the shores of the bay. I advised that Privy Councilor of the Admiralty Perels, one of the most famous living experts on international maritime law and an acknowledged authority in this domain, be asked to deliver an opinion, in order to clarify the question. This was done. The opinion tore Muravieff's contention to pieces, corroborated that of Hollmann, and completely did away with the legend about the "right of first anchorage."

Months elapsed; my August, 1897, visit to Peterhof was imminent. In agreement with the Prince, my uncle, I decided to discuss the entire matter in person and frankly with the Tsar, and, if possible, put an end to Muravieff's notes and evasions. The talk took place at Peterhof. The Tsar stated that he had no interest in the territory south of the Tientsin-Peking line, which meant that there was no reason why he should place obstacles in our path in Shantung: that his interest was concentrated upon the territory on the Yalu, around Port Arthur, etc., now that the English had made difficulties for him at Mokpo; that he would, in fact, be pleased if Germany should locate herself in future on the other side of the Gulf of Chih-li as Russia's welcome neighbor.

Afterward I had a talk with Muravieff. He employed all his arts, wriggled back and forth in his statements, and finally brought up his famous "right of first anchorage." That was all I wanted. I now passed to the offensive myself, striking out at him squarely with the opinion delivered by Perels. When I had told him, finally, as the Tsar desired, the result of the conversations between us two sovereigns, the diplomat was even more embarrassed, lost his assumed calm, and capitulated.

Thus was the soil prepared, politically speaking. In the autumn came the news from Bishop Anzer of the murder of the two German Catholic missionaries in Shantung. The entire German Catholic world, particularly the "colonials" in the Centerist party, demanded energetic measures. The Chancellor proposed to me immediate intervention. While I was engaged in the winter hunting at Lotalingen, I consulted with him, in one of the little towers of the castle there, as to what steps were to be taken. The Prince proposed to intrust Prince Henry of Prussia, who was present, with the command of the squadron that was to be sent out to reinforce the East Asiatic Division. I informed my brother of this in the presence of the Chancellor, whereat the Prince and the other gentlemen present were highly pleased. The Chancellor sent the news to the Foreign Office and to the new Secretary of State for Foreign Affairs, Herr von Bülow, who was away on a journey.

Kiao-Chau was occupied in November, 1897. In December of that year Prince Henry sailed, on board the *Deutschland,* with his squadron to Eastern Asia, where he later took over the command of the entire East Asiatic Division. On the 6th of March, 1898, the agreement with China concerning Kiao-Chau was signed. At the same time, Mr. Chamberlain in London brought up before the Japanese ambassador, Baron Kato, the idea of the conclusion of an Anglo-Japanese alliance, in order to bar Russia's advance in the East.

### QUEST FOR COALING STATIONS

One will naturally inquire why, in the discussion of our audacious move, there is no mention of England, since she was certainly deeply interested therein. Preliminaries, however, had already been gone into with England. In order to meet the necessity for German coaling stations, I had intended to found, lease, or buy some in agreement with England, so far as might be possible. In view of the fact that my uncle, the Chancellor, was, as a member of the Hohenlohe family, related to Queen Victoria, known to her personally for years and highly esteemed by her, I hoped that this might tend to facilitate the negotiations which were entered into with the English Government for the above-noted purpose. My hope was disappointed. The negotiations dragged along without any prospect of successful termination.

I took occasion, therefore, at the behest of the Chancellor, to discuss the matter with the English ambassador at Berlin. I complained of the treatment received from the English Government, which everywhere opposed German wishes, even such as were justified. The ambassador agreed frankly with this, and expressed his astonishment at England's failure to meet Germany halfway, and at English shortsightedness, since, when a young, rising nation like Germany, whose development, after all, was not to be prevented, turned directly to England in order to acquire territory with her consent, instead of going straight ahead or allying itself with other nations, it was certainly more than England could reasonably ask.

Moreover, he added that, since England already owned almost all the world, she could certainly find a place where she might permit Germany to establish a station; that he was unable to understand the gentlemen in Downing Street; that in case Germany should not succeed in obtaining England's approval, she would probably occupy, on her own account, such places as were suited to her ends, since, after all, there was no law against it.

I laid stress upon the fact that this agreed entirely with my own view and, in conclusion, I summed up my standpoint once more for the ambassador: I told him that Germany was the only country in the world which, despite its colonial possessions and its rapidly growing commerce, possessed no coaling stations; that we were quite willing to acquire these with England's consent; that, should she refuse to show a realization of our situation and fail to meet us halfway, we should be compelled to turn to some other great power, in order, with its help, to found settlements.

This talk, likewise, was fruitless. Finally, the negotiations with England were broken off, without result, in a rather impolite manner. Thereupon the Chancellor and I decided to appeal to Russia.

The occupation of Kaio-Chau aroused surprise and anger in the English Government. Having refused us her support, England had definitely reckoned on the belief that nobody would help Germany in attaining her goal. Now things had turned out differently, and there was no lack of recriminations from London. When the English ambassador took up this tone he was referred to the conversation with me, and it was made clear to him that it was solely the fault of his Government that it had come to no understanding with Germany.

England's attitude of aloofness surprised us at that time. An occurrence which, then, was unknown to me, may serve to throw light on the matter.

### FINDS SEED OF WORLD WAR[1]

In a book (*The Problem of Japan*) which appeared anonymously at The Hague in 1918 and was said to have been written by an "Ex-Diplomat from the Far East," an excerpt was published from a work of the American, Professor Usher of Washington University at St. Louis. Usher, like his former colleague, Prof. John Bassett Moore of

[1] "Once the magnitude of Pan-Germanism dawned on the English and French diplomats, once they became aware of the lengths to which Germany was willing to go, they realized the necessity of strengthening their position, and therefore made overtures to the United States, which resulted, probably before the summer of the year 1897, in an understanding between the three countries. There seems to be no doubt whatever that no papers of any sort were signed, that no pledges were given which circumstances would not justify any one of the contracting parties in denying or possibly repudiating. Nevertheless, an understanding was reached that in case of a war begun by Germany or Austria for the purpose of executing Pan-Germanism, the United States would promptly declare in favor of England and France and would do her utmost to assist them."—ROLAND G. USHER, *Pan-Germanism*, chap. x, p. 139.

Columbia University, New York, has often been called into consultation as an adviser on foreign relations by the State Department at Washington, since he had a knowledge possessed by few other Americans on international questions affecting the United States. Professor Usher, in his book published in 1913, made known, for the first time, the existence and contents of an "agreement" or "secret treaty" between *England, America,* and *France,* dating from the spring of 1897. In this it was agreed that, in case Germany or Austria, or both of them, should begin a war for the sake of "Pan-Germanism," the United States should at once declare in favor of England and France and go to the support of these powers with all its resources. Professor Usher cites at length all the reasons, including those of a colonial character, which inevitably imposed upon the United States the necessity of taking part, on the side of England and France, in a war against Germany, which Professor Usher, in 1913, prophesied as *imminent!!*

The unknown author of *The Problem of Japan* went to the trouble of publishing in tabulated form the agreements between England, France, and America in 1897, in order thereby to show, in a way easily understood, the extent of the reciprocal obligations. This chapter is extraordinarily worth reading; it gives a good glimpse into the preliminary history and *preparation of the World War* on the part of the *Entente,* which even at that time was uniting *against Germany,* although not yet appearing under the name of Entente Cordiale. The ex-diplomat remarks in this connection:

Here is a treaty that Professor Usher alleges to have been entered into as long ago as 1897, in which every phase of activity and participation in future events by England, France, and the United States is provided for, including the conquest of the Spanish dependencies, control over Mexico and Central America, the opening of China, and the annexation of coaling stations. And all these measures Professor Usher wishes us to believe were taken to defend the world against Pan-Germanism.

It is unnecessary to remind Professor Usher, or anybody else, for that matter, that Pan-Germanism, if we go so far as to assume that such a thing actually exists, had certainly never been heard of in 1897, at which time Germany had not yet adopted her program for naval construction on a large scale, the same having been bruited for the first time in 1898. If, therefore, it is true that England, France, and the United States harbored the mutual designs imputed to them by Professor Usher, and entered into an alliance to accomplish them, it will scarcely do to attribute the conception of the idea and the stimulus to its consummation to so feeble a pretext as the rise of a Pan-Germanism.[1]

Thus the ex-diplomat.

This is truly amazing. A definite treaty of partition directed against Spain, Germany, etc., arranged even to minute details, was planned between Gauls and Anglo-Saxons, in a time of the profoundest peace, and concluded without the

[1] *The Problem of Japan*, by an Ex-Counselor of Legation in the Far East, chap. viii, p. 136, note. Published by C. L. Langenhuysen, Amsterdam and Rotterdam. 1918.

slightest twinge of conscience, in order to annihilate Germany and Austria and eliminate their competition from the world market! *Seventeen years* before the beginning of the World War *this* treaty was made by the united Anglo-Saxons and its goal was systematically envisaged throughout this entire period! Now one can understand the ease with which King Edward VII could pursue his policy of encirclement; for years the principal actors had been united and in readiness. When he christened the compact "Entente Cordiale," its appearance was for the world, especially for Germany, an unpleasant novelty, but in the countries on the other side it was merely the official acknowledgment of facts long known there.

In view of this agreement, one can understand also the opposition of England in 1897 to an agreement with Germany regarding coaling stations, and the anger aroused because Germany managed, in agreement with Russia, to gain a firm foothold in China, concerning the exploitation of which land *without* German participation a tripartite treaty had already been made.

Usher talked out of school and conclusively proved *at whose door lies the guilt for the World War.* The treaty directed against Germany—sometimes called the "gentleman's agreement"—of the spring of 1897, is the basis, the point of departure, for this war, which was systematically developed by the Entente countries for seventeen years. When they had succeeded in winning over Russia and Japan likewise for their purposes, they struck the blow, after Serbia had staged the Sarajevo murder and had thus touched the match to the carefully filled powder barrel.

Professor Usher's statements are likewise a complete refutation of all those who were impelled, during the war, to find the reason for the entry of the United States in certain military acts on the part of Germany, as, for instance, the *Lusitania* case, the expansion of U-boat warfare, etc. None of that is right. The recently published, excellent book of John Kenneth Turner, *Shall It Be Again?* points out, on the basis of convincing proofs, that Wilson's alleged reasons for going to war and war aims were not the real ones. America—or rather President Wilson—was resolved probably from the start, certainly from 1915, to range herself against Germany and to fight. She did the latter, alleging the U-boat warfare as a pretext, in reality under the influence of powerful financial groups, and yielding to the pressure and prayers of her partner, France, whose resources in man power were becoming more and more exhausted. America did not wish to leave a weakened France along with England, whose annexation designs on Calais, Dunkirk, etc., were well known to her.

It was a fateful thing for Germany—let this be stated here, in a general way—that our Foreign Office was unable to meet the broad policy of encirclement of England and the cunning of Russia and France with an equal degree of diplomatic skill. This was partly because it had not really been trained under Prince Bismarck; and therefore when, after the retirement of the Prince and Count Herbert, the all-dominating will and spirit were lacking, it was not up to the task of conducting foreign affairs on its own independent initiative.

Moreover, it is difficult in Germany to train up good diplomats, since our people lack the taste and endowment for diplomacy which have shone forth brilliantly only from a few German minds, like Frederick the Great and Bismarck. Unfavorable also to the Foreign Office were the very frequent changes of Secretaries of State. Imperial Chancellors, following the example of Bismarck, maintained their influence upon the Foreign Office and suggested the Secretaries of State who should direct its affairs. I acquiesced in the proposals of the Imperial Chancellors as to these posts, since I admitted their right to choose themselves their leading collaborators in the domain of foreign affairs. That these frequent changes were not calculated to work toward the continuity of political policy was a disadvantage that had to be taken into account.

The Foreign Office was largely influenced by the axiom: "No disagreeable quarrels with other powers"—"surtout pas d'histoires" ("above all, no yarns"), as the French general said to a company of soldiers which, he had heard, wished to mutiny. One of the Secretaries of State told me once when, in placing some matter before me, I had called his attention to the apparently serious situation in connection with some foreign question, that this simply must be righted, that the Foreign Office based its acts primarily upon the maxim: "Let us have quiet."

Given this attitude, one can also understand the answer which the German representative gave to a German merchant in a South American republic who had asked him for help and intercession with the authorities, since his shop had been plundered and his property stolen: "Oh, don't bother me with these things! We have established such pleasant relations with this republic; any action undertaken in your behalf would only serve to upset them." I need scarcely add that whenever such a conception of duty came to my attention I removed the official concerned from his post.

The Foreign Office enjoyed general unpopularity both among the people and in the army. I worked continuously, during the tenure of office of various Chancellors, for thorough reform, but in vain. Every new Chancellor, especially if he himself did not come from the ranks of the foreign service, needed the Foreign Office in order to work himself into foreign affairs, and this took time. But once he had worked himself in he was under obligation to the officials, and was reluctant to make extensive changes, burdened as he was by other matters and lacking detailed knowledge regarding the Foreign Office personnel, particularly as he still believed that he needed the advice of those who were "orientated."

### DEVELOPMENT OF TSING-TAO

But let us return to Tsing-tao. Here everything was done to promote commerce and industry, and done jointly with the Chinese; the flag of the Chinese Empire, moreover, was hoisted over the Custom House at Tsing-tao. The development there was such that the port, during the years immediately preceding the war, ranked sixth among all Chinese trading centers in the commercial register of the great Chinese merchants and of the merchants' guild coming just after Tientsin. Tsing-tao was a prospering German commercial colony, where many Chinese worked side by side with Germans; it was, so to speak, a great sample warehouse of German abilities and German achievements, to which the Chinese, who formerly had not known Germany, her capabilities of achievement, or her products, could repair for selection and emulation; it was a contrast to the naval stations of Russia and England, which were purely military, directed solely toward domination and conquest.

The rapid rise of Tsing-tao as a trading center aroused the envy of the Japanese and English, but this did not prevent swarms of the latter from journeying, with their families, to the splendid beach, enjoying its cool air and the beautiful Strand Hotel, and devoting themselves to playing polo and lawn tennis after they had escaped from the heat of Hongkong, Canton, and Shanghai. Envy prompted England in 1914 to demand that Japan should take Tsing-tao, although it was *de facto* Chinese. Japan did this joyfully, promising to return it to China, but it was not returned until the beginning of 1922, after much pressure, although Japan had agreed with America that she was not to be allowed to make any territorial changes in China without previous consultation with Washington.

Thus a great German cultural work in foreign lands, which stood as a model of the method and manner which a cultured nation should employ in extending the advantages of its culture to another nation, was annihilated by English commercial envy. Some day, when Hongkong has gone the same way, England will repent of her act and bitterly reproach herself for having abandoned her old maxim, in accordance with which she has acted for so many years: "White men together against colored men." When once Japan has made a reality out of her watchword, "Asia for the Asiatics," and brought China and India under her sway, England will cast her eyes about in search of Germany and the German fleet.

As to the "yellow peril," I had the following interview with the Tsar later, after the Russo-Japanese War, at a meeting between us.

The Tsar was, at that time, visibly impressed by the growing power of Japan and its constant menace to Russia and Europe, and requested my opinion concerning this. I answered that if the Russians counted themselves among the cultured nations of Europe they must be ready to rally to the defense of these nations against the "yellow peril" and to fight for and by the side of Europe for their own and Europe's existence and culture; but that if the Russians, on the other hand, considered themselves Asiatics they would unite with the "yellow peril," and, joining forces with it, would assail Europe. The Tsar, said I, must bear this in mind in providing for the defense of his land and organizing his army.

When the Tsar asked me what course I thought the Russians would take, I replied: "The second."

The Tsar was outraged and wished to know at once on what I based this opinion. I answered that my opinion was based on Russia's construction of railways and on the arraying of the Russian army along the Prussian-Austrian frontier. Thereupon the Tsar protested that he and his house were Europeans, that his country and his Russians would certainly cleave to Europe, that he would look upon it as a matter of honor to protect Europe from the "yellow men." To this I replied that if this was the Tsar's attitude he must make his military preparations conform to it without delay. The Tsar said nothing.

At all events, I sought to utilize Tsar Nicholas II's worry at the growing power of Japan to the advantage of Germany and general European culture. Russia, despite siding with Japan, was the first nation to collapse among all those participating in the war.

### REPROACHES FOR JAPAN

The able statesmen of Japan, of whom there are quite a number, must be in some doubt as to whether they ranged their country on the right side in the war. Yes, they will perhaps ask themselves whether it would not have been more advantageous for Japan to have prevented the World War. This would have been within her powers, had she ranged herself firmly and unequivocally on the side of the Central Powers, from which in former times she had learned so willingly and so much.

Had Japan adopted soon enough such an orientation in her foreign policy, and, like Germany, fought by peaceful means for her share in world trade and activity, I should have put the "yellow peril" away in a corner and joyfully welcomed into the circle of peacefully inclined nations the progressive Japanese nation, the "Prussians of the East." Nobody regrets more than I that the "yellow peril" had not already lost its meaning when the crisis of 1914 arose. The experience derived from the World War may yet bring this about.

Germany's joint action with France and Russia at Shimonoseki was based upon Germany's situation in Europe. Wedged in between on-marching Russia, threatening Prussia's frontier, and France, fortifying her borders anew with forts and groups of fortresses, confronted with a friendship between these two nations resembling an alliance, Berlin looked with anxiety into the future. The warlike preparations of the two powers were far ahead of ours, their navies far more modern and powerful than the German navy, which consisted of a few old ships almost without fighting value. Therefore it seemed to us wise to acquiesce in the suggestion of this strong group, in order that it might not —should we decline—turn immediately to England and cause the entry of the latter into the combination. This would have meant the formation, at that time, of the combination of 1914, which would have been a serious matter for Germany. Japan, on the other hand, was about to go over anyhow to England, in her sympathies. Moreover, Germany's making common cause with the Franco-Russian group offered the possibility of achieving gradually a more trusting and less strained relationship in Europe and of living side by side with our two neighbors there in more friendliness, as a result of the common policy adopted in the Far East. The policy adopted by us at this juncture was also consistently based on the maintenance of world peace.

In the entire Kiao-Chau question, Prince Hohenlohe, despite his age, evinced a capacity for sticking steadily to his purpose and a degree of resolution which must be reckoned as greatly to his credit.

Unfortunately in the matter of the Kruger dispatch his prudence and his vision, so clear on other occasions, abandoned him: only by so assuming is his obstinate insistence on the sending of this dispatch to be understood. The influence of such an energetic and eloquent personage as Herr von Marschall, former State Attorney, may have been so powerful, the siren song of Herr von Holstein so convincing, that the Prince yielded to them. In any event, he did his country an ill turn in this matter, and damaged me seriously both in England and at home.

### THE KRUGER TELEGRAM[1]

Since the so-called Kruger dispatch made a big stir and had serious political consequences, I shall tell the story of it in detail.

The Jameson raid caused great and increasing excitement in Germany. The German nation was outraged at this attempt to overpower a little nation, which was Dutch—and, hence, Lower Saxon-German in origin—and to which we were sympathetic because of racial relationship. I was much worried at this violent excitement, which also seized upon the higher classes of society, foreseeing possible complications with England. I believed that there was no way to prevent England from conquering the Boer countries, should she so desire, although I also was convinced that such a conquest would be unjust. But I was unable to

[1] Tremendous excitement was caused in England when the incident of the Kruger message became known. On January 3, 1896, the German Emperor telegraphed as follows to the President of the South African Republic:

"I congratulate you most sincerely on having succeeded, with your people, without calling on the help of foreign powers, by opposing your own force to an armed band which broke into your country to disturb the peace, in restoring quiet and in maintaining the independence of your country against external attack."

On January 6th, in conversation with Sir Frank Lascelles, Baron von Marschall protested against the view of the English press that it was an act of hostility against England and an encroachment on English rights for the German Emperor to congratulate the head of a friendly state on his victory over an armed band that had invaded his land in defiance of international law, and had been declared to be outside the pale of the law by the English Government itself. But it was not recorded that he disavowed the Kaiser's responsibility for it.

overcome the reigning excitement, and was even harshly judged by my intimates on account of the attitude I adopted.

One day when I had gone to my uncle, the Imperial Chancellor, for a conference, at which the Secretary of State for the Navy, Admiral Hollmann, was present, Freiherr Marschall, one of the Secretaries of State, suddenly appeared in high excitement, with a sheet of paper in his hand. He declared that the excitement among the people—in the Reichstag, even—had grown to such proportions that it was absolutely necessary to give it outward expression, and that this could best be done by a telegram to Kruger, a rough draft of which he had in his hand.

I objected to this, being supported by Admiral Hollmann. At first the Imperial Chancellor remained passive in the debate. In view of the fact that I knew how ignorant Freiherr Marschall and the Foreign Office were of English national psychology, I sought to make clear to Freiherr Marschall the consequences which such a step would have among the English; in this, likewise, Admiral Hollmann seconded me. But Marschall was not to be dissuaded.

Then, finally, the Imperial Chancellor took a hand. He remarked that I, as a constitutional ruler, must not stand out against the national consciousness and against my constitutional advisers; otherwise, there was danger that the excited attitude of the German people, deeply outraged in its sense of justice and also in its sympathy for the

Dutch, might cause it to break down the barriers and turn against me personally. Already, he said, statements were flying about among the people; it was being said that the Emperor was, after all, half an Englishman, with secret English sympathies; that he was entirely under the influence of his grandmother, Queen Victoria; that the dictation emanating from England must cease once for all; that the Emperor must be freed from English tutelage, etc.

SAYS HE SIGNED AGAINST HIS WILL

In view of all this, he continued, it was his duty as Imperial Chancellor, notwithstanding he admitted the justification of my objections, to insist that I sign the telegram in the general political interest, and, above all else, in the interest of my relationship to my people. He and also Herr von Marschall, he went on, in their capacity of my constitutional advisers, would assume full responsibility for the telegram and its consequences.

Sir Valentine Chirol, at that time correspondent of the *Times,* wrote, in the *Times* of September 11th, that Herr von Marschall, directly after the sending of the dispatch, had stated to him that the dispatch did not give the personal opinion of the Emperor, but was a governmental act, for which the Chancellor and he himself assumed full responsibility.

Admiral Hollmann, when the Imperial Chancellor appealed to him for corroboration of this point of view and was asked by him to uphold it to me, declined to do so with the remark that the Anglo-Saxon world would unquestionably attribute the telegram to the Kaiser, since nobody would believe that such a provocative thing could come from His Majesty's elderly advisers, and all would consider it an "impulsive" act of the "youthful" Emperor.

Then I again tried to dissuade the gentlemen from their project. But the Imperial Chancellor and Marschall insisted that I sign, reiterating that they would be responsible for consequences. It seemed to me that I ought not to refuse after their presentation of the case. I signed.

Not long before his death Admiral Hollmann recalled the occurrence to me in full detail, as it is described here.

After the Kruger dispatch was made public the storm broke in England, as I had prophesied. I received from all circles of English society, especially from aristocratic ladies unknown to me, a veritable flood of letters containing every possible kind of reproach, some of the writers not hesitating even at slandering me personally and insulting me. Attacks and calumnies began to appear in the press, so that soon the legend of the origin of the dispatch was as firmly established as the amen at church. If Marschall had also announced in the Reichstag what he stated to Chirol, I personally would not have been drawn into the matter to such an extent.

In February, 1900, while the Boer War was in progress and while I was with the fleet at Heligoland attending the maneuvers of ships of the line, after having been present at the swearing in of recruits at Wilhelmshafen I received news by telegraph from the Wilhelmstrasse, *via* Heligoland, that Russia and France had proposed to Germany to make a joint attack on England, now that she was involved elsewhere, and cripple her sea traffic. I objected and ordered that the proposal be declined.

Since I assumed that Paris and St. Petersburg would present the matter at London in such a way as to make it appear that Berlin had made the above proposal to both of them, I immediately telegraphed from Heligoland to Queen Victoria and to the Prince of Wales (Edward) the fact of the Russo-French proposal, and its refusal by me. The Queen answered expressing her hearty thanks, the Prince of Wales with an expression of astonishment.

Later, Her Majesty let me know secretly that, shortly before the receipt of my telegram from Heligoland concerning the proposal from Paris and St. Petersburg, the false version of the matter foreseen by me had indeed been told, and that she was glad to have been able, thanks to my dispatch, to expose the intrigue to her Government and quiet it as to the loyal attitude of Germany; she added that she would not forget the service I had done England in troublous times.

### DEAL WITH CECIL RHODES

When Cecil Rhodes came to me, in order to bring about the construction of the Cape-to-Cairo

Railway and Telegraph line through the interior regions of German East Africa; his wishes were approved by me, in agreement with the Foreign Office and the Imperial Chancellor; with the proviso that a branch railway should be built *via* Tabora, and that German material should be used in the construction work on German territory. Both conditions were acquiesced in by Rhodes most willingly. He was grateful at the fulfillment of his pet ambition by Germany, only a short time after King Leopold of Belgium had refused his request.

Rhodes was full of admiration for Berlin and the tremendous German industrial plants, which he visited daily. He said that he regretted not having been in Berlin before, in order to have learned about the power and efficiency of Germany, and to have got into touch with the German Government and prominent Germans in commercial circles. He said he had wished, even before the Jameson raid, to visit Berlin, but had been prevented in London at that time from so doing; that, had he been able to inform us before of his plan to get permission to build the Cape-to-Cairo line through the Boer countries, as well as through our colonies, the German Government would probably have been able to help him by bringing persuasion to bear upon Kruger, who was unwilling to grant this permission; that "the stupid Jameson Raid" would never have been made, in that case, and the Kruger dispatch never written—as to that dispatch, he had never borne me a grudge on account of it.

He added that as we, in Germany, could not be correctly informed as to aim and actual purposes, the said raid must have looked to us like "an act of piracy," which naturally and quite rightly had excited the Germans; that all he had wanted was to have such stretches of land as were needed for his rail lines—such, in fact, as Germany had just granted to him in the interior of her colonies—a demand which was not unjust and would certainly have met with German support. I was not to worry, he added, about the dispatch and not bother myself any more about the uproar in the English press. Rhodes did not know about the origin of the Kruger dispatch and wanted to console me, imagining that I was its originator.

Rhodes went on to advise me to build the Bagdad Railway and open up Mesopotamia, after having had irrigation simultaneously introduced there. He said that this was Germany's task, just as his was the Cape-to-Cairo line. In view of the fact that the building of this line through our territory was also made dependent upon the cession to us of the Samoan Islands, Rhodes worked actively in London toward having them turned over to us.

In home politics, Prince Hohenlohe, as Chancellor, showed a mildness which was not generally favorable. Owing to his long acquaintanceship with Herr von Hertling, he was able to establish friendly relations with the Vatican. His mildness and indulgence were also exercised toward Alsace-Lorraine, in which, as an expert of long standing, he showed particular interest. But he got little thanks for this, since the French element, indirectly benefited thereby, behaved with ever-increasing arrogance.

### PEN SKETCH OF HOHENLOHE

Prince Hohenlohe loved to employ mediation, compromise, and conciliation—toward the Socialists likewise—and he employed them on some occasions when energetic measures would have been more fitting. He hailed with much joy my Far East trip to Constantinople and Jerusalem. He was pleased at the strengthening of our relations with Turkey and considered the plan for the Bagdad Railway arising from them as a great cultural work worthy of Germany.

He also gave his most enthusiastic approval to my visit to England in 1899, made by me with my wife and two sons at the desire of my royal grandmother, who, growing steadily weaker on account of her years, wished to see her oldest grandson once more. He hoped that this journey might serve to efface somewhat the consequences of the Kruger dispatch sent by him, and also to clarify some important questions by means of conferences between me and English statesmen.

In order to avoid any unpleasantness from the English press, which, angered by the Boer War and the partly unjustified attacks of certain German newspapers, had been answering in like tone, the Queen had commissioned the author of *The Life of the Prince Consort,* Sir Theodore Martin, to inform the English press of Her Majesty's desire that a friendly reception be accorded to her Imperial grandson. And that is what indeed came to pass. The visit ran its course harmoniously and caused satisfaction on all sides. I held important conferences with various leading men.

Not once in the entire visit was the Kruger dispatch mentioned. On the other hand, my royal grandmother did not conceal from her grandson how unwelcome the whole Boer War was to her; she made no secret of her disapproval and aversion for Mr. Chamberlain and all that he represented, and thanked me again for my prompt and sharp refusal of the Russo-French proposal to interfere and for my immediate announcement of this proposal. One could easily see how much the Queen loved her splendid army and how deeply she had been grieved by the heavy reverses suffered by it at the outset of the war, which had caused by no means negligible losses. Referring to these, the aged Field Marshal Duke of Cambridge coined the fine phrase: "The British nobleman and officer have shown that they can die bravely as gentlemen."

On my departure, the Queen bade me farewell with cordial and grateful greetings to her "much-cherished cousin," the Imperial Chancellor, whose ability and experience, she hoped, would continue to maintain good relations between our two countries.

My report entirely satisfied Prince Hohenlohe as to the success of my journey; at the same time, however, I was the object of the most violent attacks from a certain section of the press and from many excited "friends of the Boers." The German lacks the very thing with which the English people has been inoculated, and to which it has been trained by long political self-discipline: when a fight is on, even though it be merely upon the field of diplomacy, the Englishman unquestioningly follows the flag, in accordance with the proverb: "You can't change the jockey while running."

In the autumn of 1900 Prince Hohenlohe retired from the Chancellorship, since the work had become too arduous for a man of his advanced age. Moreover, the constant quarrels and disputes of the political parties with one another were disagreeable to him, and it went against the grain with him to make speeches before them in the Reichstag. Equally disagreeable to him was the press, part of which had taken the bit between its teeth and imagined that it could conserve the Bismarckian tradition by quoting sayings by Bismarck, and had greatly jeopardized relations with England, especially during the Boer War.

### CHANCELLOR'S RETIREMENT

The hope, aroused by the choice of Prince Hohenlohe as Chancellor and his assumption of the office, that Prince Bismarck would place less obstacles in his path, had been only partly fulfilled. The atmosphere had been much relieved and Prince Bismarck brought to a much milder frame of mind by my reconciliation with him, which had received outward expression in his solemn entry into Berlin and his staying at the old Hohenzollern palace, but his adherents and those rallying around him for the sake of opposition were not to be dissuaded from their activities. Moreover, the political representatives of the people succeeded, while I was on my way to Friedrichsruh to celebrate Bismarck's eightieth birthday, in refusing to pay homage to the old Imperial Chancellor, a thing which naturally deeply hurt the sensitive Prince Hohenlohe and filled him with indignation.

He, like myself, was deeply moved by the death of his great predecessor, and we, together with the German people, sincerely mourned Prince Bismarck as one of the greatest of the sons of Prussia and Germany, in spite of the fact that he had not always made our task easy. I insisted upon hurrying back from my trip to Norway in order to pay honor to him who, as a faithful servant of his old master, had helped the German nation to unity, and under whom I, when I was Prince, had had the proud privilege of working.

It is said that one of the reasons why Prince Hohenlohe retired from his post was the advice of his son Alexander, who was much at his father's house; he was known in society as "the Crown Prince," and was essentially different from his lovable father.

Prince Hohenlohe could look back upon a series of successes during his term as Chancellor: the overcoming of the disputes concerning the "Citizens' Book of Laws," the reform of the military punishment procedure, the Naval law, the appointment of Waldersee to the command in China at the time of the Boxer War, Tsing-tao, and the Yangste Treaty.

He bade me farewell on the 15th of October, 1900. Both of us were greatly moved, for not only was the Chancellor and faithful co-worker parting from his Emperor, but also the uncle from his nephew, who looked up with grateful esteem to the old man. At the age of seventy-five years—an age when others have long since retired to rest and contemplation—he had not hesitated to obey the summons of the Emperor to subject himself to even more exacting labors and devote his time and strength to the German fatherland. When about to leave my room, he grasped my hand once again with the request that I might grant him, during the years of life still remaining to him (which he meant to spend in Berlin), the same plain, faithful friendship which he had so long noted and admired between me and Admiral von Hollmann. I shall always preserve him faithfully in my memory.

German Postcard from World War 1

# CHAPTER IV

## Bülow

ON the day after Prince Hohenlohe's farewell, the man summoned by me as his successor—Count Bülow, Secretary of State for Foreign Affairs, arrived. His choice for the post was eminently fitting, because he was thoroughly cognizant of our foreign policy and, especially, of our relations with England—which policy was becoming constantly livelier and more complicated—and because he had already proved himself a skillful orator and ready debater in the Reichstag. The fact that the second of these qualities was lacking in his predecessor had often been painfully noticeable. When Prince Hohenlohe's intention to retire became known in the Imperial Council, the Bavarian ambassador at Berlin, Count Lerchenfeld, very pointedly remarked to me that for Heaven's sake I was not to choose another South German, since South Germans were not fitted for the leading post at Berlin; North Germans were naturally better able to fill it and, therefore, it would be better for the Empire to select a North German.

I had been acquainted personally with Bülow

for a long time, ever since the period of his ambassadorship at Rome and his work as Secretary of State. Then I had often visited him at his home and had held many a conference with him in his garden. He came into closer relationship with me when he accompanied me on my journey to the Far East, where, in co-operation with the ambassador, Freiherr Marschall, he assisted me in getting into personal touch with the leading men of the Turkish Government. Hence, the relations of the new Chancellor with me were already begun and, to a certain extent, established, since we had for years discussed all political problems and spheres. Moreover, he stood much nearer to me in age than his predecessors, most of whom could have been my grandfather. He was the first "young Chancellor" of Germany. And this made our common task easier for both of us.

When I was in Berlin, scarcely a day went by without my taking a long morning walk with the Chancellor in the garden of the Imperial Chancellor's palace, during which outstanding business was cleared up and problems of actuality discussed. I often had a meal with him and always found at his table, where I was most hospitably received by the Count, his amiable wife and a group of the most interesting men, in choosing whom the Count was a master. He was likewise unsurpassed in skillfully conducting conversation and in the witty handling of the various topics that arose. To me it was always a pleasure to be in the company of the Chancellor and enjoy his bubbling wit, to exchange views at his table with many professors, savants, and artists, as well as Government officials of all sorts, in informal, unofficial intercourse and stimulating exchange of ideas.

The Count was an excellent narrator of anecdotes, drawn both from books and his own personal experience, which he told in several languages. He liked to tell stories of the days when he was a diplomat, especially about his stay at St. Petersburg.

### BÜLOW A DISCIPLE OF BISMARCK

The Count's father was an intimate friend of Prince Bismarck and had been one of his closest co-workers. Young Bülow also had begun his career under the great Chancellor; he had been brought up on Bismarckian ideas and traditions and strongly influenced by them, but, nevertheless, had not adhered to them to such an extent as to lose his independence.

In the course of one of the first talks which I had with Bülow as Imperial Chancellor he informed himself concerning my ideas of how best to handle the English and have dealings with them. I told him that I considered absolute frankness the most important thing in dealing with England and Englishmen; that the Englishman, in presenting his point of view and working for his interests, was inconsiderate to the point of brutality, for which reason he thoroughly understood anybody who acted similarly toward him; that there must be no playing the diplomatic game, or "finessing," with an Englishman, because it made him distrust those with whom he was dealing and suspect that they were not honest and wished secretly to cheat him; that such devious methods could be successful only in dealing with Latin and Slavic nations; that, once the Englishman had become suspicious, there was nothing more to be done with him, despite the most honeyed words and most obliging concessions; that the only advice, therefore, which I could give the Chancellor was that he confine himself entirely to straightforwardness in his English policy. I said this with particular emphasis, since "finessing" was especially dear to the diplomatic character of Count Bülow and had become second nature to him.

I also took occasion, during this talk, to warn the Chancellor against Holstein. In spite of my warning—which was merely a repetition of that given me before by Bismarck—Bülow worked a great deal, or was obliged to work, with Holstein. This remarkable man had been able gradually, especially since the time that the Foreign Office had been, so to speak, orphaned by Bismarck's retirement, to create for himself a position that became steadily more influential and to maintain it under three Chancellors with such skill that he was considered indispensable.

Holstein was unquestionably possessed of great shrewdness, seconded by a phenomenal memory and a certain talent for political combinations, which, to be sure, often became a hobby in his case. His position was also based largely on the fact that he was looked upon in many quarters, especially among the older officials, as the "bearer of the Bismarckian traditions," the man who upheld these in the teeth of "the young master." His importance rested, above all, on his wide personal knowledge in the entire domain of the foreign service. Since he wielded, on account of this, an authoritative influence on all proposals relative to the appointment of officials and hence, also, on the careers of the younger officials, it may be easily understood why he, little by little, had obtained for himself a dominating position at the Foreign Office. But he sought more and more to obtain, at the same time, a decisive influence upon the conduct of foreign policy; he had, in fact, become the guiding spirit both of the Foreign Office and of German foreign policy.

#### HOLSTEIN'S SECRET POWER

The serious thing about this was that he exerted his far-reaching influence entirely from under cover and avoided all official responsibility as an adviser. He preferred to remain in the dark and exert his influence from there. He refused every responsible post—many stood open to him—every honorary title, every promotion. He lived in complete seclusion. For a long time I tried in vain to become personally acquainted with him, for which purpose I used to invite him to meals, but Holstein declined every time. Only once, in the course of many years, did he consent to dine with me at the Foreign Office, and it was characteristic of him that, whereas on this occasion all the other gentlemen present wore full evening dress, he appeared in a frock coat and excused himself on the plea that he had no dress coat.

The secrecy with which he surrounded himself in his work, so as not to be held responsible for it, became apparent also at times in the character of the memorials drawn up by him; they were unquestionably ingenious and attractive, but often as involved and ambiguous as the oracle of Delphi; there were occasions when, after a decision had been made based on the contents of one of these documents, Herr von Holstein would prove to a nicety that he meant exactly the opposite of what had been thought.

I considered it a serious matter that an irresponsible counselor should bring to bear such powerful influence, especially as he did so from under cover and, hence, in doing it, eluded the officials who were in duty bound to exert influence, and who were the responsible parties. Often, especially in the von Richthofen era, it happened that I would advise a foreign ambassador to discuss some political question, which he had taken up with me, with the Secretary of State, and he would reply: "J'en parlerai avec mon ami Holstein" ("I shall speak about it with my friend Holstein"). The fact alone that an official of the Foreign Office dealt with foreign ambassadors, going over the head of his superior, did not seem right to me; but that he should be dubbed by these foreigners "friend" seemed to me to go beyond what I deemed advisable.

Matters had, in fact, developed gradually to such a stage that Holstein conducted a good part of our foreign affairs. To be sure, he still listened to the Chancellor in connection with them, but what the Emperor thought or said about foreign affairs was rather unimportant. If things turned out successfully, the Foreign Office reaped the reward; if things went wrong, then it was the fault of the "impulsive young master."

In spite of all this, Bülow, too, apparently thought Herr von Holstein indispensable at first; he worked together with him for a long time, until at last he, too, found unbearable the pressure which this strange man exerted on everybody. To Herr von Tschirschky, during his tenure of office as Secretary of State, belongs the merit of finally bringing the unendurable situation to a head. On being questioned by me, he declared that he considered it impossible that Herr von Holstein remain at his post any longer, since he was embroiling the whole Foreign Office, seeking to eliminate him, the Secretary of State, entirely, and creating all kinds of obstacles, likewise, for the Chancellor.

### DISMISSAL—AND AN ENEMY

Thereupon I ordered Herr von Tschirschky to prepare the way for the dismissal of Herr von Holstein, which afterward took place, with the approval of the Chancellor, after the latter had recovered from the serious break-down in health which he had suffered meanwhile. Herr von Holstein himself showed what manner of man he was by going at once after his dismissal to Herr Harden and placing himself at the latter's disposal for the campaign against the Emperor.

The year 1901 gave Count Bülow plentiful opportunities to show and assert himself in dealings with England. Count Bülow still believed strongly in the Bismarckian theory of having "two irons in the fire"—*i. e.,* in making friendly agreements with another country while always remaining on good terms with Russia—in which he received support from the many pretended adherents of Bismarck.

From the midst of the Jubilee celebration of the two hundredth coronation anniversary, I was called to the deathbed of my grandmother, Queen Victoria, by a dispatch announcing to me the serious condition of the Queen. I hurriedly made the journey with my uncle, the Duke of Connaught, who was at Berlin as the Queen's representative at the festivities—he was the favorite son of the Queen and my particular friend, and a son-in-law of Prince Frederick Charles—and I was cordially received in London by the then Prince of Wales and the royal family. As my carriage drove out at a trot from the railway station a plainly dressed man stepped forward from the closely packed crowd standing there in absolute silence, to the side of the carriage, bared his head, and said: "Thank you, Kaiser." The Prince of Wales, later Edward VII, added: "That is what they all think, and they will never forget this coming of yours."

Nevertheless, they did forget it, and quickly.

After the Queen had quietly breathed her last in my arms, the curtain fell for me upon many memories of childhood. Her death signified the close of an epoch in English history and in Germany's relations with England. I now got into touch, as far as possible, with prominent personages, and noted everywhere a thoroughly sympathetic, friendly spirit, which made no secret of the wish for good relations with Germany.

At the farewell banquet impromptu speeches were made by King Edward VII and myself, which were cordial in tone and content, and did not fail to make an impression on their hearers. After the meal the English ambassador at Berlin clasped my hand and said that my speech had touched all his fellow countrymen's hearts, because what I said was sincere and simple, as was fitting for Englishmen; that the speech must at once be made public, since it would have an effect through out the country, which was grateful for my coming; and that this would be useful to the relations between the two countries. I answered that it was a matter for the British Government and the King to decide, that personally I had no objections to having the speech made public.

Nevertheless, it was not made public, and the British people never learned of my words, which were the sincere expression of my sentiments and thoughts. In another talk later on with me at Berlin the same ambassador deeply regretted this, but was unable to say what the reason was for this omission.

In concluding my remarks on my stay in England I cannot pass over the fact that a portion of the German press was unfortunately lacking both in tactful appreciation of the grief of the English royal family and people, as well as of the obligations which my family relationship and political considerations imposed upon me.

After my return home from England I was able to report to the Chancellor on the good impressions I had received, and particularly that opinion in England was apparently in favor of an understanding and of closer relations.

Bülow expressed himself as satisfied with the results of the journey, after we had talked at length about it at Homburg, and consulted as to how the situation created by the journey should be put to use. I suggested that we should unquestionably come to a good agreement, if an alliance—which I preferred—could not be brought about. In any event, a firm agreement would suffice, I said, and would suit the English; in the long run an alliance might always develop from it.

The opportunity for such an alliance came with unexpected promptness. While I was at Homburg von der Höhe in the spring of 1901, Count Metternich, who was with me as representative of the Foreign Office, brought me a notification from Berlin that *Mr. Chamberlain* had inquired there as to whether Germany was ready for an *alliance with England.* I immediately asked: "Against whom?"—since, if England so suddenly offered to make an alliance in the midst of peace, it was plain that she needed the German army, which made it worth while to find out against whom the army was needed and for what reason German troops were to fight, at England's behest, by her side. Thereupon the answer came from London that they were needed against Russia, since Russia was a menace both to India and to Constantinople.

The first thing I did was to call London's attention to the old traditional brotherhood-in-arms between the German and Russian armies, and the close family ties between the reigning dynasties of the two countries; in addition, I pointed out the dangers of a war on two fronts, in case France came in on the side of Russia, and also the fact that we had acted jointly with France and Russia in the Far East (Shimonoseki, 1895) and that there was no reason to unloose a conflict with Russia at this time, when we were in the midst of peace; that the superiority in number of the Russian army on a peace footing was very great and the eastern frontiers of Prussia seriously threatened by the grouping of the Russian forces; that England would not be in a position to protect our eastern province from a Russian attack, since her fleet could accomplish little in the Baltic and would be unable to sail into the Black Sea; that, in case of our making common cause against Russia, Germany would be the only one who would be in great danger, quite independently of the possibility of the entry of France into the fight.

Chamberlain then informed us that a firm alliance should be made, by which England would naturally bind herself to come to our aid.

### BRITISH ALLIANCE FAILS

I had also pointed out that the validity of an alliance could only be assured when the English Parliament had placed its approval upon it, since the Ministry might be driven from office by the will of the nation as expressed in Parliament, whereby signature of the Ministry might be rendered null and void and the alliance invalidated, and that we could look upon the Chamberlain suggestion, for the time being, merely as a purely personal project of his own.

To this Chamberlain replied that he would get backing from Parliament in due time and would find the way of winning the Unionists over to his idea; that all needed now was the signature of Berlin. Matters did not progress as far as that, because Parliament was not to be won over to Chamberlain's plan; therefore the "plan" came to nothing. Soon afterward England concluded her alliance with Japan (Hayashi). The Russo-Japanese War broke out, in which Japan—owing to the fact that it fitted in with her schemes—played the rôle of pawn for England's interests, which rôle had originally been reserved for Germany. By this war Russia was thrown from the east back to the west, where she might concern herself again with the Balkans, Constantinople, and India—which was to Japan's advantage—leaving to Japan a free hand in Korea and China.

In 1905 came my journey to Tangier, undertaken much against my will. It came about as follows: Toward the end of March I intended, as in the previous year, to take a Mediterranean trip for the sake of my health, for which I proposed to avail myself of some ship running empty from Cuxhaven to Naples. The *Hamburg* was destined by Ballin for this purpose. At his request that I take along some other guests, since the steamer was quite empty, I invited a number of gentlemen, among them Privy Councilor Althoc, Admiral Mensing, Count Pückler, Ambassador von Varnbuhler, Professor Schiemann, Admiral Hollmann, etc.

Soon after the proposed trip became known Bülow informed me that there was a strong desire at Lisbon to have me stop there and pay the Portuguese court a visit. To this I agreed. As the date of departure approached, Bülow expressed the additional wish that I also stop at Tangier and, by visiting that Moroccan port, strengthen the position of the Sultan of Morocco in relation to the French.

This I declined, since it seemed to me that the Morocco question was too full of explosive matter and I feared that such a visit would work out disadvantageously rather than beneficially. Bülow returned to the attack, without, however, persuading me of the necessity or advisability of the visit.

### AGAIN KAISER "GIVES IN"

During the journey I had several talks with Freiherr von Schoen, who accompanied me as representative of the Foreign Office, as to the advisability of the visit. We agreed that it would be better to drop it. I telegraphed this decision to the Chancellor from Lisbon. Bülow replied emphatically that I must take into consideration the view of the German people and of the Reichstag, which had become interested in the project, and that it was necessary that I stop at Tangier.

I gave in, with a heavy heart, for I feared that this visit, in view of the situation at Paris, might be construed as a provocation and cause an inclination in London to support France in case of war. Since I suspected that Delcassé wished to make Morocco a pretext for war, I feared that he might make use of the Tangier visit for this purpose.

The visit took place, after much difficulty had been experienced in the open roadstead of Tangier, and it met with a certain amount of friendly participation by Italian and Southern French anarchists, rogues, and adventurers. A lot of Spaniards stood upon a small square, amid waving banners and loud cries; these, according to a police official who accompanied us, were an assembly of Spanish anarchists.

The first I learned about the consequences of my Tangier visit was when I got to Gibraltar and was formally and frigidly received by the English, in marked contrast to my cordial reception the year before. What I had foreseen was justified by the facts. Embitterment and anger reigned in Paris, and Delcassé tried to rouse the nation to war; the only reason that he did not succeed was that both the Minister of War and the Minister of the Navy declared France not yet ready.

The fact that my fears were justified was also corroborated later by the conversation between Delcassé and the editor of *Le Gaulois,* in which the Minister informed an astonished world that, in case of war, England would have sided with France. Thus, even as far back as that, I ran the risk, through the Tangier visit forced upon me, of getting blamed for the unchaining of a world war. To think and act constitutionally is often a hard task for a ruler upon whom in every case responsibility is finally saddled.

In October, 1905, the Paris *Matin* reported that Delcassé had declared in the Council of Ministers that England had offered, in case of war, to land 100,000 men in Holstein and seize the Kaiser Wilhelm Canal. This English offer was repeated once more later on, with the suggestion that it be affirmed in writing. And the well-known Jaurès, who was murdered in accordance with the political ideas of Isvolsky upon the outbreak of war in 1914, knew beforehand about the statements by Delcassé published in the *Matin.*

The downfall of Delcassé and the accession of Rouvier to his post are to be ascribed partly to the influence of the Prince of Monaco. During the regatta week at Kiel the Prince had assured himself, by talks with me, the Imperial Chancellor, and Government officials, of the sincerity of our desire to compromise with France for the purpose of enabling us to live at peace with each other. He stood well with the ambassador, Prince Radolin, and worked actively toward a rapprochement between the two countries.

The Prince of Monaco himself was of the opinion that Delcassé was a menace to the maintenance of peace and hoped that he would soon fall and be replaced by Rouvier, who was a prudent politician thoroughly inclined to coming to an understanding with Germany. The Prince said that he was on good terms with Rouvier personally and would willingly place himself at the disposal of the German ambassador as a go-between.

### NEGOTIATIONS FRUITLESS

Then came Delcassé's fall, and Rouvier became Minister. At once I caused the initiation of the measures wherein I could count upon the support of the Prince of Monaco. The Chancellor was instructed to prepare a rapprochement with France. And I particularly told Prince Radolin, who personally received his instructions in Berlin, to make good use of the Rouvier régime for the purpose of eliminating all possibilities of conflict between the two countries. I added that the reports of the Prince of Monaco, with whom he was well acquainted, would be useful to him in relations with Rouvier. Prince Radolin proceeded with zeal and pleasure to the accomplishment of this worth-while task.

At first the negotiations went well, so much so that I began to hope that the important goal would be attained and the evil impression caused by the

Tangier visit effaced by an understanding. In the meantime, the negotiations concerning Morocco were continued; they were concluded, after endless trouble, by the summoning of the Algeciras Conference, based upon the circular note of Prince Bülow, which pointed out that the Most-Favored-Nation Clause No. 17 of the Madrid Convention should remain in force and that the reforms in Morocco, for which France alone was working, should be carried out, in so far as necessary, only in agreement with the signatory powers of the Madrid Conference. These events, which riveted general attention upon themselves, relegated the special negotiations with Rouvier to the background.

With regard to domestic policy, I had agreed with the Chancellor that his main task was to be the restoration of order in the relations between the parties in the Reichstag, which had got into a bad way under Hohenlohe, and, above all, to rally the Conservatives, who had been won over to the opposition by the Post-Bismarckians, once more to the support of the Government. The Chancellor accomplished this task with great patience and tenacity. He finally formed the famous "bloc," which arose from the great electoral defeat of the Socialists.

The Conservative party had many members who had direct relations with the court, and also with me personally, so that it was easier for this party than for any other to become informed as to my plans in political and other matters and to discuss my ideas with me before they took shape in projects for laws. I have not the impression that this was done to the extent that was possible; I might perhaps have come into agreement with the gentlemen, through informal conversations, in the question of the building of the Central Canal—opposed, as is well known, by the Conservatives—as well as in the less important matters of the construction of the Cathedral and the Berlin Opera House, in which I was deeply interested for the sake of the Church and of art.

I am saying nothing new if I remark that it was by no means easy to deal with the gentlemen of the Conservative party. Through their traditional services to the state they had acquired great experience and independence of judgment, and had thus formed firm political convictions, to which they held faithfully and in a genuinely conservative manner. From their ranks great statesmen, eminent Ministers, a brilliant officer corps, a model body of officials, had largely been produced. Therefore, the consciousness of their own merit was not without justification; in addition, their loyalty to their King was unshakable. The King and the country both owed them gratitude.

### FINDS FAULT WITH CONSERVATIVES

Their weakness lay in the fact that they were at times too conservative—that is, they recognized too late the demands of the time and began by opposing progress, although it might be progress advantageous to themselves. One may understand this in view of their past, but the fact remains that it worked to the detriment of their relations with me, especially during my reign, when the development of the Empire, particularly of industry and commerce, pushed rapidly forward; and I desired —and was obliged—to place no obstacles in the way of that development, but to promote it. When I said that it was not always easy, for the reasons adduced, to deal with the Conservatives, I am well aware that the same thing is maintained about me. Perhaps this is because I stood close to the Conservatives on account of my traditions, but was not a Conservative for party reasons. I was and am, indeed, in favor of progressive conservatism, which preserves what is vital, rejects what is outworn, and accepts that portion of the new which is useful.

Let me add that in discussions I was able to endure the truth, even when it was uncomfortable and bitter, better than people are aware, provided it was told to me tactfully.

So that, when it is maintained that I and the Conservatives did not get along in dealings with each other, the same reason was at the root of the difficulty on both sides. It would have been better to arrive oftener at an understanding with me in private conversations, for which I was always ready. And in the canal question, on which we could not agree, who was better qualified than the Conservative to understand and appreciate the fact that I have never subscribed to the pretty couplet, "Unser König absolut, wenn er unseren Willen tut" ("Absolute our King may be, if he does what we decree")? For, had I acted according to that principle—a very comfortable one for me—the Conservatives, in view of their belief in a strong King who really governs, would logically have been forced to oppose me. Surely the Conservatives must have respected me for having matched their honorable axiom of manly pride before the thrones of Kings with mine of kingly pride before the Conservative party's throne, just as I did with regard to all other parties.

In any event, the occasional differences with the Conservative party and with individual Conservatives cannot make me forget the services rendered by men of this very party to the House of Hohenzollern, the Prussian state, and the German Empire.

Bülow finally did the great trick of bringing Conservatives and Liberals together in Germany, thus getting a big majority for the parties siding with the Government. In doing so, the great abilities of the Chancellor, his skill, statecraft, and shrewd knowledge of men, shone forth most brilliantly. The great service rendered by him in achieving this success won him thorough appreciation and gratitude from his country and from myself; and, in addition, an increase of my trust in him. The boundless delight of the people of Berlin in the defeat of the Social Democrats at the polls led to the nocturnal demonstration, which I shall never forget, in front of my palace, in the course of which my automobile had to force a way for itself, little by little, amid a cheering crowd of many thousands surrounding it. The Lustgarten was packed with great multitudes of people, at whose tumultuous request the Empress and I had to appear on the balcony in order to receive their homage.

The Chancellor was present at the visit of King Edward VII to Kiel. Among the many guests was the former Chief Court Marshal of the Empress, Frederick, Count Seckendorff, long acquainted with Edward VII through his many visits to England, who reposed great trust in the Count. This gentleman, at the behest of Bülow, with whom he was friendly, arranged an interview between the King and the Chancellor.

It took place on board the royal English yacht after a breakfast to which I and the Chancellor were invited. Both gentlemen sat for a long time alone over their cigars. Afterward Bülow reported to me what had transpired at the interview. In discussing the possible conclusion of an alliance between Germany and England, the King, he told me, had stated that such a thing was not at all necessary in the case of our two countries, since there was no real cause for enmity or strife between them. This refusal to make an alliance was a plain sign of the English "policy of encirclement," which soon made itself felt clearly and disagreeably at the Algeciras Conference. The pro-French and anti-German attitude of England, which there came out into the open, was due to special orders from King Edward VII, who had sent Sir D. Mackenzie Wallace to Algeciras as his "supervising representative," equipped with personal instructions.

From hints given by the latter to his friends it turned out that it was the King's wish to oppose Germany strongly and support France at every opportunity. When it was pointed out to him that it might be possible, after all, to take up later with Germany this or that question and perhaps come to an understanding, he replied that, first of all came the Anglo-Russian agreement; that, once that was assured, an "arrangement" might be made with Germany also. The English "arrangement" consisted in the encirclement of Germany.

### HIS FRIENDSHIP WITH BÜLOW

The relations between me and the Chancellor remained trustful and friendly throughout this period. He was present repeatedly at the Kiel regatta. Here, he found occasion, among other matters, to confer with the Prince of Monaco and a number of influential Frenchmen, who were guests aboard the Prince's yacht, among whom doubtless the most eminent was M. Jules Roche, the leading expert on European budgets, and a great admirer of Goethe. He always carried a copy of *Faust* in his pocket.

In April, 1906, came the unfortunate collapse in the Reichstag of the overworked Chancellor. As soon as I received the news, I hurried there and was glad that Privy Councilor Renvers could give me encouraging news about Bülow's condition. While the Prince was recuperating during the summer at Norderney, I went from Heligoland, which I had been inspecting, on a torpedo boat to the island and surprised the Chancellor and his wife at their villa. I spent the day in chatting with the Chancellor, who had already recovered his health to an encouraging degree and was browned by the sea air and sunlight.

In the late autumn of 1907 the Empress and I paid a visit to Windsor, at the invitation of King Edward VII. We were most cordially received by the English royal family and the visit went off harmoniously. After this visit I went for a rest to the castle of Highcliffe, belonging to General Stewart Worthley, situated on the south coast of England, opposite The Needles.

Before my departure for England, the Chancellor, who was much pleased at the English invitation, had long talks with me as to the best way for getting on a better footing with England, and had suggested to me a number of his desires and projects, to serve me as guides in my conversations with Englishmen. During my visit I had frequent occasion to discuss the subjects agreed upon and conduct conversations as desired by the Chancellor. Cipher telegrams containing my reports on these conversations went regularly to Berlin and I repeatedly received from the Chancellor approving telegrams. I used to show these after the evening meal to my intimates who accompanied me on my visit; these men, among them the Chief Court Marshal Count Eulenberg and Prince Max Egon Fürstenberg, read them and rejoiced with me at the harmonious understanding between me and the Chancellor.

After my return from England I made a general report to the Chancellor, whereupon he expressed to me his thanks for my having personally troubled myself so much and worked so hard toward improving the relations between the two countries.

### DEFENDS FAMOUS INTERVIEW[1]

A year later came the incident about the so-called "interview," published in the *Daily Telegraph*. Its object was the improvement of German-English relations. I had sent the draft submitted to me to the Chancellor for examination through the representative of the Foreign Office, Herr von Jenisch. I had called attention, by means of notes, to certain portions which, to my way of thinking, did not belong therein and should be eliminated. Through a series of mistakes on the part of the Foreign Office, when

[1] One of the most startling incidents of the Kaiser's reign was the interview with him printed in the London *Daily Telegraph* of Oct. 28, 1908. In it he said that "Englishmen, in giving rein to suspicions unworthy of a great nation," were "mad as March hares"; and that "the prevailing sentiment among large sections of the middle and lower classes of my own people is not friendly to England. I am, therefore, so to speak, in a minority in my own land, but it is a minority of the best elements, just as it is in England with respect to Germany." German opinion was, he admitted, "bitterly hostile" to England during the Boer War, and, that the German people, if he had permitted Boer delegates in Berlin, "would have crowned them with flowers." He asserted that he had formulated a plan of campaign in South Africa which Lord Roberts adopted in substance.

The Kaiser was quoted in this interview as declaring Germany needed a large fleet chiefly on account of the Far Eastern situation.

The interview was republished in official German organs, and caused as great a stir in Germany as in England. There were many debates on it in the Reichstag and one or two "investigations."

the matter was taken up at my request, this was not done.

A storm broke loose in the press. The Chancellor spoke in the Reichstag, but did not defend the Kaiser, who was the object of attack, to the extent that I expected, declaring, on the other hand, that he wished to prevent in future the tendency toward "personal politics" which had become apparent in the last few years. The Conservative party took upon itself to address an open letter to the King through the newspapers, the contents of which are known.

During these proceedings, I was staying first at Eckartsau, with Franz Ferdinand, heir to the Austrian throne, and later with Kaiser Franz Joseph at Vienna, both of whom disapproved of the Chancellor's conduct. From Vienna I went to Donaueschingen to visit Prince Fürstenberg, to whom the press saw fit to address the demand that he should, being an honest, upright man, tell the Emperor the truth for once. When we talked over the whole matter, the Prince advised me to get together, at the Foreign Office, the dispatches from Highcliffe in 1907, and the answers to them, and have these laid before the Reichstag.

During this whole affair I underwent great mental anguish, which was heightened by the sudden death before my eyes of the intimate friend of my youth, Count Hülsen-Haeseler, chief of the Military Cabinet. The faithful, self-sacrificing friendship and care of the Prince and his family were most welcome to me in these bitter days. And letters and demonstrations from the Empire, part of which sided with me and severely censured the Chancellor, were a consolation to me during that period.

After my return, the Chancellor appeared, lectured me on my political sins, and asked that I sign the document that is already known, which was afterward communicated to the press. I signed it in silence and in silence I endured the attacks of the press against myself and the Crown.

The Chancellor struck a serious blow, by his conduct, at the firm confidence and sincere friendship which had bound me before to him. Undoubtedly Prince Bülow thought that, handling the matter as he did both in the Reichstag and with me personally, he could best serve me and the cause, especially as public excitement was running very high at that time. In this I could not agree with him, all the more so since his actions toward me in the *Daily Telegraph* affair stood out in too sharp contrast to the complaisance and recognition which Bülow had previously manifested toward me. I had become so accustomed to the amiability of the Prince that I found the treatment now accorded me incomprehensible.

### A BREAK WITH BÜLOW

The relationship between Emperor and Chancellor, excellent and amicable up to that time, was, at all events, disturbed. I gave up personal relations with the Chancellor and confined myself to official dealings. After consultation with the Minister of the Royal Household and the chief of the Cabinet, I resolved to follow Prince Fürstenberg's advice as to getting together the Highcliffe dispatches, and charged the Foreign Office with this task. It failed of accomplishment because the dispatches in question were not to be found.

Toward the end of the winter the Chancellor requested an audience with me. I walked up and down with him in the picture gallery of the palace, between the pictures of my ancestors, of the battles of the Seven Years' War, of the proclamation of the Empire at Versailles, and was amazed when the Chancellor harked back to the events of the autumn of 1908 and undertook to explain his attitude. Thereupon I took occasion to talk with him about the entire past. The frank talk and the explanations of the Prince satisfied me. The result was that he remained in office.

The Chancellor requested that I dine with him that evening, as I had so often done before, in order to show the outer world that all was again well. I did so. A pleasant evening, enlivened by the visibly delighted Princess with charming amiability, and by the Prince with his usual lively, witty talk, closed that memorable day. Alluding to the Prince's audience with me, a wag wrote later in a newspaper, parodying a famous line: "The tear flows, Germania has me again."

By this reconciliation I also wished to show that I was in the habit of sacrificing my own sensitiveness to the good of the cause. Despite Prince Bülow's attitude toward me in the Reichstag, which was calculated to pain me, I naturally never forgot his eminent gifts as a statesman and his distinguished services to the fatherland. He succeeded, by his skill, in avoiding a world war at several moments of crisis, during the period indeed, when I, together with Tirpitz, was building our protecting fleet. That was a great achievement.

A serious epilogue to the above-mentioned audience was provided by the Conservatives. The Civil Cabinet informed the party leaders of the Chancellor's audience and what happened there, with the request that the party might now take back its "Open Letter." This request—which was made solely in the interest of the Crown, not of myself personally—was declined by the party. Not until 1916, when the war was under way, did we get into touch again, through a delegate of the party, at Great General Headquarters.

Just as the Conservatives did not do enough out of respect for the Crown to satisfy me, so also the Liberals of the Left, the Democrats and the Socialists, distinguished themselves by an outburst of fury, which became, in their partisan press, a veritable orgy, in which loud demands were made for the limitation of autocratic, despotic inclinations, etc. This agitation lasted the whole winter, without hindrance or objection from high Government circles. Only after the Chancellor's audience did it stop.

Later, a coolness gradually arose between the Chancellor and the political parties. The Conservatives drew away from the Liberals—rifts appeared in the bloc. Centrists and Socialists—but, above all, the Chancellor himself—brought about its downfall, as Count Hertling repeatedly explained to me later—for the last time at Spa. He was proud to have worked energetically toward causing Bülow's downfall.

When matters had reached an impossible pass, the Chancellor drew the proper conclusions and recommended to me the choice of Herr von Bethmann as the fifth Chancellor of the Empire. After careful consultations, I decided to acquiesce in the wish of Prince Bülow, to accept his request for retirement, and to summon the man recommended by him as his successor.

German Postcard from World War 1

# CHAPTER V

## Bethmann

I HAD been well acquainted since my youth with Herr von Bethmann Hollweg. When I was in active service for the first time in 1877, as Lieutenant in the Sixth Company of the First Infantry Guard Regiment, it was quartered once at Hohenfinow, the home of old Herr von Bethmann, father of the Chancellor. I was attracted by the pleasant family circle there, which was presided over by Frau von Bethmann, a most worthy lady, born of Swiss nationality, amiable and refined.

Often, as Prince and later as Emperor, I went to Hohenfinow to visit the old gentleman, and I was received on every occasion by the young head of the rural district administration; at that time neither of us imagined that he would become Imperial Chancellor under me.

From these visits an intimate relationship sprang up little by little, which served to increase steadily my esteem for the diligence, ability, and noble character of Bethmann, which were much to my liking. These qualities clung to him throughout his career.

As Chief President and as Imperial Secretary of

State for the Interior Bethmann gave a good account of himself, and, while occupying the last-named post, made his appearance successfully before the Reichstag.

Co-operation with the Chancellor was easy for me. With Bethmann I kept up my custom of daily visits whenever possible, and of discussing fully with him, while walking in the garden of the Chancellor's palace, on politics, events of the day, special bills, and occurrences and of hearing reports from him. It was also a pleasure for me to visit the Chancellor's home, since Bethmann's spouse was the very model of a genuine German wife, one whose simple distinction earned the esteem of every visitor, while her winning kindness of heart spread around her an atmosphere of cordiality. During the Bethmann régime the custom of holding small evening receptions, instituted by Prince Bülow and most enjoyable to me, was continued, and this enabled me to keep on associating informally with men of all circles and walks of life.

In the journeys which the Chancellor had to make in order to introduce himself, he won esteem everywhere by his distinguished calm and sincere methods of expression. Such foreign countries as were not hostile to us considered him a factor making for political stability and peace, to the maintenance and strengthening of which he devoted his most zealous efforts. This was entirely to my liking.

In foreign politics he busied himself from the

start with the position of England in relation to Germany and with the "policy of encirclement" of King Edward VII, which had made itself felt more and more since Reval, and was a source of worry to Bethmann. This was likewise true of the growing desire for revenge and enmity of France, and the unreliability of Russia. During his régime as Chancellor it became clear that Italy was no longer to be reckoned with militarily; the work of Barrère in that country made "extra tours" chronic.

Upon assuming office, Herr von Bethmann found the situation with regard to France cleared up to such an extent that the German-French Morocco Agreement had been signed on February 9, 1909. By recognizing thereby the political predominance of France in Morocco Prince Bülow had put the finishing touch to the German political retreat from Morocco. The standpoint which had determined the trip to Tangier and, in addition, the Algeciras Conference, was thereby definitely abandoned. The great satisfaction of the French Government over this victory was expressed in a manner unwelcome to us by the conferring of the cross of the Legion of Honor upon Prince Radolin and Herr von Schoen.

### RECEIVES BRITISH ROYALTY

On the same day King Edward VII, with Queen Alexandra, made his first official visit to the German Emperor and his wife at their capital city of Berlin—eight years after his accession to the throne! Berlin received the exalted gentleman with rejoicing (!!) and showed no signs of dissatisfaction at his unfriendly policy.

The King did not look well; he was tired and aged, and suffered, moreover, from a severe attack of catarrh. Nevertheless, he accepted the invitation of the municipal authorities of Berlin to informal tea at the City Hall. From his description, which was corroborated by Berlin gentlemen, the function must have been satisfactory to both parties.

I informed my uncle of the signing of the German-French Morocco Agreement and the news seemed to please him. When I added, "I hope this agreement will be a stepping stone to a better understanding between the two countries," the King nodded his head approvingly and said, "May that be so!" If the King had co-operated toward this, my project would probably not have failed. Nevertheless, the visit of Their English Majesties engendered a more friendly atmosphere for the time being, which greeted Herr von Bethmann upon his assuming office.

During his term of office Herr von Bethmann had plenty of foreign matters to handle, connected with the well-known events of 1909-14. Concerning this period a mass of material has been published in different quarters, for instance, in the book, *Causes of the World War,* by Secretary of State von Jagow. In the *Belgian Documents* the attitude of the German Government in the various complications is described from a neutral standpoint. I had based this attitude on the following:

> Caution on the one hand, on the other, support of our Austro-Hungarian allies whenever there is a plain threat against their position as a world power, combined with counsels of moderation in action. Efforts in the rôle of "honest broker" everywhere, activity as a go-between wherever peace seems endangered. Firm assertion of our own interests.

In view of the "encirclement" ambitions of our opponents, we were in duty bound, for the sake of self-preservation, to work steadily at the same time toward building up our army and navy for purposes of defense, because of the central location of Germany and her open, unprotected frontiers. This period of history is also well described in Stegemann's book, and Helfferich and Friedjung also depict the prewar days interestingly.

### "EDWARD THE ENCIRCLER"

The death of the "encircler," Edward VII—of whom it was said once, in a report of the Belgian Embassy at Berlin, that "the peace of Europe was never in such danger as when the King of England concerned himself with maintaining it"—called me to London, where I shared with my close relations, the members of the English royal family, the mourning into which the passing of the King had thrown the dynasty and the nation. The entire royal family received me at the railway station as a token of their gratitude for the deference to family ties shown by my coming.

King George drove with me to Westminster Hall, where the gorgeously decorated coffin reposed upon a towering catafalque, guarded by household troops, troops of the line, and detachments from the Indian and Colonial contingents, all in the traditional attitude of mourning—heads bowed, hands crossed over the butts and hilts of their reversed arms. The old, gray hall, covered by its great Gothic wooden ceiling, towered imposingly over the catafalque, lighted merely by a few rays of the sun filtering through narrow windows. One ray flooded the magnificent coffin of the King, surmounted by the English crown, and made marvelous play with the colors of the precious stones adorning it.

Past the catafalque countless throngs of men, women, and children of all classes and strata in the nation passed in silence, many with hands folded to bid a reverent farewell to him who had been so popular as a ruler. A most impressive picture, in its marvelous medieval setting.

I went up to the catafalque, with King George, placed a cross upon it, and spoke a silent prayer, after which my right hand and that of my royal cousin found each other, quite unconsciously on our part, and met in a firm clasp. This made a deep impression on those who witnessed it, to such an extent that, in the evening, one of my relations said to me: "Your handshake with our King is all over London: the people are deeply impressed by it, and take it as a good omen for the future."

"That is the sincerest wish of my heart," I replied.

As I rode through London behind the coffin of my uncle I was a witness of the tremendous and impressive demonstration of grief on the part of the vast multitude—estimated at several millions—on streets, balconies, and roofs, every one of whom was clad in black, every man of whom stood with bared head, among all of whom reigned perfect order and absolute stillness. Upon this somber, solemn background the files of British soldiers stood out all the more gorgeously. In splendid array marched the battalions of the English Guards: Grenadiers, Scots Guards, Coldstreams, Irish Guards—in their perfectly-fitting coats, white leather facings, and heavy bearskin headgear; all picked troops of superb appearance and admirable martial bearing, a joy to any man with the heart of a soldier. And all the troops lining the path of the funeral cortège stood in the attitude of mourning already described.

During my stay I resided, at the special desire of King George, in Buckingham Palace. The widow of the dead King, Queen Alexandra, received me with moving and charming kindness, and talked much with me about bygone days; my recollections stretched back to my childhood, since I, while still a little boy, had been present at the wedding of my dead uncle.

### THE PICHON CONVERSATION

The King gave a banquet to the many princely guests and their suites, as well as for the representatives of foreign nations, at which M. Pichon was also present. He was introduced to me and, in conversation with him, I told him of the wishes which the Imperial Chancellor had communicated to me regarding our interests in Morocco and some other political matters, which M. Pichon readily agreed to carry out. All other combinations connected in various quarters with this talk, belong in the domain of fancy.

Although the period between 1909 and 1914 demanded extraordinary attention to foreign events, interior development was, nevertheless, promoted zealously, and efforts made to meet the demands of commerce, transportation, agriculture, and industry, which were growing rapidly. Unfortunately endeavors in this direction were made much more difficult by the discord among political parties.

The Chancellor wished to accomplish everything possible of accomplishment. But his inclination to get to the bottom of problems and his desire to deal only with what was, from his meticulous critical standpoint, thoroughly matured, tended, in the course of time, to hamper progress. It was difficult to bring him to make decisions before he was thoroughly convinced of their being absolutely free from objection. This made working with him tiresome and aroused in those not close to him the impression of vacillation, whereas, in reality, it was merely overconscientiousness carried too far.

In addition, the Chancellor eventually developed a strong and growing inclination toward domination; in discussions this tended to make him obstinate and caused him to lay down the law to those thinking otherwise as dogmatically as a school teacher. This brought him many enemies and often made things hard for me. A boyhood friend of the Chancellor, to whom I spoke once about this, replied, with a smile, that it had been so with him even in school; there Herr von Bethmann had constantly taught and school-mastered his fellow students, of whom my informant was one, so that finally his classmates had nicknamed him "the governess." He added that this trait was a misfortune for Bethmann, but that it had so grown into his very being that he would never be able to get rid of it.

An example of this is Bethmann's relationship to Herr von Kiderlen, whom he desired to have as Secretary of State, despite my emphatic objections. Herr von Kiderlen was an able worker and a man of strong character, who always sought to assert his independence. He had been about one year in office when Herr von Bethmann came to me one day, complained of Kiderlen's obstinacy and insubordination, and asked me to appeal to his conscience. I declined, with the observation that the Chancellor had chosen Kiderlen against my wishes and must now manage to get along with him; that the maintenance of discipline at the Foreign Office was a duty devolving upon the Chancellor, in which I had no desire to interfere.

### FINDS FAULT WITH BETHMANN

Meanwhile, Bethmann's inadequacy to the post of Chancellor became evident. Deep down in his heart he was a pacifist and was obsessed with the aberration of coming to an understanding with England. I can perfectly well understand that a man of pacifist inclinations should act thus in the hope of avoiding a war thereby. His object was entirely in accord with my policy. The ways and means whereby Bethmann sought to achieve it were, in my opinion, unsuitable. Nevertheless, I backed his endeavors. But I certainly did not believe that real success would result. It became ever more apparent, while he was Chancellor, that he was remote from political realities. Yet he always knew everything better than anybody else. Owing to this overestimation of his own powers he stuck unswervingly to his ideas, even when things all turned out differently from what he had expected.

His reports were always admirably prepared, brilliant in form, and, hence, impressive and attractive. And in this there was an element of danger. In his opinion there was always but one solution, the one which he proposed! The apparent solidity and thoroughness of his reports and suggestions, the illuminating treatment of the matters reported upon from every angle, the references to experts, to foreign and native statesmen and diplomats, etc., easily led to the impression that solely the Bethmann solution was worthy of consideration. In spite of these thorough preparations, he made mistake after mistake.

Thus he had an actual share in our misfortune. When I returned from my Norwegian trip in 1914 he did not place his resignation in my hands, to be sure, but he admitted that his political calculations had gone wrong. Nevertheless, I left him in office, even after his Reichstag speech and the English declaration of war of August 4, 1914, because I considered it most serious to change the highest official in the Empire at the most critical moment in German history. The unanimous attitude of the nation in the face of the challenge from the Entente might have been impaired by such action.

Moreover, both the Chancellor and the chief of the Civil Cabinet maintained that they had the working classes behind them. I was loath to deprive the working classes, which behaved in an exemplary manner in 1914, of the statesman whom, I had been told, they trusted.

The theory, constantly repeated to me in 1914 by the chief of the Civil Cabinet and the representative of the Foreign Office, that only Bethmann had the support of the working classes, was finally supplemented further by reports to me that the Chancellor enjoyed the confidence in foreign countries which was necessary to the conclusion of peace. Thus it came about that Bethmann always stayed in office, until, finally, the Crown Prince made the well-known investigation among the party leaders which showed that the above-mentioned theory was mistaken. This mistake was made all the clearer to me when I read, at the time of Bethmann's dismissal—to which other factors also contributed—the most unfavorable opinions of him, especially in the Social Democratic and Democratic press.

I do not wish to blame Bethmann with these frank remarks, nor to exonerate others; but, when such important matters are discussed, personal considerations must be ignored. I never doubted the nobility of Bethmann's sentiments.

May I be allowed to say a few words here concerning the reform in the Prussian franchise, since the handling of this by Herr von Bethmann is characteristic of his policy of vacillation. During the winter of 1914-15, when, following the brilliant summer campaign, the hard, severe winter trench-fighting had brought military movements to a standstill, the extraordinary achievements of all the troops and the spirit which I had found among officers and men, both at the front and in the hospitals, made such a profound impression on me that I resolved to provide, for the tried, magnificent "Nation in Arms," something in the political domain, when it returned home, which should prove that I recognized what it had done and wished to give the nation joy.

I often touched upon this theme in conversations and suggested reforms in the Prussian franchise; the man, said I, who returned home, after a struggle like this, with the Iron Cross—perhaps of both classes—must no longer be "classified" at the polls.

At this juncture a memorial was submitted to me by Herr von Loebell which proposed a reform in the Prussian franchise on similar grounds. The concise, clear, and convincing treatment of the subject pleased me so much that I had a number of gentlemen read the memorial, which took up, in its original form, only general points of view, without going into detail, and I was pleased to see that it found approval with all whom I questioned concerning it.

I had my thanks expressed to Herr von Loebell through the chief of the Cabinet, von Valentini, and caused Loebell to work out the matter in detail and make suggestions. This was done in the spring of 1915. The memorial was very thorough and dealt with a number of possibilities for the franchise, without advising any one system. It was approved by me, and sent by the chief of the Cabinet to the Chancellor, with the command that it be discussed, in the course of the year, by the Ministers, and that their vote on it—possibly, also, some suggestions from them—be laid before me. The franchise law, of course, was not to be proposed until after the conclusion of peace.

### EARLY GERMAN VICTORIES

Immediately after that I went to Pless. The battle of Gorlice-Tarnow, with its smashing victory over the enemy, brought on the Galician-Polish campaign, leading to the reconquest of Lemberg, Przemysl and the capture of Warsaw, Ivangorod, Modlin, Brest-Litovsk, etc., and completely engaged my attention.

The *Lusitania* case, too, cast its shadow over events, and Italy severed her alliance with us. So it is not to be wondered at if the franchise memorial was pushed into the background.

The next winter, and the summer of 1916, likewise, with their fighting on all fronts, the terrible battle of the Somme, and the brilliant Rumanian autumn and winter campaign, took me to all sorts of places on the western and eastern fronts, even as far as Nisch—where the first memorable meeting with the Bulgarian Tsar took place—and to Orsova, so that I had no opportunity to take up the matter of franchise reform with the care that its importance demanded.

In the spring of 1917 I asked the Chancellor to draw up an announcement of the reform, to be made to the nation at Easter, since I assumed that the Ministers had long since discussed it. The Chancellor drew up the text of the proclamation at Hamburg, in agreement with the chief of the Cabinet and myself; he proposed that the method of voting be left open for the time being, since he was not yet quite sure about this. The Easter proclamation appeared; it was based, like previous treatments of the matter, on the idea that the reform was not to be introduced until after the conclusion of peace, because most of the voters were away facing the enemy.

Party and press did what they could to postpone the accomplishment of my purpose by recriminations and strife, by bringing up the question of the Prussian Reichstag franchise, and by the demand for the introduction of the franchise bill while the war was still in progress. Thus the question embarked upon its well-known and not very pleasant course, which dragged itself out on account of the interminable negotiations in the Landtag. It was not until after the retirement of Herr von Bethmann that I learned through Loebell that the memorial of 1915 had never been submitted to the Ministers, but had lain untouched for a year and a half in a desk drawer; that the Chancellor, influenced by the desires expressed in the country, had dropped the various systems proposed and concentrated upon the general (Reichstag) franchise, of the eventual introduction of which he was, doubtless, inwardly convinced.

In any event, the original basic idea was thoroughly bungled by Bethmann's dilatoriness and the strife among the parties. What I wanted was to present a gift of honor, of my own free will, on its triumphal return home, to my victorious army, to my "Nation in Arms," my brave Prussians, with whom I had stood before the enemy.

### CHANCELLOR'S DIPLOMATIC POWER

One of the results of Bethmann's marked inclination toward control was that the Secretary of State for Foreign Affairs was, under him, a mere helper, so much so that the Foreign Office was almost affiliated with the office of the Chancellor, a state of affairs that made itself felt most especially in the use made of the press department. Bethmann likewise asserted his independence decidedly in his relations with me. Basing himself upon the fact that, constitutionally, the Chancellor alone is responsible for foreign policy, he ruled as he pleased. The Foreign Office was allowed to tell me only what the Chancellor wished, so that it happened sometimes that I was not informed concerning important occurrences.

The fact that this was possible is to be laid at the door of the Constitution of the Empire. And this is the right place for saying a word concerning the relations between the Emperor and the Chancellor. In what follows I do not refer to my relationship to Herr von Bethmann, but, quite impersonally, to the difficulties in the relationship of the German Emperor to the Imperial Chancellors, which are caused by the Imperial Constitution.

I wish to call attention to the following points:

1. According to the Constitution of the Empire, the Chancellor is the director and representative of the foreign policy of the Empire, for which he assumes full responsibility; he has this policy carried out by the Foreign Office, which is subordinated to him, after he has reported on it to the Emperor.

2. The Emperor has influence on foreign policy only in so far as the Chancellor grants it to him.

3. The Emperor can bring his influence to bear through discussions, information, suggestion, proposals, reports, and impressions received by him on his travels, which then take rank as a supplement to the political reports of the ambassadors or ministers to the countries which he has personally visited.

4. The Chancellor *may* act pursuant to such action by the Emperor, and may make it the basis of his decisions, whenever he is in agreement with the Emperor's point of view. Otherwise he is supposed to maintain *his own* point of view and carry it out (Kruger dispatch).

5. According to the Constitution, the Emperor has no means of compelling the Chancellor or the Foreign Office to accept his views. He cannot cause the Chancellor to adopt a policy for which the latter feels that he cannot assume responsibility. Should the Emperor stick to his view, the Chancellor can offer his resignation or demand that he be relieved of his post.

6. On the other hand, the Emperor has no constitutional means of hindering the Chancellor or the Foreign Office from carrying out a policy which he thinks doubtful or mistaken. All he can do, if the Chancellor insists, is to make a change in the Chancellorship.

7. Every change of Chancellors, however, is a serious matter, deeply affecting the life of the nation, and hence, at a time of political complications and high tension, an extremely serious step, an ultima ratio (last resort) which is all the more daring in that the number of men qualified to fill this abnormally difficult post is very small.

The position of the Imperial Chancellor, which was based on the towering personality of Prince Bismarck, had assumed a serious preponderance through the constantly growing number of posts under the Empire, over all of which the Chancellor was placed as chief and responsible head.

### DISCLAIMS RESPONSIBILITY

If this is borne in mind, it is absolutely impossible that anybody should still hold the Emperor alone responsible for everything, as was done formerly, especially toward the end of the war and after the war, by critical know-it-alls and carping revolutionists, both at home and in the Entente countries. That, quite apart from everything personal, is a proof of complete ignorance of the earlier Constitution of the German Empire.

The visit of the Tsar to Potsdam in November, 1910, went off to the satisfaction of all concerned, and was utilized by the Chancellor and Herr von Kiderlen to get into touch with the newly appointed Foreign Minister, Sazonoff, whom the Tsar had brought with him. Apparently, the Russian ruler enjoyed himself among us, and he took an active part in the hunt arranged in his honor, at which he proved himself an enthusiastic huntsman. The result of the conferences between the two statesmen seemed to promise well for the future; both, after they had felt each other out, harbored the hope of favorable relations between the two countries.

During my spring visit to Corfu, the Melissori troubles began, which riveted Greek attention upon themselves. Corfu was well informed of the constant smuggling of arms from Italy by way of

Valona into Albania, and there was a feeling in Greek circles that machinations from across the Adriatic, as well as from Montenegro, were not without responsibility for what was happening. It was also felt that the new Turkish Government had not been wise in its handling of the Albanians, who were very sensitive and suspicious; the former Sultan Abdul-Hamid had realized this very well and understood admirably how to get along with the Albanians and to keep them quiet. Nevertheless, there was no fear that more serious complications would ensue.

At the beginning of 1911 I received a most cordial invitation from King George of England to be present at the unveiling of the statue of Queen Victoria, the grandmother of both of us. Therefore I went in the middle of May to London with the Empress and our daughter. The reception on the part of the English royal family and the people of London was cordial.

The unveiling festivities were well arranged and very magnificent. The big, round space in front of Buckingham Palace was surrounded by grandstands, which were filled to overflowing by invited guests. In front of them were files of soldiers of all arms and all regiments of the British army, in full parade uniform, the cavalry and artillery being on foot. All the banners of the troops were arrayed at the foot of the statue.

The royal family, with their guests and their suites, was grouped around the statue. King George made a dedication speech which had a good effect, in which he made mention also of the German Imperial couple.

Then, amid salutes and greetings, the statue was unveiled; the Queen, in marble, seated upon a throne, became visible, surmounted by a golden figure of victory. It was an impressive moment. Afterward the troops marched past, the Guards in the van, then the Highlanders—who, with their gayly colored, becoming costume, gave an especially picturesque touch to the military spectacle—then the rest of the soldiers. The march past was carried out on the circular space, with all the troops constantly wheeling: the outer wings had to step out, the inner to hold back—a most difficult task for troops. The evolution was carried out brilliantly; not one man made a mistake. The Duke of Connaught, who had made all the military arrangements, deservedly won unanimous applause.

### FESTIVITIES IN ENGLAND

The remainder of our stay in England was devoted to excursions; we also enjoyed the hospitality of noble English families, at whose homes there was an opportunity to hold intercourse with many members of English nobility.

Special enjoyment in the domain of art was provided by the King to his guests by a theatrical performance at Drury Lane Theater. A well-known English play, "Money," was performed, by a company especially assembled for the occasion, consisting of the leading actors and actresses of

London. As a surprise, a curtain fell between the acts, painted especially for the occasion by a lady, which depicted King George and me, life size, on horseback, riding toward each other and saluting militarily. The picture was executed with much dash and was enthusiastically acclaimed by the audience.

The performance of the actors and actresses in "Money" was veritably masterly, since all concerned played their rôles, even the smallest, to perfection. In fact, it was a classic performance.

Another day I attended, at the Olympia track, the sports of the British army and navy, which included admirable individual feats on foot and horseback, as well as evolutions by bodies of troops in close formation.

In describing the unveiling of the statue, as well as the funeral of King Edward VII, I have concerned myself purposely with the externals and pomp that are characteristic of such occasions in England. They show that, in a land under parliamentary rule, a so-called democratic land, more importance is attached to well-nigh medieval magnificence than in the young German Empire.

The French actions in Morocco, which were no longer such as could be reconciled with the Algeciras Agreement, had once more engaged the attention of the diplomats. For this reason the Chancellor had requested me to find out, as soon as opportunity should arise, what King George thought about the situation.

I asked him if he thought that the French

methods were still in accordance with the Algeciras Agreement. The King remarked that the agreement, to tell the truth, no longer was in force, and that the best thing to do would be to forget it; that the French, fundamentally, were doing nothing different in Morocco from what the English had previously done in Egypt; that, therefore, England would place no obstacles in the path of the French, but would let them alone; that the thing to do was to recognize the "fait accompli" of the occupation of Morocco and make arrangements, for commercial protection, with France.

To the very end the visit went off well, and the inhabitants of London, of all social strata, expressed their good will every time the guests of their King showed themselves.

Thus the German Imperial couple was enabled to return home with the best of impressions. When I informed the Chancellor of these, he expressed great satisfaction. From the remarks of King George he drew the inference that England considered the Algeciras Agreement no longer valid and would not place any obstacles in the way of the French occupation of Morocco.

From this the policy followed by him and the Foreign Office arose which led to the Agadir case, the last and equally unsuccessful attempt to maintain our influence in Morocco. The situation became more serious during the Kiel regatta week. The Foreign Office informed me of its intention to send the *Panther* to Agadir. I gave expression to strong misgivings as to this step, but had to drop them in view of the urgent representations of the Foreign Office.

In the first half of 1912 came the sending of Sir Ernest Cassel with a verbal note in which England offered to remain neutral in case of an "unprovoked" attack upon Germany, provided Germany agreed to limit her naval construction program and to drop her new Naval bill, the latter being darkly hinted at. Owing to our favorable answer to this Lord Haldane was intrusted with the negotiations and sent to Berlin. The negotiations finally fell through, owing to the constantly more uncompromising attitude of England (Sir E. Grey), who finally disavowed Lord Haldane and withdrew his own verbal note, because Grey was afraid to offend the French by a German-English agreement and jeopardize the Anglo-French-Russian understanding.

Here are the details of the case:

On the morning of January 29, 1912, Herr Ballin had himself announced to me at the palace in Berlin and asked for an audience. I assumed that it was a case of a belated birthday greeting, therefore I was not a little astonished when Ballin, after a short speech of congratulation, said that he had come as an emissary of Sir Ernest Cassel, who had just arrived in Berlin on a special mission and wished to be received.

I asked whether it was a political matter, and why, if so, the meeting had not been arranged through the English ambassador. Ballin's answer was to the effect that, from hints dropped by Cassel, he knew the matter to be of great importance, and the explanation for Cassel's acting without the intervention of the ambassador was because the earnest desire had been expressed in London that the official diplomatic representatives, both the English and the German, should not be apprised of the affair.

I declared that I was ready to receive Cassel at once, but added that, should his mission have to do with political questions, I should immediately summon the Chancellor, since I was a constitutional monarch and not in a position to deal with the representative of a foreign power alone without the Chancellor.

Ballin fetched Cassel, who handed me a document which, he stated, had been prepared with the "approval and knowledge of the English Government." I read the short note through and was not a little surprised to see that I was holding in my hand a formal offer of neutrality in case Germany became involved in future warlike complications, conditioned upon certain limitations in the carrying out of our program of naval construction, which were to be the subject of mutual conferences and agreements. Walking with Ballin into the next room, I handed over the document for him to read. After he had done so both of us exclaimed in the same breath: "A verbal note!"

It was plainly apparent that this "verbal note" was aimed at the forthcoming addition to our Naval law and designed in some way to delay or frustrate it. No matter how the matter was interpreted, I found myself confronted with a peculiar situation, which also amazed Ballin. It reminded me of the situation at Cronberg-Friedrichshof in 1905, when I was obliged to decline the demand, made to me personally by the English Under Secretary, Hardinge, that we should forego our naval construction.

### SURPRISE AT BRITISH NOTE

Now, an intimate business friend of Edward VII appears, without previous announcement through official diplomatic channels, before the German Emperor with a "verbal note" inspired by the English Government, with explicit instructions to evade all the diplomatic officials of both countries. He hands over an offer from the English Government to maintain neutrality in future warlike complications provided certain agreements regarding limitation of naval construction are made. And this is done by England, the mother of "Constitutionalism"! When I pointed this out to Ballin, he exclaimed: "Holy Constitutionalism! What has become of you? That is 'personal politics' with a vengeance!"

I agreed with Ballin to send at once for Herr von Bethmann, in order that he might learn what was transpiring and decide what to do in this peculiar situation.

Bethmann was called up on the telephone and soon appeared. At first the situation aroused in him likewise a certain degree of astonishment; it was interesting to watch the play of expression on his face as he was told about the matter. The Chancellor suggested that Grand Admiral von Tirpitz also be summoned, for the proper dispatching of the business, and recommended that an answer be drawn up in English, in the same manner and form as the note delivered by Cassel, and that it be handed to Sir Ernest, who wished to return home that night. (English was chosen because there was fear of obscurity and misunderstanding if the note were translated in London.) The Chancellor asked me to draw up the note, since I knew English best. After some objection I had to make up my mind to be myself the writer of the answer.

And now the following scene took place:

I sat at the writing table in the adjutant's room; the other gentlemen stood around me. I would read a sentence from the note aloud and sketch out an answer, which was, in turn, read aloud. Then criticisms were made from right and left: one thought the sentence too complaisant, another too abrupt; it was thereupon remodeled, recast, improved, and polished. The Chancellor particularly subjected my grammar and style to much torture, owing to his habit of probing things philosophically, to his methods of profound thoroughness, which caused him to be most particular with every word, in order that it, having been studied from every angle, should later on afford nobody cause for criticism.

After hours of work the note was finally finished and, having been passed a couple of times from hand to hand and then read aloud by me half a dozen times more, it was signed.

When our group broke up, the Chancellor asked Sir Ernest who was to be expected from England to conduct the negotiations. Cassel replied that it would certainly be a Minister, which one he did not know—perhaps Mr. Winston Churchill, Minister of the Navy, since the question was a naval one. Then the Chancellor arranged further with him that the unofficial method should be retained and that Ballin should undertake to transmit all the news regarding the matter which should emanate from England.

Sir Ernest expressed his lively gratitude for his cordial reception and his satisfaction at the tenor of our reply. Later Ballin informed me from his hotel that Cassel had expressed himself as completely satisfied over the successful outcome of his mission, and that he would report to his Government the good impression made upon him.

When I thereupon conferred on the matter with Admiral von Tirpitz we both agreed that the Naval bill was in danger and, therefore, that we must be very careful.

### DIPLOMATIC PREPAREDNESS

In perfect secrecy the material was collected which Admiral von Tirpitz was to present at the negotiations; it consisted of a short historical sketch of the development of the fleet and of the increasingly difficult tasks devolving upon it; the Naval law and its aims, nature, enactment, and extension; finally, the contemplated Naval bill, its meaning and the method of putting it through.

The Chancellor asked that the main negotiations should be conducted at the palace in my presence. In addition, I agreed with Admiral von Tirpitz that he should speak English, as far as possible, and that I, in case of difficult technical expressions, would interpret.

Until England made known the name of the negotiator, our time was spent in suppositions, and Ballin informed us of combinations in connection with which a number of names, even that of Grey, came up.

At last the news arrived, through Ballin, that Haldane—the Minister of War, previously a lawyer—had been intrusted with the conduct of the negotiations and would soon arrive. General amazement! Just imagine, "mutatis mutandis," that Germany had sent her Minister of War (at that time von Heeringen) to London, instead of Admiral von Tirpitz, for the discussion of a naval matter!

When this point was discussed with Bethmann and Tirpitz a number of suppositions were advanced; the Chancellor said that Haldane was known in England as a student of Goethe and as a man versed in German philosophy and knowing the German language, so that his choice was a piece of politeness toward us. Tirpitz observed that Haldane had formerly spent some time in Berlin and worked with General von Einem at the War Ministry, and hence knew the state of affairs in Germany. I suggested that all that was very well, but that the choice of Haldane showed that England looked upon the question as purely political, since he knew only superficially about naval affairs; that the whole thing was probably directed against Germany's naval policy in general and the new Naval bill in particular; that it would be well, therefore, not to forget this, in order that the whole thing might not develop into a foreign assault upon our right of self-determination as to the strength of our defensive measures.

Haldane arrived and was received as an Imperial guest. Ballin, who accompanied him, solved the riddle of Haldane's choice on the basis of information received by him from England.

He said that when Cassel had got back to London, reported on his reception, and handed over the German reply, the impression made was so favorable that no further doubt was entertained there as to the satisfactory course of the negotiations and their conclusion in the form of an agreement; that, thereupon a keen dispute had arisen among the Ministers, especially between Churchill and Grey, as to who should go to Berlin and affix his name to this great historical document, in case the object should be achieved of making Germany completely give up the further development of her fleet; that Churchill thought himself the right man for the job, since he was at the head of the navy. But Grey and Asquith would not let their colleague reap the glory, and, for this reason, Grey stood for a while in the foreground—another proof that it was politics rather than the number of ships which was to play the leading rôle.

### SELECTION OF CHURCHILL

After a while, however, it was decided that it was more fitting to Grey's personal and official importance to appear only at the termination of the negotiations, to affix his name to the agreement, and—as it was put in the information transmitted from England to Ballin—"to get his dinner from the Emperor and to come in for his part of the festivities and fireworks"—which, in good German, means to enjoy the "Bengal light illumination."

As it had been decided that Churchill was not to get this in any event, it was necessary to choose somebody for the negotiations who was close to Asquith and Grey and who, possessing their complete confidence, was willing to conduct the negotiations as far as the beginning of the "fireworks"; one who, moreover, was already known at Berlin and not a stranger in Germany. Churchill, to be sure, qualified in this, for he had been present a few times at the Imperial maneuvers in Silesia and Württemberg as a guest of the Emperor. Ballin guaranteed the reliability of his London source of information.

Before the negotiations began I once more pointed out to Secretary of State von Tirpitz that Haldane, in spite of being just then Minister of War, probably had prepared himself for his task, and had surely received careful instructions from the English Admiralty, in which the spirit of Fisher was paramount. In his *Handbook for English Naval Officers,* Fisher had stated, among other precepts well worthy of being remembered, one which is characteristic of the Admiral, his department and its spirit, which runs, word for word, as follows: "If you tell a lie, stick to it."

Moreover, I said to Tirpitz, we must not forget what an amazing adaptability the Anglo-Saxons had, which fitted them for occupying positions which had no relation to their previous life and training. Furthermore, the interest in England in the navy was generally so intense that almost every educated man was an expert up to a certain point on naval questions.

In the course of the negotiations Haldane proved himself admirably well informed and a skillful, tenacious debater, and his brilliant qualities as a lawyer came to the fore. The conversation lasted several hours, and brought about a general clarifying, as well as a preliminary agreement as to postponement of time limits of ship construction, etc. The details concerning it are deposited in documents at the Imperial Naval Office. Tirpitz was splendid.

After some more conferences—at which, likewise, Ballin was present—Haldane returned to England. Ballin informed me that Haldane had expressed himself to him as entirely satisfied with the outcome of his mission, and had stated that in about a week or two the first draft of the agreement could be sent to us.

Time passed—the date set for the introduction of the Naval bill approached. Tirpitz suggested, in case the agreement were concluded previously, that the Naval bill be altered accordingly; otherwise, that it be introduced without alteration.

### SUSPECTS ENGLISH PURPOSES

At last we received, not the draft of the agreement, but a document asking all sorts of questions and expressing a desire for all sorts of data, a reply to which required many consultations and much reflection. Little by little the suspicion grew in me that the English were not in earnest with regard to the agreement, since question followed question and details were sought which had nothing directly to do with the agreement. England withdrew more and more from her promises, and no draft of the agreement came to hand.

In Berlin a big agitation set in against the Naval bill, Tirpitz and myself on the part of the Foreign Office, and from other quarters, both qualified and unqualified. The Chancellor also, who hoped to achieve the agreement and affix his name to a document which would free Germany from "encirclement" and bring her into a regular and better relationship with England, came out in favor of dropping the Naval bill. But that would simply have meant allowing a foreign power enormous influence in matters of German national defense and jeopardizing thereby the national right of self-determination and our readiness for battle in case of a war being forced upon us. Had we allowed this it would have amounted to our consenting to permit England, Germany's principal foe, to grant us whatever she wished, after consulting her own interests, without receiving ourselves the guaranty of any equivalent concession.

In this confused state of affairs differences of opinion and violent disputes arose, which, especially in those circles which really knew little about the navy, were conducted with much violence and not always in a practical manner. Admiral von Tirpitz, all through that winter, which was so hard a one for him and me, fought his fight like a genuine, patriotic officer, realizing the situation and seeing through his opponents with clear vision and supporting me with complete conviction to the limit of his ability. All the Government officials agreed that no foreign country could be allowed any voice in helping decide what we had or had not to do toward insuring our protection.

The hope of bringing about the agreement grew ever fainter; England continually showed lessening interest and kept eliminating important parts of her original verbal note. And so it came about that Admiral von Tirpitz and I realized that the whole proposal was merely a "maneuver."

The fight over the German Naval bill grew steadily hotter. I happened at this time to meet at Cuxhaven Doctor von Burchard, President of the Hamburg Senate, whom I respected greatly, as he was the very model of an aristocratic citizen of a Hanseatic city, and who had often been consulted by me in political matters. I described to him the entire course of the affair and the disputes in Berlin as to the introduction or nonintroduction of the bill, and asked him then to tell me, with his usual complete frankness, what he thought the right thing to do in the interest of the national welfare, since I greatly desired to hear an objective opinion, uninfluenced by the rival camps of Berlin.

Doctor Burchard replied in his clear, keen, pointed, convincing manner that it was my duty toward the people and the fatherland to stick to the bill; that whosoever spoke against its introduction was committing a sin against them; that whatever we thought necessary to our defense must be unconditionally brought into being; that, above all else, we must never permit a foreign country to have the presumption to interfere with us; that the English offer was a feint to make us drop the Naval bill; that this must, in no circumstances, be allowed; that the German nation would not understand why its right of self-determination had been sacrificed; that the bill must unquestionably be introduced; that he would work in its favor in the Federal Council (as indeed he did in a brilliant, compelling speech) and also otherwise press its acceptance in Berlin; that the English would naturally resort to abuse, but that this made no difference, since they had been doing so for a long time; that they certainly would not get into a war for such a cause; that Admiral von Tirpitz was merely doing his duty and fulfilling his obligations, and that I should support him in every way; that the Chancellor must give up opposing the measure, otherwise he would run the risk of finally forfeiting public esteem on account of being "pro-English."

Thus spoke the representative of the great commercial city, which was threatened before all others in case of war with England. The genuine Hanseatic spirit inspired his words.

Strangely enough, this opinion of Doctor Burchard concerning the English offer has recently been corroborated to me in Holland by a Dutchman who heard from Englishmen at that time the English point of view. I and Tirpitz guessed right—the offer of neutrality, in case naval expansion was curbed, was a political maneuver.

### COUNTERCHARGES OF CHEATING

Soon news also came from Ballin that the matter was not going well in England: that, according to information received, a dispute had arisen about the agreement; that there was dissatisfaction with Haldane, who, it was said, had let himself be cheated by Tirpitz! This was plain evidence of the indignation felt because Tirpitz had not walked into the trap and simply let the bill drop, and that Haldane had been unable to serve up the bill to the English Cabinet on a platter at tea time. It is useless to say that there was any "cheating" on Germany's part, but the reproach leveled at Haldane justifies the suspicion that his instructions were that *he* should seek to "cheat" the Germans.

Since his fellow countrymen thought that the reverse was true, one can but thank Admiral von Tirpitz most sincerely for having correctly asserted the German standpoint to the benefit of our fatherland.

Toward the end of March the fight about the bill took on such violence that finally the Chancellor, on the 22d, asked me for his dismissal as I stepped out of the vault in the Charlottenburg Park. After long consultation and after I had told him Doctor Burchard's view, the Chancellor withdrew his request.

When, some time afterward, I paid a visit to Herr von Bethmann in his garden, I found him quite overcome and holding in his hand a message from London. It contained the entire disavowal of the verbal note delivered by Cassel, the withdrawal of the offer of neutrality, as well as of every other offer, and at the end the advice that I dismiss Herr von Bethmann from the Imperial Chancellorship, since he enjoyed to a marked degree the confidence of the British Government! Tears of anger shone in the eyes of the Chancellor, thus badly deceived in his hopes; the praise accorded to him by a foreign government with which Germany and he had just had such painful experiences hurt him deeply. For the second time he offered me his resignation; I did not accept it, but sought to console him. I then ordered that the ambassador in London be asked how he could have accepted and forwarded such a message under any conditions.

Now the Chancellor was in favor of the bill, but it was honorably proposed with the limitation which it had been decided to impose upon it in case of the conclusion of the agreement. In England, on the other hand, the full naval construction program was carried out.

This "Haldane episode" is characteristic of England's policy. This whole maneuver, conceived on a large scale, was engineered for the sole purpose of hampering the development of the German fleet, while, simultaneously, in America, which had an almost negligible merchant fleet; in France, whose navy was superior in numbers to the German; in Italy, in Russia, which also had ships built abroad—vast construction programs were carried out without eliciting one word of protest from England. And Germany, wedged in between France and Russia, certainly had to be at least prepared to defend herself on the water against those nations.

### DEFENDS NAVAL PROGRAM

For this our naval construction program was absolutely necessary; it was never aimed against the English fleet, four or five times as strong as ours, and assuring England's superiority and security, to equal the strength of which no sensible man in Germany ever dreamed. We needed our fleet for coast defense and the protection of our commerce; for this purpose the lesser means of defense, like U-boats, torpedo boats, and mines, were not sufficient. In addition the coast batteries on the Baltic were so antiquated and miserably equipped that they would have been razed within forty-eight hours by the massed fire of the heavy guns of modern battleships. Thus, our Baltic coast was practically defenseless. To protect it the fleet was necessary.

The Skagerrak (Jutland) battle has proved what the fleet meant and what it was worth. That battle would have meant annihilation for England if the Reichstag had not refused up to 1900 all proposals for strengthening the navy. Those twelve lost years were destined never to be retrieved.

Before we take our leave of Haldane I wish to touch upon another episode in his activities. In 1906 he came, with the permission of the German Government, to Berlin, to inform himself concerning the Prussian defense conditions, recruiting, General Staff, etc. He busied himself at the Ministry of War, where the Minister, General von Einem, personally gave him information. After about two or three weeks' work there he returned, well satisfied, to England.

When, after the outbreak of the World War, the "pro-German" Haldane, the friend of Goethe, was boycotted and treated with such hostility that he could no longer show himself in public, he had a defense written of his term of office as Minister of War by the well-known littérateur and journalist, Mr. Begbie, entitled *Vindication of Great Britain.* Therein his services toward forming a regular General Staff and preparing the British army for the World War are placed in a bright light and emphasis is laid on the skill with which he utilized the permission obtained from the Prussian War Ministry in order to learn in Germany about military matters and to reorganize the British army and General Staff, to the minutest detail and on the German model, for the coming war against the erstwhile German hosts.

Here we see the sly, adroit lawyer, who, sheltered under the hospitality of a foreign country, studies its military arrangements in order to forge weapons against it out of the material and knowledge thus acquired. Quite characteristically the book is dedicated to King Edward VII, whose intimate, emissary, and tool Haldane was. In those days Berlin saw in Haldane's mission a "rapprochement" with England, toward which Germans were always bending their efforts; in reality, however, it was a "reconnoitering expedition" under the very roof of the German cousin. England showed her gratitude by the World War, which Haldane helped to prepare; in this case Haldane "cheated" the Germans!

That is the history of the Haldane mission. Later it was summarily maintained by all sorts of ignorant dabblers in politics, belonging to the press and the general public, that the promising "rapprochement" with England through Haldane had been wrecked by the obstinacy of the Emperor and Admiral von Tirpitz and by their clinging to the Naval bill against the wishes of all "sensible counselors!"

### KINGSHIP OF ALBANIA

At that time [in 1912] the question of the establishment of an independent Albanian state and the choice by the Powers of a head for it, was brought to my attention also. A number of candidates lusting for a crown had already presented themselves before the tribunal of the Powers, without getting themselves accepted; a number of candidates, considered by the Powers, were declined by the Albanians. I looked upon the matter in itself with indifference, and was of the opinion that—as in the case of every "creation of a nation"—the greatest possible attention should be paid to historical development, also to geographical peculiarities and the customs of the inhabitants.

In this peculiar land there has never been any united nation under one ruler and one dynasty. In valleys, encircled and cut off by high mountain ranges, the Albanian tribes live separated to a considerable degree from one another. Their political system is not unlike the clan system of the Scotch. Christians and Mohammedans are represented in equal numbers.

The custom of "vendetta" is an ancient one, sanctified by tradition, which is no less true of robbery and cattle stealing. Agriculture is still in a backward stage of development, farming is in its infancy, the implements used therein date from before the flood.

The head man of the clan dispenses justice in the open, under the village tree, as it used to be done once upon a time among the ancient Germans. Every man is armed and most are excellent shots. Whenever the head man of the clan turns up while on a horseback tour through his territory in some hamlet, the inhabitants expect a blessing from him in the form of jingling coins, which sometimes are scattered about by him from the saddle. This, of course, is particularly customary at the outset of a new Government's term, and great is the dissatisfaction when it does not happen.

Up to the time of the Balkan War many Albanians entered the Turkish service, where they rose to high importance, being greatly prized on account of their diligence and keen intelligence, as well as their tenacious energy. They supplied the Turkish administration with a large number of officials, also with a certain percentage in the diplomatic corps and the army. The young Albanian nobles were proud to serve in a splendid company of palace guards of the Sultan, which scarcely had an equal for size, martial appearance, and manly beauty. These were partly relatives of the Sultan, since the latter used to have noble Albanian women of the principal clans in his harem in order that he—protected by blood brotherhood—might be safe from the "vendettas" of the clans, and, also, that he might find out everything that might serve to influence the feelings of the Albanian chieftains. The desires of the Albanians which reached him by this road—for instance, as to supplies of arms and ammunition, school houses, building of highways, etc.—were thereupon granted in an inconspicuous manner. Thus the Sultan was enabled to keep the usually turbulent Albanians quiet and loyal by means of "family ties."

With this knowledge of the state of affairs as a foundation, I sought to bring my influence to bear toward having a Mohammedan Prince chosen, if possible—perhaps an Egyptian Prince—not forgetting that he should have a well-lined purse, which is an absolute necessity in Albania. My advice was not heeded by the "Areopagus of the Powers," whose members were not bothering themselves with the interests of the Albanians, but seeking, first of all, for pretexts and opportunities for fishing in the troubled Albanian waters in such a way as to benefit their own countries.

### OPPOSED CHOICE OF GERMAN

Therefore, I was not at all pleased when the choice fell upon Prince William of Wied. I esteemed him as a distinguished, knightly man of lofty sentiments, but considered him unfitted for the post. The Prince knew altogether too little about Balkan affairs to be able to undertake this thorny task with hope of success. It was particularly unpleasant to me that a German Prince should make a fool of himself there, since it was apparent from the start that the Entente would place all sorts of obstacles in his path. Upon being questioned by the Prince, I told my cousin all my doubts, laying stress upon the difficulties awaiting him, and advised him urgently to decline. I could not command him, since the Prince of Wied, as head of the family, had the final word in the matter.

After the Prince's acceptance of the candidacy offered him by the Powers, I received him in the presence of the Chancellor. A certain irresolution in the bearing of the Prince, who contemplated his new task with anything but enthusiasm, strengthened the resolve in me and the Chancellor to try hard once more to dissuade the young candidate from ascending the recently invented Albanian "throne." But in vain. The ambitious, mystically excited wife of the Prince saw in Albania the fulfillment of her wishes. And "ce que femme veut, Dieu le veut" ("what woman wishes, God wishes").

Carmen Sylva [the Queen of Rumania] also worked toward having him accept; she went so far, in fact, as to publish an article in the newspapers beginning "Fairyland Wants Its Prince."

So even the best meant warnings were useless. I had also strongly advised the Prince not to go to Albania before the settlement of the financial question, since the reasons which had led me to suggest the selection of a rich ruler now came to the fore. The Prince was not very wealthy and the Powers had to supply him with a "donation," concerning the amount of which, and the method of paying it by installments, an unpleasant quarrel arose. At last a part payment was made.

Danger lurked for the Prince and his eventual

Government in the person of Essad Pasha, an unreliable, intriguing, greedy soldier of fortune, who himself had designs on the Albanian throne and held sway over a certain number of armed adherents. From the start he was an opponent of the new Prince and he plotted secretly with Italy, which was not favorably inclined toward the Prince of Wied. Now, it would have been quite natural and a matter of course if the new ruler had taken with him in his suite men from Germany whom he knew and who were faithful to him. But he did not. An Englishman and an Italian were attached to his person as "secretaries" and they had nothing better to do than to work against his interests, to give him bad advice and to intrigue against him.

### REQUIREMENTS OF A RULER

During the time that the Prince of Wied was making his preparations the excellently written pamphlet of an Austrian General Staff officer, dealing with his travels in Albania, appeared. The officer described, in a lively and clear style, the geographical and climatic drawbacks, the population and customs, the general poverty and backwardness of the land.

He pointed out that a future ruler of the land must in no circumstances reside on the coast, but must show himself to the inhabitants and travel about in the country. Owing to the primitive means of transportation, he went on, the lord of the land must sit all day on horseback and ride through his domain, having at his saddle bow the famous "bag of sequins" mentioned in all Oriental tales and legends, in order to sway public opinion in his favor in the places visited by the expected shower of gold. The ruler must be sure, the author continued, to bind some of the clans of the region closely to himself, so as to have at his beck and call an armed force for asserting his will and overcoming any opponents wishing to rebel, since this was the only way to maintain his power, in view of the utter lack of "troops" or an "army" in the European sense of the word.

This meant that the ruler of Albania must lead at first a nomadic, horseback life, and, in addition, provide himself with a wandering camp, with tents and other accessories and the necessary horses. Plenty of men adapted to this sort of life might have been found in his squadron of the Third Guard Uhlan Regiment, since many of his Uhlans, who were very fond of the Prince, had declared that they were ready to accompany him as volunteers. Surely, they would have served him better and been more useful to him than what he did in preparing to take over the overlordship of Albania, without knowledge of the country.

I advised my cousin urgently to study this pamphlet and to follow its recommendations, especially with regard to his residence, which should be fixed at some point as far as possible from the warships of the Powers, in order that he might not be forced to act under their pressure and arouse suspicion among the Albanians that their ruler needed these ships for protection against his subjects. Did the Prince ever read the pamphlet? In any event, the course adopted by him subsequently was contrary to its advice and the advice given him by me.

The Prince and his wife journeyed to Albania, and things turned out as I had foreseen. According to reports describing the arrival of the sovereign couple, the Princess, although she was a German, addressed the assembled Albanians from her balcony in French, since they understood no German! The "court" remained at Durazzo under the guns of the foreign ships. The Prince did not travel on horseback through the land, nor did he scatter gold sequins about—not even from his balcony on the day of his arrival—nor did he push Essad out of the way. So the adventure ended as one might imagine.

I have gone into some detail in describing my opinion and attitude toward the question of the choice of the ruler of Albania because, from every possible quarter, false rumors have been circulated for the purpose of imputing to me motives which were utterly foreign to me. In this matter, also, I gave honest advice when questioned, based on sound knowledge of mankind.

The year 1912 also witnessed the meeting with the Tsar at Baltisch-Port, whither I repaired on board my yacht at the invitation of Nicholas II. Our two yachts anchored side by side, so that visiting from ship to ship was easy. The Tsar, his children, and his entire entourage vied with one another in evidences of good will and hospitality. The Russian and German escorting squadrons were inspected, turn and turn about, by the Tsar and myself together, and we took our meals either at the Tsar's table or mine.

We spent one morning on land near Baltisch-Port. The Eighty-fifth "Viborg" Infantry Regiment, whose commander I was, had been drawn up in a field and was inspected first in parade formation, then in company and battalion exercises, which were carried out in as satisfactory a manner as was the parade with which the evolutions were brought to a close.

The regiment, composed of four battalions, made an excellent impression. It was in field equipment—brown-gray blouses and caps—and the latter, worn jauntily cocked over one ear by all, gave to the sun-browned, martial faces of the strong young soldiers a bold air which brought joy to the heart of every soldier who gazed upon them.

In the course of the brilliant and uncommonly amiable reception which I met with on this occasion I received no hint of the Balkan alliance, concluded a short time before.

It was my last visit in Russia before the outbreak of the war.

German Postcard from World War 1

# CHAPTER VI

## My Co-workers in the Administration

IT behooves me to remark that I found particular pleasure in working with His Excellency von Stephan and in dealing with him. He was a man of the old school, who fitted in so well with me that he always grasped my ideas and suggestions and afterward carried them out with energy and power, owing to his firm belief in them. A man of iron energy and unflagging capacity for work and joyousness; endowed, moreover, with refreshing humor, quick to perceive new possibilities, never at a loss for expedients, well versed in political and technical matters, he seemed to have been born especially for creative co-operation. I trusted him implicitly, and my trust in him was never betrayed. I learned much from my association with this stimulating, shrewd counselor.

The Post-Office Department reached an unimagined degree of excellence and aroused the admiration of the whole world. The great invention of the telephone was utilized to the limit, was applied extensively to the public service, and was developed so as to facilitate it. Likewise in the domain of building Stephan brought about a decided improvement, which received my approval and support.

All great state building projects depended on the vote of the investigating "Academy of Building," which, at that time, was a slow-moving, cumbrous, and backward body. I had already had experiences of my own with it. The "White Drawing Room," originally merely provisional, had been put up without much attention to style—it had been intended at first for an Indian masquerade, a "Lalla Rookh" festival, in honor of the Grand Duchess Charlotte, daughter of Frederick William III, and her husband, later Tsar Nicholas I. An investigation instituted at my order showed the material to be spurious and inferior; the structure was in the worst possible state of decay and in danger of collapse; a new one was needed.

With the co-operation and collaboration of the Empress Frederick, projects and plans were made, and, finally, a big model was provided by Building Councilor Inne—the "modern Schlüter," as the Empress Frederick used to call him—which won unanimous approval. Only the Building Academy opposed wearisome objections, stating that the "White Drawing Room" ought to be preserved "in its old historical beauty," and required no alterations. When the new structure was completed, however, it also met with the approval of the gentlemen who had been formerly so critical.

Herr von Stephan also was at loggerheads with the Academy of Building. He wanted to alter many post offices, or build entirely new ones, especially in the big cities, but, in view of the fearful slowness and devotion to red tape of the aforesaid official body, he used to receive no answers at all, or else refusals, when he brought these matters to its attention. The rule of thumb was supreme there. Herr von Stephan was of the opinion that, in its buildings as well as in other directions, the youthful German Empire must give an impression of power, and that the Imperial post offices must be built accordingly; he believed that they should harmonize with the general style of the towns where they were located, or, at least, conform to the style of the oldest and most important buildings there. Nor could I do otherwise than agree with such a view.

### ACADEMY'S SHACKLES BROKEN

At last there came a rupture with the aforementioned Academy. His Excellency von Stephan lost patience and informed me that he had freed his office, and the buildings erected by it, from the supervision of the Academy; that he had even formed a committee from among his own architects and officials for supervising purposes; and that all he asked of me was to subject the more important plans for buildings to a final inspection. I did so willingly.

Stephan was an enthusiastic huntsman, so that I had additional opportunities, while on the court hunts, to enjoy association with this refreshing, unchanging, faithful official and counselor.

Among the Ministers whom I particularly esteemed His Excellency Miquel took first place. He it was who, as my Finance Minister, put through for Prussia the great reform which placed the land on a sound basis and helped it toward prosperity. Intercourse with this astute political expert gave me great pleasure, and a wealth of teaching and stimulus.

The degree to which Miquel was versed in all possible matters was astounding. In conversation he was brisk, humorous, and keen in elucidating and arguing on a subject, in addition to which a strong historical bent ran, like a red thread, through his quotations. In history and ancient languages he was marvelously well equipped, so that, in his reports, he was able often to hark back to the times of the Romans and quote from his store of knowledge—not out of Büchmann[1]—pieces of Latin in support of his arguments. Even when he was instructing he was never tiresome on account of his brilliant dialectics, but used to hold his hearers spellbound to the very end.

It was His Excellency Miquel likewise who incited me to favor the great canal projects and supported me when the Prussian Conservatives opposed the Central [Rhine-Weser-Elbe] Canal, and caused the failure of the plan to build it. He lent strength to the King and made the latter decide not to let up in this fight until victory was won. He knew, as I did, what blessings the canals

[1] A German philologist who compiled a well-known book of quotations.

in Holland and the splendid canal network of France had brought to those lands and what a relief they were to the ever more hard-pressed railways. In the World War we might have had a splendid east-to-west artery of transportation for ammunition, wounded, siege material, supplies, and the like, which would have made it possible, by thus relieving the railways, for the latter to transport troops on an even greater scale—moreover, this would have lessened the shortage of coal. In time of peace also, for which the canal was destined, it would have been most beneficial.

Minister von Miquel was a most ardent enthusiast for the Imperial German idea and the German Empire of the Hohenzollerns: I lent an attentive ear to his spirited handling of this theme. He was a man who, clinging to the old tradition, thought in a great German, Imperial way; he was fully adequate to the requirements and demands of the new era, rightly appreciating when these were of value.

From the start I concerned myself with the completion of the railway system. From the reports relating to national defense and the complaints of the General Staff, as well as from personal observation, I knew of the absolutely incredible neglect suffered by East Prussia in the matter of railways. The state of affairs was absolutely dangerous, in view of the steady, though gradual, reinforcing of the Russian troops facing our frontier, and the development of the Russian railway system.

During the last years of his reign Emperor William the Great had commanded Field Marshal Moltke to report on the situation, since the Russian armies, under the influence of France, were being posted ever more conspicuously on the eastern frontier of Prussia, arousing apprehension as to the possibility of irruptions of great masses of Russian cavalry into Prussia, Posen, and Silesia. Quartermaster-General Count Waldersee and I were present at the reading of this report. From it came the resolve to shift Prussian troops eastward and to push toward completion the neglected railway system.

The measures ordained by Emperor William I and begun by him required time, particularly as the new railway bridges over the Vistula and Nogat had to be built by the military authorities in the teeth of strong official opposition (Maybach). Since the railways were considered a "national pocketbook," there was a desire to build only "paying" lines, which caused prejudice against outlays for military lines designed for the defense of the fatherland, since it diminished the fine surplus funds by which such great store was laid.

Not until my reign were the plans of Emperor William I brought to realization. Anyone taking up a railway map of 1888 will be amazed at the lack of railway connection in the east, particularly in East Prussia, especially if he compares it with a 1914 map showing the development in the intervening years. If we had had the old network, we should have lost our eastern territory in 1914.

Unquestionably, Minister von Maybach rendered valuable services in the promotion and development of the railway system. He had to take into account the wishes and demands of the rapidly developing industrial sections of Western Germany, in doing which he naturally considered military desires also, as far as he could. But during his régime Eastern Germany was very badly treated with regard to railway lines, bridges, and rolling stock. Had there been mobilization at that time, it would have been necessary to transfer hundreds of locomotives to the east in order to maintain schedules capable of meeting even part of the requirements of the General Staff. The only means of communication with the east were the two antiquated trestle bridges at Dirschau and Marienburg. The General Staff became insistent, which brought quarrels between it and Maybach.

Not until Minister Thielen came into office was there a change, occasioned by his self-sacrificing work, for which thanks are due him. Realizing correctly what the military requirements were, he pushed forward the completion of the eastern railways. Thielen was an able, diligent, thoroughly reliable official of the old Prussian type, faithful to me and enjoying my high esteem. In common with Miquel, he stood faithfully by the side of his sovereign in the fight for the Central Canal. Characteristic of him were the words which he said in my presence, before a big assembly of people, at the opening of the Elbe-Trave Canal: "The Central Canal must and will be built." Relations between him and me remained harmonious until his retirement.

Despite the railway construction work in the western part of Germany, there were in that region likewise serious gaps in the network of railways, from the point of view of mobilization and deployment of troops, which had long since needed remedying. The Rhine, as far up as Mainz, was crossed by one railway bridge only; the Main could be crossed only at Frankfort. For a long time the General Staff had been demanding the remedying of these conditions. Fortunately, general traffic moved in the same direction—for instance, if a traveler coming from the west wished to reach one of the watering places in the Taunus Mountains, or some place on the railway along the right bank of the Rhine, he had to go as far as Frankfort, and then return in the same direction whence he had come, although at Mainz he had almost been opposite Wiesbaden.

Minister Budde was the man chosen for the accomplishment of this work. As chief of the railway department of the General Staff he had long since attracted my attention by his extraordinary capacity for work, his energy, and his promptness in making decisions. He had often reported to me on the gaps in our railway system, which would hamper quick deployment of troops on two fronts, and always pointed out the preparations being made by Russia and France, which we were in duty bound to meet with preparations of equal scope, in the interests of the national defense.

The first consideration, of course, in railway construction had been the improvement and facilitation of industry and commerce, but it had not been able to meet the immeasurably increased demands of these, since the great network of canals, designed to relieve the railways, was not in existence. The war on two fronts, which threatened us more and more—and for which our railways were, technically speaking, not yet ready, partly from financial-technical reasons—made necessary that more careful attention should be paid to military requirements. Russia was building, with French billions, an enormous network of railways against us, while in France the railways destined to facilitate the deployment of forces against Germany were being indefatigably extended by the completion of three-track lines—something as yet totally unknown in Germany.

Minister Budde set to work without delay. The second great railway bridge over the Rhine at Mainz was constructed, likewise the bridge over the Main at Costheim, and the necessary switches and loops for establishing communication with the line along the right bank of the Rhine, and with Wiesbaden; also the triangle at Biebrich-Mosbach was completed. Budde's talents found brilliant scope in the organization and training of the railway employees, whose numbers had grown until they formed a large army, and in his far-sighted care for his subordinates.

I respected this vigorous, active man with all my heart, and deeply regretted that a treacherous ailment put an end to his career in the very midst of his work.

In His Excellency von Breitenbach I acquired a new and valuable aid and co-worker in my plans regarding the railways. In the course of years he developed into a personage of high eminence. Distinguished and obliging, of comprehensive attainments, keen political insight, great capacity for work and untiring industry, he stood in close relationship to me.

His co-operation with the General Staff in military matters was due to his thorough belief in the necessity of strengthening our means of defense against possible hostile attacks. Plans were made for the construction of three new Rhine bridges, at Rüdesheim, Neuwied, and the Loreley, which were not completed until during the war—they were named, respectively, after the Crown Prince, Hindenburg, and Ludendorff. In the east, great extensions of railway stations, bridges, and new railway lines were built, some of them while the war was in progress.

Other important works carried out by Breitenbach in the west were the great railway bridge at Cologne, to replace the old trestle bridge; a new bridge, by the Beyen Tower, for freight traffic; and new railways in the Eiffel Mountains. Moreover, at my special suggestion, a through line was built from Giessen to Wiesbaden, which included reconstruction of the stations at Homburg and

Wiesbaden and the building of a loop around Frankfort and Höchst. In addition, trains were provided with through cars from Flushing to the Taunus.

To show that it is impossible to please everybody, I wish to observe in passing that we were violently attacked by the hotel proprietors of Frankfort, who were naturally not at all pleased at this elimination of Frankfort and of the necessity, existing previously, for passengers to change trains there, since they lost thereby many customers formerly obliged to spend a night in some Frankfort hotel. This element brought particularly strong opposition to bear against the loop line around Höchst.

The battle concerning the Central Canal was decided at last in favor of my plans. Under Breitenbach, construction on it was pushed forward by sections with great energy. Those portions of this canal which it had been possible to place in operation have fully met expectations.

During this period, also, the extraordinarily difficult extension and deepening of the Kaiser Wilhelm Canal, almost equivalent to building an entirely new waterway, was brought to completion, likewise the great Emden sea lock. These were remarkable achievements in the domain of bridge and lock construction, which aroused the admiration of the world; in the matter of locks, for instance, those built at this time far surpassed the locks of the Panama Canal in size. The difficult tasks were brilliantly and thoroughly completed by the officials in charge; in so far as the construction work was in the hands of the Empire, it was carried out mostly with the supervising co-operation of the Prussian Ministry of Transportation.

I often went to Breitenbach's home, where I had an opportunity, thanks to him, of having interesting talks on commercial-political and economic subjects with a highly intelligent circle, of meeting a lot of eminent men and discussing important questions. The plans and sketches of all the larger railway stations, locks, and bridges were submitted to me before the work of building or rebuilding them was begun, and reports concerning them were made to me.

I have intentionally gone into detail in this matter in order to show the following: First, how a monarch can and must influence the development of his realm by personal participation; second, how, if he makes his selections quite independently of party reasons, he can place able men at the head of the various departments; third, how, by the honest co-operation of these men with the sovereign, whose complete confidence they enjoy, brilliant results can be achieved. Everything that we did together was aboveboard and honest; nothing mattered but the welfare and development of the fatherland, its strengthening and equipment for competition in the world market.

As was natural, I had close and lasting relations in the regular course of events with the Ministry of Public Worship and Instruction. Herr von

Gossler and Herr von Trott may surely be considered the most important and prominent occupants of this post. In this Ministry a co-worker almost without equal arose in the person of Ministry Director Althoff, a man of genius.

I had been made acquainted with the dark side of the high-school system of education by my own school experiences. The predominantly philological character of the training led, in the whole educational system as well, to a certain one-sidedness.

When I was at the Cassel High School in 1874-77 I had observed that, although there was great enthusiasm for 1870-71 and the new Empire among the boys, there was, nevertheless, a distinct lack of the right conception of the German idea, of the feeling "civis Germanus sum" ("I am a German citizen")—which I impressed later upon my people at the laying of the foundation-stone of the Saalburg. To create such sentiments and awaken them in the rising generation and to lay the foundations for them firmly in the young hearts was a task somewhat beyond the powers of the teaching staff, in view of the fossilized, antiquated philological curriculum.

There was great neglect in the department of German history, which is exactly the study through which young hearts may be made to glow, through which the love of one's native country, its future and greatness, may be aroused. But little was taught of more recent history, covering the years since 1815. Young philologists were produced, but no German citizens qualified for practical co-operation toward building up the flourishing young Empire.

In other words, no *youths who were consciously Germans* were being turned out. In a small reading club composed of my classmates I often tried to inculcate the idea of the Greater Germany, in order to eliminate parochial and similar conceptions which hampered the German idea. Admiral Werner's *Book of the German Fleet* was one of the few works by means of which the living feeling for the German Empire could be fanned into flame.

Another thing that struck me, in addition to the one-sidedness of the education in the schools, was the tendency, among youths planning their careers in those days, to turn their attention to becoming Government officials, and always consider the profession of lawyer or judge the most worthy goal.

This was doubtless due to the fact that the conditions obtaining in the Prussia of olden days still had their effect in the youthful German Empire. As long as the state consisted, so to speak, of government and administration, this tendency among German youths in the shaping of their lives was understandable and justified; since we were living in a country of officials, the right road for a young man to select was the service of the state. British youths of that time, self-reliant and made robust by sports, were already talking, to be sure, of colonial conquests, of expeditions to explore new regions of the earth, of extending British commerce; and they were trying, in the guise of pioneers of their country, to make Great Britain still stronger and greater, by practical, free action, not as paid hirelings of the state. But England had long been a world empire when we were still a land of officials; therefore, the youth of Britain could seek more remote and important goals than the German.

Now that Germany had entered into world economics and world politics, however, as a by no means negligible factor, the aspirations of German youth should have undergone a more prompt transformation. For this reason it was that I, during the later years of my reign, used to compare, with a heavy heart, the proud young Britons, who had learned much less Latin and Greek than was required among us, with the children of Germany, pale from overstudy. To be sure, there were even then enterprising men in Germany—brilliant names can be cited among them—but the conception of serving the fatherland, not by traveling along a definite, officially certified road, but by independent competition, had not yet become sufficiently generalized. Therefore I held up the English as an example, for it seems to me better to take the good where one finds it, without prejudice, than to go through the world wearing blinkers.

With these considerations as a basis I won for my German youths the *School Reform* against desperate opposition from the philologists, inside and outside the Ministry and school circles. Unfortunately, the reform did not take the shape which I hoped, and did not lead to the results which I had expected.

The Germanic idea in all its splendor was first revealed and preached to the astonished German people by Chamberlain in his *Foundations of the Nineteenth Century*. But, as is proved by the collapse of the German people, this was in vain. To be sure, there was much singing of "Deutschland über alles," but Germans, obeying the commands of their enemies, allowed the Emperor to fall and the Empire to be broken to pieces; and, placing themselves under the orders of Russian criminals vastly inferior to them in culture, they stabbed their own army in the back while it was still fighting valiantly.

Had Germans of all classes and conditions been educated to feel joy and pride in their fatherland, such a degradation of a great nation would have been unimaginable.

This degradation—which, it must be admitted, occurred under remarkable, extremely difficult circumstances—is all the more difficult to understand in view of the fact that the youth of Germany, although it was impaired in health by overstudy, and not so toughened by sports as the English, achieved brilliant feats in the World War, such as were nowhere equaled before.

The years 1914-18 showed what might have been made out of the German people had it only developed its admirable qualities in the right direction. The 4th of August, 1914, the heroes of Langemark, countless splendid figures from all classes, rise up from the chaos of the long war to show what the German can do when he throws away Philistinism and devotes himself, with the enthusiasm which so seldom reveals itself completely in him, to a great cause. May the German people never forget these incarnations of its better self; may it emulate them with its full strength by inculcating in itself the true German spirit!

In the post of Minister of Justice I found His Excellency Friedberg, the intimate, faithful friend of my father, whom I had known ever since my youth, when he was a welcome guest in the home of my parents. This simple, affable man enjoyed with me the same consideration which had been shown him by my parents.

In later years I had frequent and welcome dealings with His Excellency Beseler, who also enabled me to hear informal discussion at his house of many an interesting legal problem by prominent lawyers, and to come into touch with legal luminaries. I felt no particular inclination toward the lawyers in themselves—since pedantry, remoteness from actualities and doctrinaire leanings often assert themselves in the domain of the law altogether too much for my taste—but the compilation of the *Citizens' Law Book* interested me greatly. I was present at sessions dealing with it, and was proud that this fundamental German work should have been brought to completion in my reign.

When I met the Lord Chief Justice of England, while I was on a visit to that country, at the home of Lord Haldane, I asked that great jurist what he thought of the administration and interpretation of the law in Germany. His answer ran thus: "You pronounce judgment too much according to the letter of the law; we according to the spirit and content of the law."

I have ofter pointed out how unfortunate it was that we have not been able to introduce, in police cases—connected with traffic, streets, etc.—the prompt procedure of the English "police court." For, in England, punishment in such cases is meted out on the very next day, whereas in Germany months often elapse, what with gathering of evidence and examination of witnesses, until, finally, some insignificant sentence is pronounced long after the case has been forgotten. I should also have liked to introduce into Germany the heavy penalties for libels published in the press which are customary in England.

I have often pointed out how unfortunate it was Prince, with Minister of Finance Scholz, and had taken part in sessions wherein that famous man, His Excellency Meinecke, figured. Meinecke was Under Secretary of State in the Finance Ministry and had, therefore, much to do with other Ministers, since finances were an important thing everywhere. He had achieved a certain degree of fame because he—as he thought—was always able smilingly to find the best way out of tight places.

Scholz was faithful to his duty and able, but he

did not succeed in making the dry substance of taxes and the like particularly interesting and pleasant to me, nor was there any change in this state of affairs until the versatile Miquel took charge of the Finance Ministry. When Miquel reported to me concerning the Prussian financial reform, he suggested three plans: one modest, one medium, one ambitious. To the delight of the Minister I decided, without hesitation, for the third. Both the monarch and the Minister were filled with satisfaction when the reform was carried out.

The Minister of the Interior, Herr von Puttkamer, had been forced to retire during the ninety-nine days, to the great sorrow of him who was then Crown Prince. He was an able, tried old Prussian official; one of those Pomeranians of the old school, filled with loyalty to the King—a nobleman through and through. Rumor had it that the Empress Frederick had driven him from office by a plot, but this is not true. The Empress, with her inclination to English Liberalism, doubtless did not like the old-time Prussian Conservative, yet she was not at all to blame for his going. Prince Bismarck pushed him aside, perhaps out of consideration for the Empress Frederick.

I was deeply interested in forestry and its improvement along practical lines, especially as new gold reserves could be created for the state by reforestation.

Next to Herr von Podbielski, the ablest Minister of Agriculture and Forests was Freiherr von

Schorlemer. Just as Herr von Podbielski bent his efforts toward creating great stretches of forests in the east, in order to keep off the east wind by a compact forest zone and thus improve our climate, and, at the same time, provide a natural protection against Russian attacks, so Herr von Schorlemer opened up the eastern forest reservations by extensive construction of roads, and by thus facilitating the transportation of wood helped Germany greatly in making headway in competition against wood from Russia.

Both Ministers sought, in co-operation with me, to improve our splendid Prussian forestry personnel and better living conditions among them, and to help toward promotions in their ranks—all of which these officials, zealous in their work and faithful to their King, fully deserved.

The influx of large sums into the state's pocketbook depended indeed on the honesty, industry, and reliability of these men. I expected much toward the restoration of the fatherland from the statesmanlike shrewdness and ability of Herr von Schorlemer, who was always quite conscious of the goal at which he was aiming.[1]

I learned much about forestry from Head Foresters Freiherr von Hövel (Joachimsthal, Schorfheide) and Freiherr Speck von Sternburg (Szittkohnen, Rominten) on my many hunting expeditions with these excellent huntsmen and administrators.

[1] His recent death, which snatched him away in the midst of beneficial labors, is a serious loss to the fatherland.

Let me say a word here regarding a Russian curiosity in the domain of preserving wild game. The Tsar, who had heard a great deal about the fine antlers of the stags at Rominten, wished to have some of the same sort at Spala, in Poland. Freiherr von Sternburg was sent to the Spala hunting lodge one summer in order to give advice regarding this project.

He was received very cordially by a general, who had charge of the hunting there and lived at the lodge. Sternburg noticed that all the apartments, even those not inhabited, were always kept heated. When he spoke of the enormous waste of wood occasioned by this, the general shrugged his shoulders and remarked that one never could tell, the Tsar might put in an appearance some day, after all. A gamekeeper, who was a German, was assigned to Sternburg, since the general did not know his way about on the reservation and was quite ignorant of game feeding.

In the course of his tours about the place Sternburg observed a number of places where meadows could be turned into pastures or good feeding places could be installed. He drew attention to the need of such arrangements, having noticed that the deer had already begun to shed their horns to a considerable extent, thereby causing much damage to the trees.

But the gamekeeper shook his head sadly and remarked that he had already reported all that, but in vain, since the hay for the deer had to be brought by rail from the Black Sea and the shipments sometimes either did not arrive at all or were greatly delayed and arrived spoiled. But nothing would be done to alter this, continued the gamekeeper, since too many people made a good thing out of this transporting of the hay, which was paid for at huge prices.

He also told how—after he had called attention to the many splinters of wood found in the intestines of the deer, in order to prove that they were insufficiently fed and that feeding places must be provided—a committee of animal doctors had been brought from St. Petersburg to investigate the matter. The said committee lived and ate for weeks in Spala at the Tsar's expense, shot many deer, examined them, and held sessions; and the upshot of all this was a report that the animals had wood in their stomachs, which proved that they could live on wood, for which reason feeding places would be superfluous and the hay from the Black Sea would suffice to supplement the wood. And there the matter remained, in spite of Sternburg's visit!

When I heard this yarn, I involuntarily thought of an anecdote which Prince Bülow especially delighted to tell in connection with his sojourn at St. Petersburg. While there, he had attended the salon of Madame Durnovo, where society used often to gather. One day a prominent general was complaining to the hostess that he had been trapped in a money matter, which had brought him much unpleasantness from "above." Apparently he wished, by his mournful description, to arouse sympathy for his bad luck, but Madame Durnovo retorted, in her rough way: "Mon cher Général, quand on fait des sâletés, il faut qu'elles réussissent!" ("My dear General, when you play dirty tricks it is necessary that they be successful!")

As Secretary of State in the Imperial Postal Department likewise, Herr von Podbielski, after I had chosen him and declined a number of other candidates, did excellent work, treading worthily in the footsteps of Stephan. Very practical; endowed with the business sense and a great knowledge of business; well versed and clever in financial matters; of innate administrative talent, and, at the same time, quick to fight; caustically witty; a good speaker and debater—he worked with zeal and skill, often as a pioneer, particularly in matters of world postal service, wireless telegraphy, etc. This former colonel in the Ziethen Hussars made a name for himself in the service of his fatherland which will never be forgotten.

An amusing contrast to his career is that of a Russian Hussar officer under Nicholas I. This Tsar, being full of anger against the Holy Synod, had driven away the man at the head of it. Shortly afterward he inspected the Hussar Body Guard Regiment, commanded by Colonel Count Protassoff. The immense satisfaction of the Tsar at the splendid appearance and maneuvering of the fine regiment found expression in the words, amazing alike to the commander and his men: "Thou hast maneuvered thy regiment magnificently, and, as a token of my satisfaction, I name thee Procurator of the Holy Synod, which thou must put into good shape for me!"

Mention must be made here of another excellent and worthy man, Minister Möller. He came from Bielefeld, like Hinzpeter, and was bound to my old teacher by lasting ties of friendship. In the legislature he was one of the leaders of the National Liberals, by whom he was highly esteemed, as he was in the Reichstag, on account of his upright, distinguished Westphalian characteristics and his great experience in the commercial-political domain.

When Imperial Chancellor Bülow suggested Möller to me as Minister I remarked that he was a party man and member of the Reichstag. The Chancellor said that the National Liberals would be pleased at Möller's appointment. I observed that the state Ministry of the Prussian King could not and must not be a party Ministry, but must stand above the parties in entire independence of them; that I esteemed Möller personally very much, but, should he become Minister, every member of the legislature would have the ambition to become one likewise; that, through Möller's appointment, the ambitions of the other parties to obtain ministerial chairs would also be aroused and nobody could foresee the consequences; that, moreover, Möller would be greatly missed in the Reichstag, from which I did not wish to take him on account of his influence with all parties.

Despite these objections and my advice against it, Bülow stuck to his idea. Möller became Minister, and, as such, stood very well with me. But what I had prophesied occurred comparatively soon: Minister Möller was obliged to retire by circumstances partially connected with the inner workings of his party.

German Postcard from World War 1

## CHAPTER VII

### Science and Art

THE broad and many-sided field whose care devolved upon the Ministry of Public Worship and Instruction—embracing art, science, research, medical matters, etc.—always aroused my lively interest and enlisted my efforts in its behalf.

Special pleasure was afforded me by the development of the Technical High School. The increasing importance of technical matters drew ever larger numbers of the ablest youths to institutions of learning of this description, and the achievements of the teachers there and of the young engineers who were graduated constantly brought new laurels to the German name.

Among the teachers at Charlottenburg one of the most prominent and best known all over the world was Professor Doctor Slaby. Until his death he had constant dealings with me and kept me informed concerning the newest inventions by means of captivating discourses. These were given not only in his laboratory, but also in the quiet hunting lodge in the forests of Brandenburg, where I, together with the Empress, surrounded by a few intimates, used to listen eagerly to Slaby's words. Slaby was also dear to me as an individual and caused me much mental enjoyment by his simple, clear views on every possible sort of thing in this world, which he could always express in the most stimulating and enthralling manner. Slaby meant much to me, and I felt grateful affection for him up to the time of his death.

Influenced by the achievements of the technical high schools and of such men as Slaby, Intze, and so on, I resolved to grant the high schools the same privilege of representation in the Prussian upper house as was enjoyed by the universities. But the universities protested vehemently against this to the Minister of Public Worship and Instruction, and there ensued a violent fight against the classical-scientific arrogance of the savants, until I finally enforced my will by a decree. Slaby received the news from me by telegraph in his laboratory while he was delivering a lecture, and gave it to the students, who burst into wild cheers. The technical high schools have shown themselves worthy of the honor conferred upon them.

In view of the constantly more violent fight for the markets of the world and its outlets, it became necessary, in order to utilize the wisdom of the leaders of German science in this direction, to provide them with more freedom, quiet, possibility for working, and materials. Many savants of importance were hampered in research work by their activities as teachers, so that the only time they had left over for research was their vacation. This state of affairs resulted in overwork and overburdening, which had to be stopped.

### CHEMICAL RESEARCH

Attention was turned first to improvements in the domain of chemistry. Minister von Trott and Director of the Ministry Althoff, having grasped the state of affairs with clear understanding, made possible for me the establishment of the Kaiser Wilhelm Society and drew up the statutes governing it. In the short time of its existence it has achieved brilliant results and given me an opportunity, at its general meetings, to become acquainted with eminent men in all branches of knowledge with whom I thereafter entered into regular intercourse. I also visited their laboratories, where I could follow the progress of their labors. New laboratories were founded, others subsidized from the contributions of the senate and members of the organization.

I was proud of this creation of mine, since it proved a boon to the fatherland. The inventions due to the research of its members benefited the entire nation. It was a peace-time achievement with a great and most promising future, which, under the guidance of Herr von Trott, was in most excellent hands; unfortunately, the war robbed me of this joy, along with all others. Nowadays I must do without the intercourse with my men of learning of my association, and that is a cruel blow to me. May it continue to live and labor for the benefit of research and the good of the fatherland!

I had to face a severe fight in getting Professor Harnack summoned to Berlin. The theologians of the Right and the Orthodox element protested vehemently. After I had again obtained full information from Hinzpeter and he had closed his opinion with the words that it would be most regrettable for Berlin and Prussia if I backed down, I insisted upon the summoning of Harnack, and summoned he was.

Nowadays it is impossible to understand the opposition to him. What a man Harnack is! What an authoritative position he has won for himself in the world of the mind! What benefit, what knowledge, intercourse with this fiery intellect has brought to me! What wonders he has achieved, as head of the Royal Library and dean of the senate of the Kaiser Wilhelm Society, where he, the theologian, delivered the most learned and most substantial talks on exact sciences, research, inventions, and chemistry. I shall always look back with pleasure on the personality of Harnack and on his labors.

Professor Erich Schmidt of the University of Berlin was also a friend of mine and was often at my home; I owe many an enjoyable evening to the learned discourses of this savant.

Professor Schiemann enjoyed my particular confidence. An upright man, a native of the Baltic Provinces, a champion of the Germanic idea against Slavic arrogance, a clear-sighted politician and brilliant historian and writer, Schiemann was constantly asked by me for advice on political and historical questions. To him I owe much good counsel, especially regarding the East. He was often at my home and often accompanied me on journeys—as, for instance, to Tangier—and he heard from me in our talks much important confidential matter not yet known to others on political questions. His unshakable capacity for keeping his mouth shut justified my trust in him. It was a source of satisfaction to me to appoint this tried man curator of the University of Dorpat, after the liberation of the Baltic Provinces.

### KAISER'S RUSSIAN FORESIGHT

How well he and I agreed in our political views regarding Russia is illustrated by the following incident: After the Peace of Portsmouth, between Russia and Japan, brought about by me in conjunction with President Roosevelt in 1905, there was much official (Foreign Office) and unofficial puzzling of heads at Berlin as to what political line Russia would take. In general it was thought that Russia, angered at her defeat, would lean toward the West—and hence toward Germany—in order to find there new connections and strength to help her in striking a blow for revenge against Japan and reconquest of her lost territory and prestige.

My opinion was quite different—but I could not make the official world share it. I emphasized the following points: That the Russians were

Asiatics and Slavs; being the first, they would be inclined to favor Japan, in spite of their defeat; being the second, they would like to ally themselves with those who had proved themselves strong. Hence I thought that, after a while, Russia, despite the Bjökö Agreement, would join Japan, not Germany, and turn later against Germany. On account of these "fantastic" ideas, I was actually ridiculed, officially and unofficially.

I summoned Schiemann and questioned him on this subject, without revealing to him what I thought about it. I was much pleased when his answer agreed absolutely with the views held by me. For a long time Schiemann and I stood almost alone when this weighty matter of foreign politics came up in discussions.

The event justified us. The so-called "Russian experts" of Berlin, as well as the official world, were mistaken.

During the very first years of my reign there was occasion for much important building work.

First, there was the question of erecting a worthy monument over the tomb of my grandparents. Since the old mausoleum at Charlottenburg was inadequate, it was necessary to erect an addition. Unfortunately, the funds left by Emperor William the Great for such "extra construction"—the so-called Extra Construction Fund—had been used up during the ninety-nine days on something else. Hence I was obliged to burden the Crown revenues with unforeseen building expenses. The mausoleum of my parents at Marly was erected by the

Empress Frederick, according to her own sketches and designs, and for this, too, I had to provide the funds.

A thorough examination of the royal palaces—including those in the provinces—had revealed, particularly at the palace in Berlin, such deplorable conditions in sanitation, comfort, and so on, that there could be no more delay in remedying them. In the course of my thirty years' reign I restored these palaces to good condition—working in accordance with carefully prepared budgets, examined, corrected, and supervised by myself with the help of architects (such as Ihne), and of artists, with due regard for the traditions of my ancestors—all of which gave me much trouble and tried my patience, but also provided me with a great deal of enjoyment.

### ARCHITECTURAL INTERESTS

In restoring the Berlin palace, the Empress Frederick, with her sure, keen eye for the proper style and her sound judgment, helped materially in offsetting the harm and neglect dating from bygone days. My mother's expression of her view ought surely to be of general interest: "Any style is good so long as it is pure." Ihne used to call the eclecticism of the 'nineties "a peu près style" (the "almost style"). The restoration of the Picture Gallery, the last work of Herr Ihne—who died, unfortunately, all too soon—was not completed until during the first half of the war. The palace of my forefathers, erected at much pains and a source of pride to me, was later bombarded, stormed, sacked, and devastated by revolutionary hordes.

These artistic building enterprises, as well as the already-mentioned restoration of the White Drawing Room, belong among the duties of representation devolving upon every Government, be it absolute, constitutional, or democratic in form. They afford a criterion of the national culture and are a means of encouraging artists and, through them, the development of art.

During my vacations I busied myself with archæology and was active in excavation work. Here I kept in view one basic idea: to discover the roots from which ancient Greek art developed and to erect or find a bridge in the endeavor to establish the cultural influence of the East on the West. It appeared to me that Assyriology was important, since from it might be expected an elucidation and vitalizing of the Old Testament, and, hence, of the Holy Scriptures. Therefore, I accepted with pleasure the offer of the presidency of the German Orient Society and devoted myself to the study of its work, which I promoted to the best of my ability, never missing one of its public lectures on the results of its explorations. I had much to do with those at the head of it, and caused detailed reports to be made to me of the excavations at Nineveh, Assur, and Babylon, in Egypt and in Syria, for the protection and facilitation of which I often personally brought influence to bear on the Turkish Government.

Professor Delitzsch, a member of the society gave his well-known and much-attacked lecture on "Babel and Bible," which, unfortunately, fell upon the ears of a public as yet too ignorant and unprepared, and led to all sorts of misinterpretations, some of them in church circles.

I strove hard to clear up the matter. Since I realized that the importance of Assyriology, then enlisting the efforts of many prominent men, including clergymen of both religions, was not yet understood and appreciated by the general public, I had my trusted friend and brilliant theater director, Count Hülsen-Haesler, produce the play "Assurbanipal," after long preparation, under the auspices of the German Orient Society. Assyriologists of all countries were invited to the dress rehearsal; in the boxes, all mixed up together, were professors, Protestant and Catholic clergymen, Jews and Christians. Many expressed to me their thanks for having shown, by this performance, how far research work had already progressed and for having, at the same time, revealed more clearly to the general public the importance of Assyriology.

My sojourn at Corfu likewise afforded me the pleasure of serving archæology and of busying myself personally with excavation. The accidental discovery of a relief head of a Gorgon near the town of Corfu led me to take charge of the work myself. I called to my aid the experienced excavator and expert in Greek antiques, Professor Dörpfeld, who took over the direction of the excavation work. This savant, who was as enthusiastic as I for the ancient Hellenic world, became in the course of time a faithful friend of mine and an invaluable source of instruction in questions relating to architecture, styles, and so on among the ancient Greeks and Achæans.

### "ILIAD" AS A GUIDE BOOK

It was a joy to hear Dörpfeld read and elucidate the old Homeric poems, and establish, by means of a map and following the hints and descriptions of the poet, the location of the old Achæan settlements destroyed later by the Doric migration. It appeared that the names of the old places had often been transferred by the dispossessed inhabitants to the new places. This made the identification of the location more difficult. Nevertheless, Dörpfeld had rediscovered the location of a whole series of them, with the help of his Homer, which he carried in his hand like a Baedeker, hitting upon it by following the minute geographical descriptions given by Homer.

This interested me so much that I took a trip by water, with the Empress, in the company of Dörpfeld, in order to put the matter to the test. We went to Leukas (Ithaca) and visited, one after another, the places made famous by the "Odyssey," while Dörpfeld read from his Homer the descriptive text referring to each. I was amazed and had to admit that the region and the description tallied exactly.

The excavations begun by me in Corfu under

Dörpfeld's direction had valuable archæological results, since they produced evidence of an extremely remote epoch of the earliest Doric art. The relief of the Gorgon has given rise already to many theories—probable and improbable—combined, unfortunately, with a lot of superfluous acrimonious discussion. From all this, it seems to me, one of the piers for the bridge sought by me between Asia and Europe is assuming shape.

I sent reports regularly to the Archæological Society, and I also brought the well-known Professor Caro from Athens to work with me. I was busy with preparations for lectures to be delivered before the society during the winter of 1914-15, and with searching discussions on many disputed questions, which I hoped to bring toward a solution "sine ira et studio." It was a pleasure to me to be visited almost regularly, at Corfu, by English and American archæologists, former pupils of Dörpfeld, who helped zealously in throwing light on the difficult problems which often came up. Since they were at work in Asia Minor, I was deeply interested in hearing what importance they attached to the Asiatic influence on early Greek art—as a result of their discoveries—and how readily they recognized a connection with the East in the finds made at Corfu. In 1914, Professor Duhn of Heidelberg visited the excavations at Corfu and, after thorough investigation, gave his support to the views held by Dörpfeld and me. I shall tell in a separate piece of writing about the result of my Corfu excavations.

That was the sort of thing which, in the spring of 1914, occupied the thoughts of the German Emperor, who, lusting for robbery and conquest, is accused of having bloodthirstily brought on the World War. While I was exploring and discussing Gorgons, Doric columns, and Homer, they were already mobilizing against us in the Caucasus and Russia. And the Tsar, at the beginning of the year, when asked about his travel plans, had replied: "Je resterai chez moi cette année, car nous aurons la guerre!" ("I shall stay at home this year, for we are going to have war!").

# CHAPTER VIII

## My Relations with the Church

MUCH has been written and said about my relations with the Church. Even when I was still a prince and a student at Bonn, I realized the harmful influence of the "Kulturkampf" in its last phase. The religious rift did so much toward antagonism that once, for example, I was directly boycotted, while on a hunting expedition, by members of leading noble Rhenish-Westphalian families of the Rhineland belonging to the Ultra-Montane party. Even as far back as that I resolved, in the interests of the national welfare, to work toward creating a modus vivendi such as would make it possible for people professing the two creeds to live peacefully with each other. The "Kulturkampf," as such, had come to an end before the beginning of my reign.

I strove patiently and earnestly to be on good terms with the Bishops, and I was on very friendly terms with several, especially Cardinal Kopp, Archbishop Simar, Doctor Schulte, Prince-Bishop Bertram, Bishop Thiel, and, last but not least, Archbishop Faulhaber and Cardinal von Hartmann. All of these were men far above the average and an ornament to the episcopate, who gave proof during the war of their patriotic devotion to Emperor and Empire. This shows that I had succeeded in clearing away the mists of the "Kulturkampf" and enabling my Catholic subjects, like others, to rejoice in the Empire, in accordance with the motto, "suum cuique" ("to each his own").

I was bound particularly closely all my life to Cardinal Kopp, Prince-Bishop of Breslau. He always served me loyally, so that my relationship to him was most trusting. Of much value to me was his mediation in dealings with the Vatican, where he stood in high honor, although he championed absolutely the German point of view.

### FRIENDSHIP FOR POPE LEO XIII

Probably little is known by the general public of the friendly, trusting relationship that existed between me and Pope Leo XIII. A prelate who was close to him told me later that I had won the confidence of the Pope on my first visit by the absolute frankness which I showed toward him and with which I told him things which others intentionally kept from his ears.

Receptions by the Pope were conducted with tremendous pomp. Swiss and Noble Guards, in brilliant uniforms, servants, chamberlains, and ecclesiastical dignitaries, were present in large numbers—a miniature representation of the might of the Roman Catholic Church.

After I had traversed the courts, halls, and drawing-rooms, in which all these men had arrayed themselves, I seated myself opposite the Pope himself, in his little, one-windowed study. The distinguished gentleman, with the fine, noble-featured old face, whose eyes gazed piercingly at his visitor, made a deep impression upon me. We discussed many timely subjects. I was greatly pleased that the Pope spoke appreciatively and gratefully of the position occupied in Germany by the Catholic religion and its adherents, adding the assurance that he, for his part, would contribute toward having the German Catholics yield to no other Germans in love for their fatherland and in loyalty.

Pope Leo XIII gave evidences of friendliness toward me whenever he could. For instance, on the occasion of one of my visits to Rome, he accorded my suite and servants the honor of a special audience; he sent Prince-Bishop Kopp as Papal Delegate on the occasion of the consecration by me of the portal which I had had added to the cathedral at Metz, and was so kind as to inform me of the naming of Archbishop Fischer of Cologne as Cardinal, which was done to celebrate that day.

On the occasion of the Papal Jubilee in 1903 to celebrate the twenty-fifth anniversary of his accession to the Papacy, I sent a special mission to convey my congratulations to the Pope, at the head of which was Freiherr von Loe, for many years intimately acquainted with him.

Not long after that—and only a few months before his death—I paid my third and last visit to the Pope. Though he was very weak, this ninety-three-year-old man came up to me, holding both his hands outstretched. Concerning this visit, which was characterized by great cordiality on both sides, I immediately jotted down some notes, which recently came into my possession again.

The Pope said, among other things, that he could not but give his full approval to the principles according to which I governed; that he had followed with interest my methods of governing and recognized with pleasure that I had built up my rule on a foundation of firm Christianity; that such lofty religious principles underlay it that it behooved him to ask the blessing of Heaven upon myself, my dynasty, and the German Empire, and to grant me his apostolic benediction.

### "SWORD OF CATHOLIC CHURCH"

It was of interest to me that the Pope said to me on this occasion that Germany must become the sword of the Catholic Church. I remarked that the old Roman Empire of the German nation no longer existed and that conditions had changed. But he stuck to his words.

Then the Pope went on to say that he must thank me once more for my unflagging attention to the welfare of my Catholic subjects; that he had heard about this from so many sources that he was glad to tell me personally how grateful both he and the German Catholics were for this attention to their interests; that he could assure me that my Catholic subjects would stand by me, in good and bad times, with absolute fidelity. "Ils resteront absolument et infailliblement fidèles" ("They will remain absolutely and infallibly faithful").

I rejoiced greatly at these words of appreciation from such an exalted source. I answered that I considered it the duty of a Christian sovereign to care for his subjects to the best of his ability, irrespective of creed; that I could assure him that, during my reign, everybody could profess his religion without interference and fulfill his duties toward his ecclesiastical overlord; that this was a fundamental principle of my life, from which I could not be swerved.

Because I showed my Catholic fellow countrymen from the very beginning that I wished to allow them complete freedom in the exercise of their religion, a quieter spirit was engendered in the land and the aftermath of the "Kulturkampf" disappeared more and more. But I did not conceal from myself the fact that, despite all politeness and friendliness, the prelates, with the sole exception of Cardinal Kopp, still continued to look upon me as the Emperor, and I was compelled to take into account that, in the Catholic south and west, this idea would never quite vanish. Grateful acknowledgment has repeatedly been made to me of the fact that the Catholics were as well off, during my reign, as they could possibly desire; but the constantly more uncompromising attitude of the Church on mixed marriages, and that of the Centrist party in politics, were certainly a sign that the antiheretical tendency still lived beneath the peaceful surface.

This made all the more intense my desire for the firm union of the *Protestant Churches*—first, in Prussia, then in Germany, finally, in all Europe. My endeavors, in conjunction with the Chief Ecclesiastical Councilor, the General Superintendent, and so on, to find means of effecting this union, were most earnest. I hailed the Eisenach Conference with joy and followed its proceedings with interest. I assembled all the General Superintendents for the consecration of the Church at Jerusalem and also was able to greet invited deputations from Sweden, Norway, and so forth; and I did likewise on the occasion of the consecration of the Berlin cathedral, where, among many other deputations, the Church of England was represented by the Bishop of Ripon (W. Boyd-Carpenter), the pastor of Queen Victoria of England, equally prominent as a writer and preacher.

Whenever possible, I worked toward compromise, closer relations and union, yet nothing definite resulted. Though church union in Prussia has been a success, Lutherans and Reformists kept apart in other sections of the fatherland. Many local rulers kept sharp watch over their rights in relation to religions and, owing to this, were hostile to a closer union of the different creeds within their territory. Therefore, despite my endeavors, the German Protestant Church was not able to unite and make common cause against the elements hostile to it. Only through the emergency brought on by the revolution was this made possible. On Ascension Day, 1922, to my great joy, the "German Evangelical Church Union" was solemnly formed at the Schloss Church at Wittenberg.

### DOCTOR DRYANDER'S INFLUENCE

During the first years of my military service at Potsdam I had felt deeply the inadequacy of the sermons, which often dealt only with dry dogmatic matter and paid too little attention to the person of Christ. In Bonn I became acquainted with Doctor Dryander, who made an impression on me lasting throughout my life. His sermons were free from dogma, the person of Christ was their pivotal point, and "practical Christianity" was brought into the foreground.

Later I brought him to Berlin and soon had him appointed to a post at the Cathedral and in my palace. Dryander was by my side for years, until long after the 9th of November, standing close to me spiritually, and bringing to me spiritual consolation. We often talked on religious matters and thrashed out thoroughly the tasks and the future of the Protestant Church. The views of Dryander—mild, yet powerful, clear, and of truly evangelical strength—made of him a pillar and an ornament of his Church, and a faithful coworker with the Emperor, to whom he was closely bound, in the interests of the Church and its development.

Since the 9th of November, Doctor Dryander also has been exposed to persecutions, but he has stood his ground courageously; the hopes, beliefs, and trust of his King are with him and the Evangelical Church! The Church must again raise up the broken nation inwardly according to the gospel of "Ein'feste Burg ist unser Gott."

I cannot allow to pass without remark the influence exerted by the work—translated at my instigation—of the English missionary Bernard Lucas, entitled *Conversations with Christ;* as well as the sermons on Jesus by Pastor Schneller (Jerusalem), and the collections of sermons called *The Old God Still Lives* and *From Deep Trouble,* by Consistorial Councilor Conrad. These brought us much inspiration and comfort by their vital ability to absorb and hold readers and hearers.

The fact that I could deal with religious and church questions with complete objectivity "sine ira et studio" is due to my excellent teacher, Professor Doctor Hinzpeter, a Westphalian Calvinist. He caused his pupil to grow up and live with the Bible, eliminating, at the same time, all dogmatic and polemical questions; owing to this, polemics in religion have remained alien to me, and expressions like that autocratic one, "orthodox," are repulsive to me. As to my own religious convictions, I set forth what they were years ago, in a letter to my friend, Admiral Hollmann, made public at the time, part of which is reproduced at the end of this chapter.

I was enabled to bring joy to the hearts of my Catholic subjects when I presented the plot of ground known as the "Dormition," acquired by me from the Sultan in 1898 as a result of my sojourn in Jerusalem, to the German Catholics there. The worthy, faithful Father Peter Schmitz, representative of the Catholic Society in Jerusalem, expressed to me the heartfelt thanks of the German Catholics on the spot in eloquent words at the ceremony of taking possession.

### THE CHURCH IN JERUSALEM

When I conferred with him as to future building operations and as to the selection of persons to occupy the place, the old expert on Jerusalem advised me to select none of the order of monks there, since all were more or less mixed up in the intrigues and quarrels concerning the "loci sacri" (sacred spots). After my return a delegation of the German Knights of Malta, under Count Praschma, appeared before me to express their gratitude. The design for the church, made by a very talented Cologne architect and skillfully adapted to the local style, was submitted to me. After the completion of the church I decided that the Benedictine monks of Beuron should take over the "Dormition"; they did so in 1906, also taking over the monastery built next the new St. Mary's Church.

I was on friendly terms for many years with the Benedictine monks of the Beuron Congregation, with whose Archabbot, Wolter, I had become acquainted at Sigmaringen. In mediæval times the order always stood well with the German Emperors, of whom scarcely one failed to visit, in connection with his journeys to Rome, the magnificently situated Monte Cassino. When the Benedictine monks asked permission to establish a settlement on the Rhine I had the splendid Romanesque abbey of Maria Laach—unused at the time—turned over to them. The order, which counts among its members excellent artists, including Father Desiderius, has brought new glory to the abbey, which had fallen into neglect and decay, by magnificent interior decorations. Often have I visited Maria Laach and rejoiced in the progress of its restoration, as well as in conversations with the intelligent abbots and in the hearty, simple reception on the part of the faithful brethren.

When I visited the monastery of Monte Cassino I became acquainted, in the person of Archabbot Monsignor Krug, with a man of extraordinary mental gifts and comprehensive culture, who had traveled a great deal about the world. He could express himself with equal fluency in Italian, English, and French, and his mother tongue, German. In his address to King Victor Emmanuel of Italy and me, he pointed out that nearly all the German Emperors, as well as the Lombard Kings before them, had paid visits to Monte Cassino. He presented me with a magnificent collection of copies of documents of the time of the Emperor Frederick II, taken from the library of the order, and I reciprocated by presenting him with the works of Frederick the Great.

Agriculture flourishes in the environs of the monasteries maintained by the Benedictine Order, being carried on by the lay brothers with all the latest improvements, to the benefit of the backward peasantry of the region; and in the country and town communities of the order church singing and organ playing are zealously cultivated by the monks, who have attained a high degree of artistic skill. The art of the goldsmith also flourishes among the monks, likewise art embroidery among the Benedictine nuns.

I caused to be reproduced in its full size the Labarum (standard) of the Emperor Constantine the Great, designed in accordance with the researches made by Monsignor Wilpert: one copy I presented to the Pope, another to my Palace Chapel at Berlin. The latter was stolen from the chapel by the mob during the days of the revolution. The metal work was done entirely by monks, the embroidery by nuns of the order, both excellently. One of the places inhabited by nuns of this order is the convent of Saint Hildegard, above Rüdesheim, which I visited in 1917.

My letter to Admiral Hollmann was due to the excitement aroused by a lecture entitled "Babel and Bible," delivered by Professor Delitzsch before the German Orient Society, of which Admiral Hollmann was one of the Board of Managers.

### SCHOLARSHIP AND RELIGION

The first part of the letter, which deals primarily with Professor Delitzsch's statements, has been omitted from the reproduction of the letter printed below:

*Feb. 15, 1903.*

MY DEAR HOLLMANN:

I should now like to return once again to my own standpoint regarding the doctrine or view of revelation, as I have often set it forth to you, my dear Hollman, and other gentlemen. I distinguish between two different kinds of revelation: a progressive, to a certain extent historical revelation, and a purely religious one, paving the way to the future coming of the Messiah.

Of the first, this is to be said: There is not the smallest doubt in my mind that God constantly reveals Himself through the human race created by Him. He has "breathed His breath into mankind," or, in other words, given it a piece of Himself, a soul. He follows the development of the human race with a Father's love and interest; for the purpose of leading it forward and benefiting it, he "reveals" Himself in some great savant or priest or king, whether among the heathens, Jews, or Christians.

Hammurabi was one of these, likewise Moses, Abraham, Homer, Charlemagne, Luther, Shakespeare, Goethe, Kant, Emperor William the Great. These men were selected by Him and made worthy of His grace; of achieving for their people, both in the spiritual and the physical domain, splendid and imperishable things, in accordance with His will. How often did my grandfather clearly emphasize that he was but an instrument in the hand of the Lord.

The works of great minds are gifts of God to the peoples of the earth, in order that they may improve themselves on these models and grope forward, by means of them, through the confusion of that which is still unexplored here below. God has certainly revealed Himself in different ways to different peoples, according to their standing and degree of culture, and He is still doing it now. For, just as we are overcome most by the greatness and majesty of the splendor of Creation when we contemplate it, and are amazed at the greatness of God as revealed therein, so also may we, in contemplating whatever is great or splendid in the works of a man or a people, recognize therein with gratitude the splendor of the revelation of God. He works directly upon us and among us! The second kind of revelation, the more religious kind, is that which leads to the coming of the Lord. It is introduced from Abraham onward, slowly but with foresight, all-wise and all-knowing; for without it mankind would have been doomed.

And now begins the most astounding influence, the revelation of God. The tribe of Abraham, and the people descended from it, consider the holiest thing of all, unescapable in its logical consequences, the belief in one God. This belief they must have and cultivate. Scattered by the captivity in Egypt, the separate parts are welded together by Moses for the second time, and still they try to maintain their "monotheism." The direct intervention of God is what brings regeneration to this people.

### KAISER'S THEOLOGY

And thus it goes through the centuries, until the Messiah announced and foreshadowed by the Prophets and Psalmists shall at last appear. The greatest revelation of God in the world! For He Himself appeared in the body of His Son; Christ is God, God in human form. He saved us. He inspires us, we are led to follow Him, we feel His fire burning within us, His pity strengthening us, His dissatisfaction destroying us, but also His intercession saving us. Sure of victory, building solely upon His word, we go through work, scorn, grief, misery, and death, for in Him we have the revealed word of God, and God never lies.

That is my view of this question. The Word, especially for us of the Evangelical faith, has become everything on account of Luther; and Delitzsch, as a good theologian, should not forget that our great Luther taught us to sing and believe: "Das Wort sie sollen lassen stehn" ("The Word they must allow to stand").

It is self-evident that the Old Testament contains a large number of parts which are of purely human-historical character and not "God's revealed Word." These are purely historical descriptions of events of all sorts, which occur in the life of the people of Israel in the domain of politics, religion, morals, and spiritual life.

For instance, the giving out of the Law on Mount Sinai can be looked upon only symbolically as having been inspired by God, since Moses had to turn to a revival of laws perhaps known of old (possibly drawn from the Code of Hammurabi), in order to bring coherence and solidarity to the framework of his people, which was loose and little capable of resistance. Here the historian may perhaps find a connection, either in sense or words, with the laws of Hammurabi, the friend of Abraham, which may be logically right; but this can never affect the fact that God had inspired Moses to act thus, and, to that extent, had revealed Himself to the people of Israel.

Therefore, my view is that our good professor should rather avoid introducing and treating of religion as such in his lectures before our association, but that he may continue, unhindered, to describe whatever brings the religion, customs, and so on of the Babylonians, and so on, into relation with the Old Testament.

As far as I am concerned, I am led by the above to the following conclusion:

(a) I believe in one only God.

(b) We men need, in order to teach Him, a *Form*, especially for our children.

(c) This *Form* has been, up to now, the Old Testament, as we now know it. This *Form* will be essentially changed by research, inscriptions, and excavations; but that will cause no harm, nor will the fact that, thereby, much of the halo of the Chosen People will disappear, cause any harm. The kernel and content remain always the same: God and His influence.

Religion was never a result of science, but something flowing from the heart and being of man, through his relations with God.

With heartiest thanks and many greetings, I remain always

Your sincere friend,

(Signed) WILHELM I. R.

# CHAPTER IX

## Army and Navy

MY close relations with the army are a matter of common knowledge. In this direction I conformed to the tradition of my family. Prussia's kings did not chase cosmopolitan mirages, but realized that the welfare of their land could only be assured by means of a real power protecting industry and commerce. If, in a number of utterances, I admonished my people to "keep their powder dry" and "their swords sharp," the warning was addressed alike to foe and friend. I wished our foes to pause and think a long time before they dared to engage with us. I wished to cultivate a manly spirit in the German people; I wished to make sure that, when the hour struck for us to defend the fruits of our industry against an enemy's lust of conquest, it should find a strong race.

In view of this I attached high value to the educational duty of the army. General compulsory military service has a social influence upon men in the mass equaled by nothing else. It brings together rich and poor, sons of the soil and of the city; it brings acquaintanceship and mutual understanding among young people whose roads, otherwise, would lead them far apart; the feeling that they are serving one idea unites them.

And think what we made out of our young men! Pale town boys were transformed into erect, healthy, sport-hardened men; limbs grown stiff through labor were made adroit and pliable.

I stepped direct from brigade commander to king—to repeat the well-known words of King Frederick William III. Up to then I had climbed the steps of an officer's career. I still think with pleasure of my pride when, on the 2d of May, 1869, during the spring parade, I first stood in the ranks before my grandfather. Relations with the individual man have always seemed valuable to me, and, therefore, I particularly treasured the assignments, during my military service, where I could cultivate such relations. My activities as commander of a company, a squadron, and a battery, likewise as head of a regiment, are unforgetable to me.

I felt at home among my soldiers. In them I placed unlimited trust. The painful experiences of the autumn of 1918 have not diminished this trust. I do not forget that a part of the German people, after four years of unprecedented achievements and privations, had become too ill to withstand being corrupted by foes within and without. Moreover, the best of the Germans lay under the green sod; the others were thrown into such consternation by the events of the revolution which had been held to be impossible that they could not spur themselves to act.

Compulsory military service was the best school for the physical and moral toughening of our people. It created for us free men who knew their own value. From these an excellent corps of non-commissioned officers was formed; from the latter, in turn, we drew our Government officials, the like of whom, in ability, incorruptibility and fidelity to duty no other nation on earth can show.

### BELIEVES OFFICERS STILL LOYAL

And it is from these very elements that I receive nowadays signs of loyalty, every one of which does me good. My old Second Company of the First Infantry Guard Regiment has shared, through good and evil days, the vicissitudes of its old captain. I saw them for the last time in 1913, in close formation—still one hundred twenty-five strong—under that excellent sergeant, Hartmann, on the occasion of the celebration of the twenty-fifth anniversary of my accession to the throne.

In view of its proud duty as an educator and leader of the nation in arms, the officer corps occupied a particularly important position in the German Empire. The method of replacement, which, by adoption of the officers' vote, had been lodged in the hands of the various bodies of officers themselves, guaranteed the needed homogeneity. Harmful outcroppings of the idea of caste were merely sporadic; wherever they made themselves felt they were instantly rooted out.

I entered much and willingly into relations with the various officer corps and felt like a comrade among them. The materialistic spirit of our age, to be sure, had not passed over the officer corps without leaving traces; but, on the whole, it must be admitted that nowhere else were self-discipline, fidelity to duty, and simplicity cultivated to such an extent as among the officers.

A process of weeding out such as existed in no other profession allowed only the ablest and best to reach positions of influence. The commanding generals were men of a high degree of attainment and ability and—what is even more important—men of character. It is a difficult matter to single out individuals from among them.

Though the man in the ranks at the front was always particularly close to my heart, I must, nevertheless, give special prominence to the General Staff as a school for the officer corps. I have already remarked that Field Marshal Count Moltke had known how by careful training to build up men who were not only up to requirements, technically speaking, but also qualified for action demanding willingness to assume responsibility, independence of judgment, and far-sightedness. "To be more than you seem" is written in the preface to the *Pocket Manual for the General Staff Officer.*

Field Marshal Count Moltke laid the foundations for this training; and his successors—Count Waldersee, that great genius, Count Schlieffen, and General von Moltke—built upon them. The result was the General Staff, which accomplished unprecedented feats in the World War, and aroused admiration throughout the world.

I soon realized that the greatest possible improvement of our highly developed technical department was absolutely necessary and would save precious blood. Wherever possible, I worked toward the perfection of our armament and sought to place machinery in the service of our army.

Among new creations, the very first place is taken by the heavy artillery of the army in the field. In bringing this into being I was obliged to overcome much opposition—particularly, strange to relate, in the ranks of the artillery itself. It is a source of great satisfaction to me that I put this matter through. It laid the foundation for the carrying out of operations on a large scale, and it was long before our foes could catch up with us in this direction.

### BETTER MILITARY EQUIPMENT

Mention must also be made of the machine gun, which developed from modest beginnings to being the backbone of the infantry's fighting powers; the replacement of the rifle by the machine gun multiplied the firing power of the infantry while, at the same time, diminishing its losses.

Nor can I pass over without mention the introduction of the movable field kitchen, which I had seen for the first time at some maneuvers of the Russian army. It was of the greatest value in maintaining the fighting efficiency of the army, since the possibility of getting sufficient nourishment kept our troops fresh and healthy.

All human work remains unfinished. Nevertheless, it may be said, without exaggeration, that the German army which marched to battle in 1914 was an instrument of warfare without an equal.

Whereas, at my accession to the throne, I had found the army in a condition which merely required development upon the foundations already laid, the navy, on the other hand, was in the first stage of development. After the failure of all the attempts of Admiral Hollmann to move the recalcitrant Reichstag to adopt a slowly progressing, systematic strengthening of German sea power—largely due to the cheap catchwords of Deputy Richter and the lack of understanding of the Liberals of the Left, who were fooled by them—the Admiral requested me to retire him. Deeply moved, I acceded to his request; this plain, loyal man, the son of a genuine Berlin bourgeois family, had become dear to me through his upright character, his devotion to duty, and his attachment to me. My friendship with him, based upon this estimate, lasted for many years up to the moment of the Admiral's sudden death; it often caused me to visit this faithful man, endowed with fine Berlin wit, at his home, and there to associate with him as head of the German Orient Society, as well as to see him, in a small circle of intimates, at my own home, or to take him with me as a treasured traveling companion. He was one of the most faithful of my faithful friends, always remaining the same in his disinterestedness, never asking anything for himself. Happy the city which can produce such citizens! I preserve a grateful memory of this tried and trusted friend.

Admiral Tirpitz succeeded Hollmann. In his very first reports, which laid the foundation of the first Naval law, he showed himself thoroughly in accord with me in the belief that the sanction of the Reichstag for the building of warships was not to be gained by the old form of procedure. As I have already pointed out, the opposition was not to be convinced; the tone of the debates conducted by Richter was unworthy of the importance of the subject; for instance, the gunboat obtained in the Reichstag by the Poles, under Herr von Koscielsky, was jokingly dubbed *Koscielska.* Ridicule was the weapon used, though the future of the fatherland was in question.

It was necessary that the representative of the navy should have a solid phalanx behind him, both among the Ministers of State and in the Reichstag, and that it should, from absolute conviction, energetically support him and the cause. Therefore, there was need of communicating to the Reichstag members, still rather ignorant in naval matters, the details of the great work; moreover, a great movement must be engineered among the people, among the "general public," indifferent as yet, to arouse its interest and enthusiasm for the navy, in order that pressure from the people itself might be brought to bear upon the Reichstag members. To this end, an energetic propaganda was needed, through a well-organized and well-directed press, as well as through eminent men of science at the universities and technical high schools.

### FIGHT IN THE REICHSTAG

There was need of a complete change in the whole method of handling the matter in the Reichstag. There must be no more bickerings about individual ships and docks. In making up the military budget, no arguments arose over the strength of the army, unless it was a matter of new formations. The makeup of the navy, like that of the army, must be settled by law once for all, its right of existence recognized and protected. The units composing it must no longer be a matter for debate. Moreover, not only the officer corps but that of noncommissioned officers must be strengthened and trained, in order to be ready for service on the new ships. At the beginning of my reign, sixty to eighty cadets, at the most, were enrolled every year; in the last few years before the war several hundred asked admission. Twelve precious years, never to be retrieved, were lost by the failure of the Reichstag; it is even harder to create a navy overnight than an army.

The goal to be striven for was implied in the law, which expressed the "idea of risk"; the aim was to cause even the strongest hostile fleet to think seriously before it came to blows with the German fleet, in view of the heavy losses that were to be feared in a battle, which put the foe in danger of becoming too weak for other tasks. The "idea of risk" was brilliantly vindicated in the Skager-Rak (Jutland) battle; the enemy, in spite of his immense superiority, dared not risk a second battle. Trafalgar was already dim; its laurels must not be completely lost.

The total number of units (ships) on hand—it was principally a matter of ships of the line—was taken as a basis for the Naval law, although these, with the exception of the four ships of the *Brandenburg* class, were little better than old iron.

The Naval law was looked upon by many laymen, in view of the numbers involved, as a naval increase. In reality, however, this was a false view, since the so-called existing fleet was absolutely no longer a fleet. It was slowly dying of old age—as Hollmann said when he retired; included in it were almost the oldest ships still in service in all Europe.

Now that the Naval law was gradually coming into force, lively building operations set in, launchings were reported in the press, and there was joy among those under the dominion of the "rage du nombre" at the growing number of ships. But when it was made clear to them that as soon as the new ships were ready the old ones must be eliminated, so that, as a matter of fact, the total number of ships of fighting value would, at first, not be increased, they were greatly disillusioned. Had the necessary ships been built in time during the wasted twelve years the Naval law would have found a quite different, usable basis already in existence. But as matters now stood it was really a question of the complete rebuilding of the entire German fleet.

The large number of ships, to which those which had to be eliminated were added, was a fallacy. Therefore the English made a mistake when they merely took account of the number of ships—since that fitted in well with the propaganda against Germany—but paid no attention to age or type, arriving thus at a total that was far too high, and, by such misleading methods, artificially nourishing the so-called apprehension at the growth of the German navy.

Admiral Tirpitz now went ahead with the program approved by me. With iron energy and merciless sacrifice of his health and strength he soon was able to inject efficiency and power into the handling of the naval question. At my command he went, after the drafting of the Naval law, to Friedrichsruh, the residence of Prince Bismarck, in order to convince the latter of the necessity for having a German navy.

The press worked zealously toward the introduction of the Naval law, and political economists, experts on commerce and politics and so forth, placed their pens at the service of the great national cause, the necessity for a navy having been by now widely realized.

In the meantime the English, too, helped—though quite unconsciously—toward bettering the

Naval law's chance of being passed. The Boer War had broken out, and had aroused among the German people much sympathy for the little country and much indignation on account of England's violent assault upon it. Thereupon the news came of the utterly unjustified capture of two German steamers on the East African coast by English warships. Indignation was general.

The news of the stopping of the second steamer happened to be received by the Secretary of State, von Bülow, at the very moment when Tirpitz and I were with him. As soon as Bülow had read the dispatch aloud, I quoted the old English proverb, "It's an ill wind that blows nobody good," and Tirpitz exclaimed, "Now we have the wind we need for bringing our ship into port. The Naval law will go through. Your Majesty must present a medal to the captain of the English ship in gratitude for having put it through."

The Imperial Chancellor ordered up champagne and the three of us drank joyously to the new law, its acceptance, and the future German fleet, not forgetting to express our thanks to the English navy, which had proved so helpful to us.

Many years later, on my return from Lowther Castle, where I had been hunting with Lord Lonsdale, I was invited to dine with Lord Rosebery, the great Liberal statesman and former Minister of Foreign Affairs, also known through his researches in the history of Napoleon, at his beautiful country estate of Dalmeny Castle, situated close to the sea, not far from the great Forth bridge.

Among the guests was General Sir Ian Hamilton, a Scotchman, well known on account of his part in the Boer War, with whom I had become acquainted when he was a guest at the Imperial German maneuvers, the Lord Provost of Edinburgh, and a captain of the English navy, who was commander of the naval station there.

The last sat next Admiral Freiherr von Senden, directly across the table from me, and attracted my attention by the obvious embarrassment which he manifested in his talk with the Admiral, which he conducted in a low voice. After dinner Admiral von Senden introduced the captain to me, whereat the Englishman's embarrassment caused him to behave even more awkwardly than before, and aroused my attention because of the worried look of his eyes and his pale face.

After the conversation, which turned on various maritime topics, had come to an end, I asked Freiherr von Senden what the matter was with the man; the Admiral laughed and replied that he had elicited from his neighbor, during the meal, that he had been the commander of the ship which had captured the two German steamers in the Boer War, and that he had been afraid that I might find this out. Senden had thereupon told him that he was entirely mistaken about this; that had His Majesty learned who he was he could rest assured that he would have been very well treated and thanked into the bargain.

"Thanked? What for?" queried the Englishman.

"For having made the passage of the Naval law so much easier for the Emperor!"

One of the prime considerations in the passage of the Naval law—as also for all later additions, and, in general, for the whole question of warship construction—was the question whether the German shipbuilding industry would be in a position to keep pace with the naval program; whether, in fact, it would be able to carry it out at all. Here, too, Admiral von Tirpitz worked with tireless energy. Encouraged and fired with enthusiasm by him, the German shipbuilding yards went at the great problem, filled with German audacity, and solved it with positively brilliant results, greatly distancing their foreign competitors. The admirable technical endowment of the German engineers, as well as the better education of the German working classes, contributed in full measure toward this achievement.

### FEVERISH HASTE FOR NAVY

Consultations, conferences, reports to me, service trips to all shipbuilding yards, were the daily bread of the indefatigable Tirpitz. But the tremendous trouble and work were richly rewarded. The people woke up, began to have a thought for the value of the colonies (raw materials provided by ourselves without foreign middlemen!) and for commercial relations, and to feel interest in commerce, navigation, shipping, etc.

And, at last, the derisive opposition stopped

cracking its jokes. Tirpitz, always ready for battle, wielded a sharp blade in fighting, never joked and allowed nobody to joke with him, so that his opponents no longer felt like laughing. Things went particularly badly with Deputy Richter when Tirpitz brilliantly snubbed and silenced him by quoting a patriotic saying, dating from the 'forties, of old Harkort—whose district Richter represented—concerning the need for a German fleet. Now it was the turn of the other side of the Reichstag to laugh.

And so the great day dawned. The law was passed, after much fighting and talking, by a great majority. The strength of the German navy was assured; naval construction was to be accomplished.

By means of construction and keeping an increased number of ships in service a fleet soon sprang into being. In order to maneuver, lead, and train its personnel a new book of regulations and signal code were needed—at the beginning of my reign these had been worked out merely for one division—four ships—since at that time a larger number of units never navigated together in the German navy—*i. e.,* a larger number were not kept in service. And even these were out of service in the autumn, so that, in winter, there was (with the exception of cruisers in foreign waters) absolutely no German navy. All the care expended during the summer season on training of crews, officers, noncommissioned officers, engine-room crews, and stokers, as well as on rigging and upkeep of ships, was as good as wasted when the ships were retired from service in the autumn; and when spring came and they were put back into commission things had to be started at the beginning again. The result was that any degree of continuity in training and of coherence among the crews with relation to each other and their ships—of "ship spirit," in short—could not be maintained. This was maintained only on board the ships stationed in foreign waters. Therefore, after the necessary heating equipment, etc., had been put in, I ordered that ships be kept in service also through the winter, which was a veritable boon to the development of the fleet.

In order to obtain the necessary number of units needed by the new regulations, Admiral von Tirpitz, in view of the shortage of ships of the line, had already formed into divisions all the sorts of vessels available, including gunboats and dispatch boats, and carried out evolutions with them, so that when the replacement of line ships began to take place the foundations for the new regulations had already been laid. The latter were then constantly developed with the greatest energy by all the officials concerned and kept pace with the growth of the fleet.

Hard work was done on the development of that important weapon, the torpedo boat. At that time we were filled with joyful pride that a German torpedo-boat division was the first united torpedo squadron ever to cross the North Sea. It sailed, under the command of my brother, Prince Henry, to take part in the celebration of Queen Victoria's Golden Jubilee (1887).

### COLONEL GOETHAL'S VISIT

The development of Heligoland and its fortifications as a point of support for small cruisers and torpedo boats—also, later on, for U-boats—was also taken in hand, after the necessary protective work for preserving the island had been constructed by the state—in connection with which work the Empire and Prussia fought like cat and dog.

On account of the growth of the fleet it became necessary to widen the Kaiser Wilhelm Canal. After a hard struggle we caused the new locks to be built of the largest possible size, capable of meeting the development of dreadnaughts for a long time to come. There the far-sighted policy of the Admiral was brilliantly vindicated.

This found unexpected corroboration by a foreigner. Colonel Goethals, the builder of the Panama Canal, requested through the United States Government permission to inspect the Kaiser Wilhelm Canal and its new locks. Permission was most willingly granted. After a meal with me, at which Admiral von Tirpitz was present, the Admiral questioned the American engineer (who was enthusiastic over our construction work) concerning the measurements of the Panama locks, whereupon it transpired that the measurements of the locks of the Panama Canal were much smaller than those of the Kaiser Wilhelm Canal.

To my astonished question as to how that could be possible, Goethals replied that the Navy Department, upon inquiry by him, had given those measurements for ships of the line. Admiral von Tirpitz then remarked that this size would be far from adequate for the future, and that the newer type of dreadnaughts and superdreadnaughts would not be able to go through the locks, consequently the canal would soon be useless for American and other big battleships. The Colonel agreed, and remarked that this was already true of the newest ships under construction, and he congratulated His Excellency upon having had the courage to demand and put through the big locks of the Kaiser Wilhelm Canal, which he had looked upon with admiration and envy.

In like manner the very backward and antiquated Imperial docks [the old tinker's shops, as Tirpitz called them] were rebuilt and developed into model modern plants and the arrangements for the workers were developed so as to further the welfare of the latter along the most approved lines. Only those who, like myself, have followed and seen with their own eyes from the very beginning the origin and development of all these factors necessary to the building up—nay, the creation anew—of the fleet can form anything like a proper idea of the enormous achievement of Admiral von Tirpitz and his entire corps of assistants.

The office of the Imperial Naval Department was also a new creation; the old "Oberkommando" was eliminated when it was divided into the two main branches of Admiralty Staff and Imperial Naval Department. Both of these (as in the army) were directly under the supreme war commander in chief—this meant that there was no longer any official between the Emperor and his navy.

### COMING OF THE DREADNAUGHT

When Admiral Fisher evolved an entirely new type of ship for England in the shape of the "dreadnaught"—thereby surprising the world as if he had launched a sudden assault upon it—and thought that he had thus given England, once for all, an unapproachable naval superiority which the rest of the powers could never meet, there was naturally great excitement in all naval circles. The idea, to be sure, did not originate with Fisher, but came—in the form of an appeal to shipbuilders of the whole world—from the famous Italian engineer Cuniberti, who had made public a sketch in Fred Jane's *Illustrated Naval Atlas.*

At the first conference regarding the introduction of the "dreadnaught" type of big fighting ship by England I at once agreed with Admiral von Tirpitz that it had robbed all pre-dreadnaughts of their value and consigned them to the scrap heap, especially the German ships, which it had been necessary to keep considerably smaller, on account of the measurements of our old locks, than the ships of other navies, particularly the English.

Thereupon Admiral von Tirpitz remarked that

this would also apply to the English fleet itself as soon as the other nations had followed Fisher's example; that England had robbed her enormous pre-dreadnaught force, upon which her great superiority lasted, of its fighting value, which would necessitate her building an entirely new fleet of big fighting ships, in competition with the entire world, which would do likewise; that this would be exceedingly costly; that England, in order to maintain her notorious "two-Power standard," would have to exert herself to such an extent that she would look with more disfavor than ever on new warships built by other nations, toward whom she was unfriendly, and begin to make objections; then this would be especially true if we started building, but would be in vain, since, with the existing types of ships in our fleet, we could not expect to fight against big battleships, but were forced, "nolens volens," to follow England along this road.

The war fully confirmed Admiral Tirpitz's opinion. Every one of our ships not in the big fighting-ship class had to be retired from service.

When the first German big fighting ship was placed in service there was a loud outcry in the land of the British. The conviction gradually dawned that Fisher and his shipbuilders had counted absolutely on the belief that Germany would not be able to build any big fighting ships. Therefore the disappointment was all the greater. Why such an assumption was made is beyond comprehension, since, even at that time, German shipbuilders had already built the great ocean greyhounds, far surpassing our warships of the line in tonnage, which had occasioned painfully noticeable competition to the English steamship lines. Our big fighting ships, despite their small number, showed themselves, at the Skager-Rak (Jutland) battle, not only equal to their English opponents, but superior to them both in seaworthiness and in standing up under gunfire.

### IMPATIENT FOR U-BOATS

The building of U-boats, unfortunately, could not be pushed forward before the war to an extent commensurate with my desires. On the one hand, it was necessary not to overburden the naval budget during the carrying out of the Naval law; moreover, most important of all, it was necessary to collect further data from experiments.

Tirpitz believed that the types with which other nations were experimenting were too small and fit only for coast defense; that Germany must build "seagoing" submarines capable of navigating in the open sea; that this necessitated a larger type—which, however, must first be systematically developed. This took a long time and required careful experiments with models.

The result was that, at first, in 1914, there were only a small number of seaworthy submarines in readiness. Even then more pressure might have been brought to bear upon England with the available submarines had not the Chancellor been so concerned lest England be provoked thereby.

The number and efficiency of the submarines rose rapidly in the course of the war; in considering numbers, however, one must always remember that in wartime, U-boats are to be reckoned as follows: One third of the total in active service, one third on the outward or return journey, one third undergoing repairs. The achievements of the U-boats aroused the admiration of the entire world and won the ardent gratitude of the fatherland.

Admiral von Tirpitz's tremendous success in creating the commercial colony of Tsing-tao must never be forgotten. Here he gave proof once more of his brilliant talent for administration and organization in all directions. Those talents of his created, out of a place that was previously almost unknown and entirely without importance, a commercial center which, within a few years, showed a turnover of between fifty and sixty millions.

The dealings with Reichstag members, the press, and big industrial and world-commercial elements gradually increased the Admiral's interest in political matters, particularly in foreign affairs, which were always bound up with the utilization of ships. The clear world-vision acquired by him as a traveled sailor, well acquainted with foreign parts, qualified Tirpitz to make quick decisions, which his fiery temperament wished to see translated promptly into action.

The opposition and slowness of officialdom irritated him greatly. A certain tendency to distrust, perhaps strengthened by many an experience, often misled him to harbor suspicion—sometimes justified, sometimes not—against individuals. This caused a strong tinge of reserve in Tirpitz's character and "hampered the joyful workings of the heart" in others. He was also capable of bringing to bear new views on a matter with great decision, when, after renewed reflection or study of new facts, he had altered his previous view. This made working with him not always exactly agreeable or easy. The tremendous results of his achievements, of which he was justly proud, gave him a consciousness of the power of his personality, which sometimes made itself apparent even to his friends.

During the war Tirpitz's tendency to mix in politics got the upper hand with him so much that it eventually led to differences of opinion which finally caused his retirement, since von Bethmann, the Imperial Chancellor, demanded the dismissal of the Admiral-in-chief with the observation that the Imperial Secretaries of State were his subordinates and that the political policy must be conducted by himself alone.

It was with a heavy heart that I acquiesced in the departure of this energetic, strong-willed man, who had carried out my plans with genius and who was indefatigable as a co-worker. Tirpitz may always rest assured of my Imperial gratitude. If only this source of strength might stand soon again by the side of the unfortunate German fatherland in its misery and distress! Tirpitz can do and dares to do what many others do not dare. The saying of the poet most certainly applies to Admiral von Tirpitz: "The greatest blessing to the children of earth is, after all, personality!"

The criticisms which the Admiral felt constrained to make of me, in his book—which is well worth reading—cannot change, in the slightest, my opinion of him.

# CHAPTER X

## The Outbreak of War

AFTER the arrival of the news of the assassination of my friend, the Archduke Franz Ferdinand, I gave up going to Kiel for the regatta week and went back home, since I intended to go to Vienna for his funeral. But I was asked from there to give up this plan. Later I heard that one of the reasons for this was consideration for my personal safety; to this I naturally would have paid no attention.

Greatly worried on account of the turn which matters might now take, I decided to give up my intended journey to Norway and remain at home. The Imperial Chancellor and the Foreign Office held a view contrary to mine and wished me to undertake the journey, as they considered that it would have a quieting effect on all Europe. For a long time I argued against going away from my country at a time when the future was so unsettled, but Imperial Chancellor von Bethmann told me, in short and concise terms, that if I were now to give up my travel plans, which were already widely known, this would make the situation appear more serious than it had been up to that moment and possibly lead to the outbreak of war, for which I might be held responsible; that the whole world was merely waiting to be put out of suspense by the news that I, in spite of the situation, had quietly gone on my trip.

Thereupon I consulted the Chief of the General Staff, and, when he also proved to be calm and unworried regarding the state of affairs and himself asked for a summer leave of absence to go to Carlsbad, I decided, though with a heavy heart, upon my departure.

The much-discussed so-called Potsdam Crown Council of July 5th in reality never took place. It is an invention of malevolent persons. Naturally, before my departure, I received, as was my custom, some of the Ministers individually, in order to hear from them reports concerning their departments. Neither was there any council of Ministers and there was no talk about war preparations at a single one of the conferences.

My fleet was cruising in the Norwegian fjords, as usual, while I was on my summer vacation trip. During my stay at Balholm I received only meager news from the Foreign Office and was obliged to rely principally on the Norwegian newspapers, from which I got the impression that the situation was growing worse. I telegraphed repeatedly to the Chancellor and the Foreign Office that I considered it advisable to return home, but was asked each time not to interrupt my journey.

When I learned that the English fleet had not dispersed after the review at Spithead, but had remained concentrated, I telegraphed again to Berlin that I considered my return necessary. My opinion was not shared there.

But when, after that, I learned from the Norwegian newspapers—not from Berlin—about the Austrian ultimatum to Serbia, and, immediately thereafter, about the Serbian note to Austria, I started without further ado upon my return journey and commanded the fleet to repair to Wilhelmshaven. Upon my departure I learned from a Norwegian source that it was said that a part of the English fleet had left secretly for Norway in order to capture me (though peace still reigned!). It is significant that Sir Edward Goschen, the English ambassador, was informed on July 26th at the Foreign Office that my return journey, undertaken on my own initiative, was to be regretted, since agitating rumors might be caused by it.

### SAYS WAR WAS NOT FORESEEN

Upon my arrival at Potsdam I found the Chancellor and the Foreign Office in conflict with the Chief of the General Staff, since General von Moltke was of the opinion that war was sure to break out, whereas the other two stuck firmly to their view that things would not get to such a bad pass, that there would be some way of avoiding war, provided I did not order mobilization. This dispute kept up steadily. Not until General von Moltke announced that the Russians had set fire to their frontier posts, torn up the frontier railway tracks, and posted red mobilization notices did a light break upon the diplomats in the Wilhelmstrasse and bring about both their own collapse and that of their powers of resistance. They had not *wished* to *believe* in the war.

This shows plainly how little we had expected—much less prepared for—war in July, 1914. When, in the spring of 1914, Tsar Nicholas II was questioned by his Court Marshal as to his spring and summer plans, he replied: "Je resterai chez moi cette année parceque nous aurons la guerre" ("I shall stay at home this year because we shall have war"). (This fact, it is said, was reported to Imperial Chancellor von Bethmann; I heard nothing about it then and learned about it for the first time in November, 1918.) This was the same Tsar who gave me, on two separate occasions—at Björkö and Baltisch-Port—entirely without being pressed by me and in a way that surprised me, his word of honor as a sovereign, to which he added weight by a clasp of the hand and an embrace, that he would never draw his sword against the German Emperor—least of all as an ally of England—in case a war should break out in Europe, owing to his gratitude to the German Emperor for his attitude in the Russo-Japanese War, in which England alone had involved Russia, adding that he hated England, since she had done him and Russia a great wrong by inciting Japan against them.

At the very time that the Tsar was announcing his summer war program I was busy at Corfu excavating antiquities; then I went to Wiesbaden, and, finally, to Norway. A monarch who wishes war and prepares it in such a way that he can suddenly fall upon his neighbors—a task requiring long secret mobilization preparations and concentration of troops—does not spend months outside his own country and does not allow his Chief of the General Staff to go to Carlsbad on leave of absence. My enemies, in the meantime, planned their preparations for an attack.

Our entire diplomatic machine failed. The menace of war was not seen because the Foreign Office was so hypnotized with its idea of "surtout pas d'histoires" ("above all, no stories"), its belief in peace at any cost, that it had completely eliminated war as a possible instrument of Entente statesmanship from its calculations, and, therefore, did not rightly estimate the importance of the signs of war.

Herein also is proof of Germany's peaceful inclinations. The above-mentioned standpoint of the Foreign Office brought it to a certain extent into conflict with the General Staff and the Admiralty Staff, who uttered warnings, as was their duty, and wished to make preparations for defense. This conflict in views showed its effect for a long time; the army could not forget that, by the fault of the Foreign Office, it had been taken by surprise, and the diplomats were piqued because, in spite of their stratagems, war had ensued, after all.

Innumerable are the pieces of evidence that as early as the spring and summer of 1914, when nobody in Germany believed as yet in the Entente's attack, war had been prepared for in Russia, France, Belgium, and England.

I included the most important proofs of this, in so far as they are known to me, in the *Comparative Historical Tables* compiled by me. On account of their great number, I shall cite only a few here. If in so doing I do not mention all names, this is done for reasons easily understood. Let me remark furthermore that this whole mass of material became known to me only little by little, partly during the war, mostly after the war.

1. As far back as April, 1914, the accumulation of gold reserves in the English banks began. On the other hand, Germany, as late as July, was still exporting gold and grain; to the Entente countries, among others.

2. In April, 1914, the German Naval Attaché in Tokyo, Captain von Knorr, reported that he was greatly struck by the certainty with which everyone there foresaw a war of the Triple Alliance against Germany in the near future . . . that there was a something in the air as if, so to speak, people were expressing their condolences over a death sentence not yet pronounced.

3. At the end of March, 1914, General Sherbatsheff, director of the St. Petersburg War Academy, made an address to his officers, wherein, among other things, he said: That war with the powers forming the Triple Alliance had become unavoidable on account of Austria's anti-Russian Balkan policy; that there existed the strongest sort of probability that it would break out as early as that same summer; that, for Russia, it was a point of honor to assume the offensive immediately.

4. In the report of the Belgian ambassador at

Berlin regarding a Japanese military mission which had arrived from St. Petersburg in April, 1914, it was stated, among other things: At the regimental messes the Japanese officers had heard quite open talk of an imminent war against Austria-Hungary and Germany; it was stated, however, that the army was ready to take the field, and that the moment was as auspicious for the Russians as for their allies, the French.

5. According to the memoirs of the then French ambassador at St. Petersburg, M. Paléologue, published in 1921, in the *Revue des Deux Mondes*, the Grand Duchesses Anastasia and Militza told him on July 22, 1914, at Tsarskoe Selo, that their father, the King of Montenegro, had informed them, in a cipher telegram, that "we shall have war before the end of the month [that is, before the 13th of August, Russian style]; . . . nothing will be left of Austria. . . . You will take back Alsace-Lorraine. . . . Our armies will meet in Berlin. . . . Germany will be annihilated."

6. The former Serbian Chargé d'Affaires at Berlin, Bogitshevich, tells in his book, *Causes of the War*, published in 1919, of the following statement which Cambon, the then French ambassador at Berlin, made to him on the 26th or 27th of July, 1914: "If Germany wishes matters to come to a war, she will have England also against her. The English fleet will take Hamburg. We shall thoroughly beat the Germans." Bogitshevich states that this talk made him sure that the war had been decided upon at the time of the meeting of Poincaré with the Russian Tsar at St. Petersburg, if not sooner.

#### RUSSIAN CROWN COUNCIL

7. Another Russian of high rank, a member of the Duma and a good friend of Sazonoff, told me later about the secret Crown Council held, with the Tsar presiding, in February, 1914; moreover, I obtained

corroboration, from other Russian sources mentioned in my *Historical Tables*, of the following: At this Crown Council Sazonoff made an address wherein he suggested to the Tsar to seize Constantinople, which, since the Triple Alliance would not acquiesce in it, would cause a war against Germany and Austria. He added that Italy would break away from these two, in the natural course of events; that France was to be trusted absolutely and England probably.

The Tsar had agreed, it was said, and given orders to take the necessary preliminary steps. The Russian Finance Minister, Count Kokovzeff, wrote to the Tsar advising against this course—I was informed of this by Count Mirbach after the peace of Brest-Litovsk—recommending a firm union with Germany and warning against war, which, he said, would be unfavorable to Russia and lead to revolution and the fall of the dynasty. The Tsar did not follow this advice, but pushed on toward war.

The same gentleman told me this: *Two* days after the outbreak of war he had been invited by Sazonoff to breakfast. The latter came up to him, beaming with joy, and, rubbing his hands together, asked: "Come now, my dear Baron, you must admit that I have chosen the moment for war excellently, haven't I?" When the Baron, rather worried, asked him what stand England would take, the Minister smote his pocket, and, with a sly wink, whispered: "I have something in my pocket which, within the next few weeks, will bring joy to all Russia and astound the entire world; I have received the English promise that England will go with Russia against Germany!"

9. Russian prisoners belonging to the *Siberian* Corps, who were taken in East Prussia, said that they had been transported by rail in the summer of 1913, to the vicinity of Moscow, since maneuvers were to be held there by the Tsar. The maneuvers did not take place, but the troops were not taken back. They were

stationed for the winter in the vicinity of Moscow. In the summer of 1914 they were brought forward to the vicinity of Vilna, since big maneuvers were to be held there by the Tsar; at and near Vilna they were deployed and then, suddenly, the sharp cartridges (war ammunition) were distributed and they were informed that there was a war against Germany; they were unable to say why and wherefore.

10. In a report, made public in the press, during the winter of 1914-15; by an American, concerning his trip through the Caucasus in the spring of 1914, the following was stated: When he arrived in the Caucasus, at the beginning of *May,* 1914, he met, while on his way to Tiflis, long columns of troops of all arms, in war equipment. He had feared that a revolt had broken out in the Caucasus. When he made inquiries of the authorities at Tiflis, while having his passport inspected, he received the quieting news that the Caucasus was quite peaceful, that he might travel wheresoever he wished, that what he had seen had to do only with practice marching and maneuvers.

At the close of his trip at the end of May, 1914, he wished to embark at a Caucasian port, but all the vessels there were so filled with troops that only after much trouble could he manage to get a cabin for himself and his wife. The Russian officers told him that they were to land at Odessa and march from there to take part in some great maneuvers.

### THE COSSACK'S TESTIMONY

11. Prince Tundutoff, Hetman of the Calmuck Cossacks living between Tsaritsin and Astrakhan, who was, before and during the war, personal aid of the Grand Duke Nicholas Nicholaievitch, came to General Headquarters at Bosmont in 1918, seeking to establish connection with Germany, since the Cossacks were not Slavs at all and thoroughly hostile to the Bolsheviki.

He stated that he had been sent by Nicholas Nicholaievitch, before the outbreak of war, to the General Staff, in order to keep the Grand Duke posted on happenings there and that he had been a witness of the notorious telephone talks between the Tsar and the Chief of the General Staff, General Januskevitch; that the Tsar, deeply impressed by the earnest telegram of the German Emperor, had resolved to forbid mobilization and had ordered Januskevitch by telephone not to carry out mobilization, *i. e.,* to break it off; that the latter had not obeyed the unmistakable order, but had inquired by telephone of Sazonoff, Minister of Foreign Affairs—with whom, for weeks, he had kept in touch, intrigued and incited to war—what he was to do now; that Sazonoff had answered that the Tsar's order was nonsense, that all the General need do was to carry out mobilization, that he [Sazonoff] would bring the Tsar around again next day and talk him out of heeding the stupid telegram from the German Emperor; that, thereupon, Januskevitch had informed the Tsar that mobilization was already under way and could no longer be broken off.

Prince Tundutoff added: "This was a lie, for I myself saw the mobilization order lying beside Januskevitch on his writing table, which shows that it had not as yet been given out at all."

The psychologically interesting point about the above is that Tsar Nicholas, who helped prepare the World War and had already ordered mobilization, wished to recede at the last moment. My earnest, warning telegram, it seems, made him realize clearly for the first time the colossal responsibility which he was bringing upon himself by his warlike preparations. Therefore, he wished to stop the war machine, the murderer of entire peoples, which he had just set in motion. This would have been possible and peace might have been preserved if Sazonoff had not frustrated his wish.

When I asked whether the Grand Duke, who was known as a German-hater, had incited much to war, the Cossack chief replied that the Grand Duke had certainly worked zealously for war, but that incitement on his part would have been superfluous, since there was already a strong sentiment against Germany all through the Russian officer corps; that this spirit was transmitted, principally, from the French army to the Russian officers; that there had been a desire, in fact, to go to war in 1908-09 (Bosnian Question), but France was not then ready; that, in 1914, Russia, likewise, was not quite ready; that Januskevitch and Sukhomlinoff had really planned the war for 1917, but Sazonoff and Isvolsky, as well as the French, could not be restrained any longer; that the former two were afraid of revolution in Russia and of the influence of the German Emperor on the Tsar, which might dissuade the Tsar from the idea of waging war; and that the French, who were sure, for the time being, of England's help, were afraid that England might come to an understanding later on with Germany at the expense of France.

When I asked whether the Tsar had been aware of the warlike spirit in Russia and had tolerated it, the Cossack Prince answered that it was worthy of note that the Tsar had forbidden once for all, as a matter of precaution, the inviting of German diplomats or military attachés to luncheons or evening meals given by Russian officers at which he himself was to be present.

### STORES OF ENGLISH COATS

(12) When our troops advanced in 1914 they found, in northern France and along the Belgian frontier, great stores of English soldiers' greatcoats. According to statements by the inhabitants, these were placed there during the *last years of peace.* Most of the English infantrymen who were made prisoners by

us in the summer of 1914 had no greatcoats; when asked why, they answered, quite naïvely: "We are to find our greatcoats in the stores at Maubeuge, Le Quesnoy, etc., in the north of France and in Belgium."

It was the same regarding maps. In Maubeuge great quantities of English military maps of northern France and Belgium were found by our men; copies of these have been shown to me. The names of places were printed in French and English, and all sorts of words were translated in the margin for the convenience of soldiers; for instance: moulin=mill, pont=bridge, maison=house, ville=town, bois=wood, etc. These maps date from 1911 and were engraved at Southampton.

The stores were established by England, with the permission of the French and Belgian Governments, *before* the war, in the midst of peace. What a tempest of horror would have broken out in Belgium, the "neutral country," and what a rumpus England and France would have kicked up, if we had wished to establish stores of German soldiers' greatcoats and maps in Spa, Liège, and Namur!

Among the statesmen who, besides Poincaré, particularly helped unleash the World War, the Sazonoff-Isvolsky group probably should take first rank. Isvolsky, it is said, when at Paris, proudly placed his hand upon his breast and declared: "I made the war. Je suis le père de cette guerre" ("I am the father of this war").

Delcassé also has a large share in the guilt for the World War, and Grey an even larger share, since he was the spiritual leader of the "encirclement policy," which he faithfully pushed forward and brought to completion, as the "legacy" of his dead sovereign.

I have been informed that an important rôle was played in the preparation of the World War directed against the monarchical Central Powers by the policy of the international "Great Orient Lodge"; a policy extending over many years and always envisaging the goal at which it aimed. But the German Great Lodges, I was furthermore told —with two exceptions wherein non-German financial interests are paramount and which maintain secret connection with the "Great Orient" in Paris —had no relationship to the "Great Orient." They were entirely loyal and faithful, according to the assurance given me by the distinguished German Freemason who explained to me this whole interrelationship, which had, until then, been unknown to me. He said that in 1917 an international meeting of the lodges of the "Great Orient" was held, after which there was a subsequent conference in Switzerland; at this the following program was adopted: Dismemberment of Austria-Hungary, democratization of Germany, elimination of the House of Hapsburg, abdication of the German Emperor, restitution of Alsace-Lorraine to France, union of Galicia with Poland, elimination of the Pope and the Catholic Church, elimination of every state Church in Europe.

I am not now in a position to investigate the very damaging information which has been transmitted to me, in the best of faith, concerning the organization and activities of the Great Orient Lodges. Secret and public political organizations have played important parts in the life of peoples and states, ever since history has existed. Some of them have been beneficial: most of them have been destructive, if they had to have secret passwords which shunned the light of day. The most dangerous of these organizations hide under the cloak of some ideal object or other—such as active love of their neighbors, readiness to help the weak, and poor, and so forth—in order that, with such pretexts as a blind, they may work for their real secret ends. It is certainly advisable to study the activities of the Great Orient Lodges, since one cannot adopt a final attitude toward this world-wide organization until it has been thoroughly investigated.

I shall not take up the war operations in this work. I shall leave this task all the more readily to my officers and to the historians, since I, writing as I am without a single document, would be able to describe events only in very broad outline.

When I look back upon the four arduous war years, with their hopes and fears, their brilliant victories and losses in precious blood, what is uppermost in my mind is the feeling of ardent gratitude and undying admiration for the unequaled achievements of the German Nation in arms.

### PROUD OF GERMAN ARMY

Just as no sacrifice in endurance and privation was too great for those staying at home, so also the army, in defending itself during the war criminally forced upon us, did not merely overcome the crushing superiority of twenty-eight hostile nations, but likewise, on land and water and in the air, won victories whose glory may have paled a bit in the mists of the present day, but, for that very reason, will shine forth all the more brightly in the light of history. Nor is that all. Wherever there was distress among our allies, German intervention, often with weak forces, always restored the situation and often won noteworthy successes. Germans fought on all the battlefields of the far-flung World War.

Surely the heroic bravery of the German nation deserved a better fate than to fall a victim to the dagger that treacherously stabbed it from behind; it seems to be the German destiny that Germans shall always be defeated by Germans. Recently I read the unfortunately not entirely unjustified words: "In Germany every Siegfried has his Hödur behind him."

Finally, let me say a word concerning the German "atrocities" and give two instances thereof!

After our advance into northern France I immediately ordered that art treasures be protected. Art historians and professors were assigned to each army, who traveled about inspecting, photographing, and describing churches, châteaux, and castles. Among them Professor Clemen, Curator of the Rhine Province, especially distinguishel himself and reported to me, when I was at the front, on the protection of art treasures.

All the collections in towns, museums, and castles were catalogued and numbered; whenever they seemed to be imperiled by the fighting they were taken away and assembled, at Valenciennes and Maubeuge, in two splendid museums. There they were carefully preserved and the name of the owner marked on each article.

The old windows of the cathedral of St. Quentin were removed by German soldiers, at the risk of their lives, under English shell-fire. The story of the destruction of the church by the English was told by a German Catholic priest, who published it with photographs, and it was sent, by my orders, to the Pope.

At the château of Pinon, which belongs to the Princess of Poix, who had been a guest of mine and the Empress, the headquarters of the general commanding the Third Army Corps was located. I visited the château and lived there. Previously the English had been quartered there and had ravaged the place terribly. The commanding general, von Lochow, and his staff had a great deal of trouble getting it into some sort of shape again after the devastation wrought by the English.

Accompanied by the general, I visited the private apartments of the Princess, which, up to then, our soldiers had been forbidden to enter. I found that her entire wardrobe had been thrown out of the clothes presses by the English soldiers and, together with her hats, was lying about on the floor. I had every garment carefully cleaned, hung in the presses, and locked up. The writing desk had also been broken into and the Princess's correspondence was scattered about. At my command, all the letters were gathered together, sealed in a package, placed in the writing desk, and locked up.

Afterward, al! the silverware was found buried

in the garden. According to the villagers this had been ordered as early as the *beginning of July,* so the Princess had known about the war long before its outbreak! I at once ordered that the silver be inventoried, deposited in the bank at Aix-la-Chapelle, and returned to the Princess after the war. Through neutral channels I caused news to be transmitted to the Princess in Switzerland, by my Court Marshal, Freiherr von Reischach, concerning Pinon, her silverware, and my care for her property. No answer was received. Instead, the Princess had published in the French press a letter to the effect that General von Kluck had stolen all her silver.

On account of my care and the self-sacrificing work of German art experts and soldiers—partly at the risk of their lives—art treasures worth billions were preserved for their French owners and for French towns. This was done by the Huns, the boches!

# CHAPTER XI

## The Pope and Peace

IN the summer of 1917 I received at Krueznach a visit from the Papal Nuncio, Pacelli, who was accompanied by a chaplain. Pacelli is a distinguished, likable man, of high intelligence and excellent manners, the perfect pattern of an eminent prelate of the Catholic Church. He knows German well enough to understand it easily when he hears it, but not sufficiently to speak it with fluency.

Our conversation was conducted in French, but the Nuncio now and then employed German expressions of speech. The chaplain spoke German fluently and took part—even when not asked—in the conversation, whenever he feared that the Nuncio was becoming too much influenced by what I said.

Very soon the conversation turned on the possibility of peace mediation and the bringing about of peace, in which connection all sorts of projects and possibilities were touched upon, discussed, and dismissed.

Finally, I suggested that the Pope should make an effort, seeing that my peace offer of December

12, 1916, had been rejected in such an unprecedented manner. The Nuncio remarked that he thought such a step would be attended with great difficulties; that the Pope had already been rebuffed when he had made certain advances in this direction; that, aside from this, the Pope was absolutely in despair on account of the slaughter and wondered ceaselessly how he might help toward freeing the world and European culture from the scourge of war. Any suggestion as to this, he added, would be most valuable to the Vatican.

I stated that the Pope, as the highest in rank among all the priests of the Roman Catholic Christians and Church, should, first of all, seek to issue instructions to his priests in all countries to banish hate, once for all, from their minds, since hate was the greatest obstacle in the path of the peace idea; that it was, unfortunately, true that the clergy in the Entente countries were, to a positively frightful extent, the standard-bearers and instigators of hate and fighting.

I called attention to the numerous reports from soldiers at the beginning of the war concerning abbés and parish priests captured with arms in their hands; to the machinations of Cardinal Mercier and the Belgian clergy, members of which often worked spies; to the sermon of the Protestant Bishop London, who, from the pulpit, glorified the "Baralong" murderers; and to other similar cases. I added that it would be, therefore, a great achievement if the Pope should succeed in having the Roman Catholic clergy in all the countries at war condemn hatred and recommend peace, as was already being done by the German clergy, be it from the pulpit or by means of pastoral letters.

### URGES PAPAL INTERCESSION

Pacelli found this idea excellent and worthy of attention, but he remarked that it would be difficult to enlist the efforts of the various prelates in its support. I replied that, in view of the severe discipline of the hierarchy of the Roman Catholic Church, I could not imagine that, if the Pope should solemnly call upon the prelates of the Church to preach reconciliation and consideration for the foe, those of any country whatsoever should refuse obedience; that the prelates, on account of their eminent rank, were above all parties, and, since reconciliation and love of our neighbor were fundamental principles of the Christian religion, they were absolutely in duty bound to work toward making people observe these principles.

Pacelli agreed to this and promised to give the idea his earnest attention and report upon it to the Vatican. In the further course of the conversation, the Nuncio asked what form—beyond the purely ecclesiastical step suggested by me—the bringing about of peace possibilities through the intervention of the Pope might take. I pointed out that Italy and Austria were two Roman Catholic states, upon which the Pope could bring influence to bear easily and effectively; that one of these lands was his native country and place of residence, in which he was greatly revered by the people and exerted direct influence upon his fellow countrymen; that Austria was ruled by a sovereign who actually bore the title "apostolic"; who, with all his family, had direct relations with the Vatican and was among the most faithful adherents of the Catholic Church; that I was, therefore, of the opinion that it would not be difficult for the Pope to try at least to make a beginning with these two countries and cause them to talk peace.

I added that the diplomatic skill and wide vision of the Vatican were known the world over; that, if once a beginning were made in this way—and it had a good chance of success—the other Powers could scarcely refuse an invitation from the Vatican later on to an exchange of views, which should be, at first, not binding upon them.

The Nuncio remarked that it would be difficult for the Vatican to make the Italian Government agree to such a thing, since it had no direct relation with the said Government and no influence upon its members; that the Italian Government would never look with favor upon an invitation, even to mere conferences.

Here the chaplain interposed that such a step by the Pope was absolutely out of the question, since it would entail consequences which might be actually dangerous to the Vatican; the Government would at once mobilize the "piazza" ("man in the street") against the Vatican, and the Vatican certainly could not expose itself to that. When I refused to attach importance to this objection, the chaplain grew more and more excited. He said that I did not know the Romans; that, when they were incited they were simply terrible; that just as soon as the "piazza" got into action things would get disagreeable; that, if it did, there was even a possibility of an attack on the Vatican, which might actually imperil the life of the Pope himself.

### SCOUTS DANGER FROM "PIAZZA"

I replied that I, too, was well acquainted with the Vatican; that no rabble or "piazza" could storm it; that, in addition, the Pope had a strong party of adherents in society circles and among the people, which would at once be ready to defend him. The Nuncio agreed with me, but the chaplain continued unabashed to expatiate upon the terrors of the "piazza" and paint the risks run by the Pope in the blackest of colors.

I then remarked that anyone wishing to capture the Vatican must first get a battery of heavy mortars and howitzers, as well as pioneers and storm troops, and institute a regular siege; that all this was scarcely possible for the "piazza"; that, therefore, it was highly improbable that the latter would undertake anything. Moreover, I mentioned having heard that measures had already been taken in the Vatican to guard against such an emergency. At this the priest was silent.

The Nuncio then remarked that it was difficult for the Pope to do anything really practical toward peace without giving offense and arousing opposition in lay Italy, which would place him in danger; that it must be borne in mind that he was, unfortunately, not free; that had the Pope a country, or at least a district of his own where he could govern autonomously and do as he pleased, the situation would be quite different; that, as matters stood, he was too dependent upon lay Rome and not able to act according to his own free will.

I remarked that the aim of bringing peace to the world was so holy and great that it was impossible for the Pope to be frightened away, by purely wordly considerations, from accomplishing such a task, which seemed created especially for him; that, should he succeed in it, the grateful world would assuredly bring influence to bear upon the Italian Government in support of his wishes and of his independence.

This made an impression on the Nuncio; he remarked that I was right, after all; that the Pope must do something in the matter.

Then I called the attention of the Nuncio to the following point: He must have noticed, I said, how the Socialists of all countries were zealously working in favor of peace efforts. I told him that we had always allowed the German Socialists to travel to foreign parts in order to discuss the question of making peace at conferences, because I believed them to be acquainted with the desires and views of the lower classes; that we placed no obstacles in the path of anybody desiring to work honestly and without veiled purpose in the interests of peace; that the same desires for peace also existed among the Entente nations and among their Socialists, but that the latter were prevented by refusal of passports from attending congresses in neutral lands; that the desire for peace was gaining strength in the world, nations were acquiring it more and more, and if nobody in any Government should be found willing to work for peace—I, unfortunately, had failed in my attempt—the peoples would finally take the matter into their own hands. I added that this would not occur without serious shocks and revolutions, as history proved, through which the Roman Church and the Pope would not come unscathed.

### WINS PROMISE OF ACTION

What must a Catholic soldier think, I asked, when he reads always of efforts by Socialists only, never of an effort by the Pope, to free him from the horrors of war? If the Pope did nothing, I continued, there was danger of peace being forced upon the world by the Socialists, which would mean the end of the power of the Pope and the Roman Church, even among Catholics!

This argument struck home to the Nuncio. He stated that he would at once report it to the Vatican and give it his support; that the Pope would have to act.

Greatly worried, the chaplain again interposed, remarking that the Pope would endanger himself by such a course; that the "piazza" would attack him.

To this I replied that I was a Protestant, and, hence, a heretic in the chaplain's eyes, notwithstanding which I was obliged to point out that the Pope was designated the "Viceroy of Christ upon earth" by the Catholic Church and world; that I had, in studying the Holy Scriptures, occupied myself earnestly and carefully with the person of the Saviour and sought to immerse myself profoundly therein; that the Lord had never feared the "piazza," although no fortresslike building, with guards and weapons, was at His disposal; that the Lord had always walked into the midst of the "piazza," spoken to it, and finally gone to His death on the Cross for the sake of this hostile "piazza."

Was I now to believe, I asked, that His "Viceroy upon earth" was afraid of the possibility of becoming a martyr, like his Lord, in order to bring peace to the bleeding world, all on account of the ragged Roman "piazza"? I, the Protestant, thought far too highly of a Roman priest, particularly of the Pope, to believe such a thing. Nothing could be more glorious for him, I went on, than to devote himself unreservedly, body and soul, to the great cause of peace, even despite the remote danger of thus becoming a martyr!

With shining eyes, the Nuncio grasped my hand and said, deeply moved: "Vous avez parfaitement raison! C'est le devoir du Pape; il faut qu'il agisse; c'est par lui que le monde doit être régagné à la paix. Je transmettrai vos paroles à Sa Sainteté" ("You are absolutely right! It is the duty of the Pope; he must act; it is through him that the world must be won back to peace. I shall transmit your words to His Holiness").

The chaplain turned away, shaking his head, and murmured to himself: "Ah, la piazza, la piazza!"

ROTOPHOT-BERLIN · 1904
KAISER WILHELM II.
9592

## CHAPTER XII

### End of the War and My Abdication

A FEW days after August 8, 1918, I summoned a Crown Council, in order to get a clear conception of the situation and to draw therefrom the necessary conclusions upon which to base the policy to be followed by Count Hertling. The Chief Military Command approved the idea that the Imperial Chancellor should keep in sight the possibility of getting into closer touch with the enemy, but laid stress on the necessity of first occupying the Siegfried line and there thoroughly beating off the foe, and on the fact that negotiations must not begin before this occurred. Thereupon I directed that the Chancellor get into communication with a neutral power—the Netherlands—in order to ascertain whether it was ready to undertake such a step toward mediation.

What rendered the contemplated action through Dutch channels very difficult was that Austria could not be brought to a definite agreement, but continually postponed the declaration which had been requested of her. Even a verbal agreement given to me by the Emperor Charles was afterward broken by him under Burian's influence.

The Dutch government had already been informed by me and had signified its readiness to act. Meanwhile, Austria, without notifying us, made her first separate peace offer, which set the ball rolling. The Emperor Charles had indeed got into touch secretly with the Entente and had long since resolved to abandon us. He acted according to the plan which he had explained thus to his entourage: "When I go to the Germans, I agree to everything they say, and when I return home, I do whatever I please."

Thus it happened that my government and I were constantly deceived by actions in Vienna, without being able to do anything against it, since from there we constantly received the hint: "If you make things hard for us, we shall leave you in the lurch; in other words, our army will no longer fight by your side." In view of our situation, such action on Austria's part had to be avoided in any way possible, both on military and political grounds.

The defection of Hungary and Austria brought a crisis upon us. Had Emperor Charles kept control of his nerves for three weeks longer, many things would have turned out differently. But Andrassy—as he himself admitted—had been negotiating for a long time in Switzerland, behind our backs, with the Entente. Thus Emperor Charles believed that he would assure himself of good treatment at the hands of the Entente.

After our failure of August 8th, General Ludendorff had declared that he could no longer guarantee a military victory. Therefore, the preparation of peace negotiations was necessary. Since diplomacy had not succeeded in initiating any promising negotiations and the military situation had become even worse in the meantime, on account of revolutionary agitation, Ludendorff, on the 29th of September, demanded that preparations be made for an armistice instead of for peace negotiations.

### MOVEMENT FOR ABDICATION

At this critical time a strong movement began at home in favor of setting up a new government for the now necessary termination of the war. I could not ignore this movement, since the old government, during the seven weeks from August 8th to the end of September, had not managed to initiate peace negotiations offering any hope of success.

Meanwhile, General von Gallwitz and General von Mudra, summoned from the front, appeared before me. They gave a picture of the inner situation of the army, laying due emphasis upon the great number of shirkers behind the front, the frequency of insubordination, the displaying of the red flag upon trains filled with soldiers returning from furloughs at home and other similar phenomena.

The two generals considered that the principal cause of the bad conditions was to be sought in the unfavorble influence exerted upon the soldiers by the spirit predominating behind the front and in the general desire for ending the fighting and getting peace, which was spreading from the homeland along the lines of communication behind the front and was already becoming noticeable even among some of the troops at the front itself. The generals advanced the opinion that, owing to these reasons, the army must immediately be withdrawn behind the Antwerp-Meuse line.

On that same day I commanded Field Marshal von Hindenburg by telephone to effect as soon as possible the retreat to the Antwerp-Meuse line. The falling back of the tired, but nowhere decisively beaten, army to this position merely signified occupying an essentially shorter line, possessing far greater natural advantages. It was not yet completed, to be sure, but the fact was to be borne in mind that we had engaged in battle on the Somme while occupying positions composed largely of shell craters. What we had to do was to regain operative freedom, which, to my way of thinking, was by no means impossible; in the course of the war, had we not often retreated in order to put ourselves in a situation that was more advantageous from the military point of view?

The army, to be sure, was no longer the old army. The new 1918 troops particularly were badly tainted with revolutionary propaganda and often took advantage of the darkness at night to sneak away from the firing and vanish to the rear.

But the majority of my divisions fought flawlessly to the very end and preserved their discipline and military spirit. To the very end they were always a match for the foe in morale; despite superiority in numbers, cannon, munitions, tanks, and airplanes, the foe invariably succumbed when he ran up against serious resistance. Therefore, the associations of our ex-fighters at the front are right in bearing upon their banners the motto: "Unbeaten on land and sea!"

### SAYS ARMY WAS STILL STRONG

The achievements of the German fighters at the front and of the German Nation in arms, during four and a half years of war, are beyond all praise. One does not know what to admire most: the enthusiasm with which the magnificent youth of 1914, without waiting for our artillery fire to take effect, joyfully charged on the enemy, or the self-sacrificing fidelity to duty and tenacity with which our men in field gray, sparingly fed and seldom relieved, year in, year out, digging by night, living in dugouts and earthholes by day, or crouching in shell holes, defied the hail of steel from the enemy artillery, flyers, and tanks. And this army, which one might have expected was to be rated as utterly fought to a finish, was able, after nearly four years of war, to carry out successful offensive operations such as our foes could nowhere boast of, despite their colossal superiority.

In spite of all this, it was not right to believe the German army capable of accomplishing the superhuman; it was necessary for us to fall back, in order to get breath.

The Field Marshal balked at the order to retreat; the army, he thought, should stay were it was, for political reasons (peace negotiations and so on); he also pointed out, among other things, that it was necessary, first, to arrange for the withdrawal to the rear of war materials, etc.

I now resolved to go to the front, acquiescing in the desire expressed to me by the army that I might be with my hard-fighting troops and convince myself personally of their spirit and condition.

I could carry out this resolve all the sooner in view of the fact that, ever since the new Government had been set up, no further claims were made upon my time either by it or by the Imperial Chancellor, which made my staying at home seem useless.

The notes to Wilson were discussed and written by Solf, the War Cabinet, and the Reichstag, after sessions lasting hours, without my being informed thereof; until, finally, on the occasion of the last note to Wilson, I caused Solf to be given to understand very plainly, through my chief of Cabinet, that I demanded to know about the note *before* it was sent.

Solf appeared and showed the note; he was proud of his antithesis between *laying down* of arms ("Waffenstreckung"), which was demanded by Wilson, and *armistice* ("Waffenstillstand"), which was proposed. When I spoke about the rumors of abdication and demanded that the Foreign Office adopt an attitude, through the press, against what was unworthy in the newspaper polemics, Solf replied that already everybody on every street corner was talking about abdication and that, even in the best circles, people were discussing it quite unreservedly.

When I expressed my indignation at this, Solf sought to console me by observing that, should His Majesty go, he also would, since he could serve no longer under such conditions. I went, or—to put it much more correctly—I was overthrown by my own Government, and—Herr Solf remained.

When the Imperial Chancellor, Prince Max, heard of my resolve to go to the front, he did all he could to prevent it. He asked why I wished to go and received the answer that I considered it my duty, as Supreme Commander, to return to the front, since I had been separated for almost a month from the hard-fighting army. When the Chancellor objected that I was indispensable at home, I retorted that we were at war, that the Emperor belonged to his soldiers. Finally, I declared, once for all, that I would go; that in case Wilson's armistice note arrived, it would have to be discussed, anyhow, at the General Headquarters of the army, for which purpose the Chancellor and other members of the Government would be obliged to go to Spa for the conferences.

### "JOYFULLY RECEIVED" BY ARMY

I went to the army in Flanders, after having once more given the General Staff at Spa definite orders to fall back as quickly as possible to the

Antwerp-Meuse line, in order that the troops might finally be taken out of the fighting and given a rest. Despite objections that this would demand time, that the position was not yet ready, that the war material must first be taken back, and so forth, I stood by the order. The retreat was begun.

In Flanders I saw delegations from the different divisions, spoke with the soldiers, distributed decorations, and was everywhere joyfully received by officers and men. Particularly ardent enthusiasm reigned among the soldiers of a royal Saxon recruit depot, who greeted me with wild cheers at the railway station when I was returning to my train. While I was giving out decorations to members of the Reserve Guard Division, an enemy bombing squadron, followed by heavy fire from anti-aircraft guns and machine guns, flew directly over us and dropped bombs near the special train.

The commanders of the army were unanimous in declaring that the spirit of the troops at the front was good and reliable; that, further to the rear, among the supply columns, it was not so good; that the worst of all were the soldiers back from leave, who, it was plain to be seen, had been worked upon and infected at home, whence they had brought back a poor spirit. The young recruits at the depots, it was stated, furthermore, were good.

At Spa, whither I now went, news came constantly from home about the ever more violent agitation and hostile attitude against the Emperor and the growing slackness and helplessness of the Government, which, without initiative or strength, was letting itself be pushed around at will. It was alluded to contemptuously in the newspapers as the "debating society" and Prince Max was called by leading newspapers the "Revolution Chancellor." As I learned afterward, he lay in bed for ten days, suffering from grippe and incapable of really directing affairs. His Excellency von Payer and Solf, with the so-called War Cabinet, which was in permanent session, governed the German Empire.

At such a critical time, to my way of thinking, the imperiled ship of state should not be steered by representatives of the Imperial Chancellor, since they certainly cannot have the authority possessed by the responsible head of the Government. What was particularly needed at this juncture was authority; yet, so far as I know, no wide powers to act had been conferred upon the Vice Chancellor.

The right solution—*i. e.,* the one that those concerned were in duty bound to adopt—would have been to remove Prince Max actually from the post of Chancellor and summon in his place some man of strong personality. Since we had the parliamentary form of government it devolved upon the political parties to bring about the change in the Chancellorship and present me with a successor to Prince Max. This did not take place.

Now the efforts of the Government and the Imperial Chancellor to induce me to abdicate began. Drews, the Minister of the Interior, came to me at the behest of the Chancellor, in order to supply me with information concerning the spirit in the country. He described the well-known happenings in press, high finance, and public, and laid emphasis on the fact that the Imperial Chancellor himself adopted no attitude toward the question of my abdication, but, nevertheless, had sent him to me. Drews, in short, was to suggest to me that I myself should decide to abdicate, in order that it might not appear that the Government had exerted pressure upon me.

I spoke to the Minister about the fateful consequences of my abdication and asked how he, as a Prussian official, could reconcile such a supposition with his oath as an official to his King. The Minister grew embarrassed and excused himself by reference to the command of the Imperial Chancellor, who had been unable to find any other man for the task. I was informed later that Drews was one of the first officials who spoke of the abdication of his master and King.

I refused to abdicate and declared that I would gather troops together and return with them in order to help the Government to maintain order in the land.

After that, Drews was received, in my presence, by Field Marshal von Hindenburg and General Gröner, whom he informed of the mission intrusted to him by the Imperial Chancellor and by both of whom he was very sharply rebuked in the name of the army. Gröner's characterization of Prince

Max, in particular, was expressed in such plain terms that I had to appease and comfort the Minister.

The Field Marshal also called Drews's attention to the fact that, in the event of my abdication, the army would not go on fighting, but would disperse, and that the majority of the officers, in particular, would probably resign and thus leave the army without leaders.

Soon after that I learned from one of my sons that the Imperial Chancellor had tried to ascertain whether he was prepared to undertake the mission which subsequently was undertaken by Drews. My son indignantly declined to suggest abdication to his father.

In the meantime I had sent the chief of Cabinet, von Delbrück, to Berlin, in order to lay before the Chancellor a general address, also intended for publication, which should take the place of my address to the Ministry (not published by the Chancellor), deal more broadly with the matters taken up therein, and make clear my attitude toward the Government and toward the new direction taken by public opinion. At first the Chancellor failed to publish this. Not until several days later did he find himself forced to permit publication, owing to a letter written to him, as I learned afterward, by the Empress.

Thereupon Herr von Delbrück informed me that the address had made a good impression in Berlin and in the press, relieved the situation, and tended to quiet the people, so that the idea of abdication had begun to disappear and even the Socialists of the Right had decided to postpone action concerning it.

### SOCIALIST ACTIVITY

During the next few days there were constant reports that the Socialists in Berlin were planning trouble and that the Chancellor was growing steadily more nervous. The report given by Drews to the Government, after his return from Spa, had not failed to cause an impression; the gentlemen wished to get rid of me, to be sure, but for the time being they were afraid of the consequences.

Their point of view was as obscure as their conduct. They acted as if they did not want a republic, yet failed completely to realize that their course was bound to lead straight to a republic. Many, in fact, explained the actions of the Government by maintaining that the creation of a republic was the very end that its members had in view; plenty of people drew the conclusion, from the puzzling conduct of the Chancellor toward me, that he was working to eliminate me in order to become himself President of the German Republic, after being, in the interim, the administrator of the Empire.

To believe this is undoubtedly to do the Prince an injustice; such a train of thought is impossible in a man belonging to an old German princely family.

General Gröner, who had gone to Berlin to study the situation, reported on his return that he had received very bad impressions regarding the Government and the sentiment prevailing in the country; that things were approaching revolution; that the Government was merely tearing down without setting up anything positive; that the people wanted peace at last, at any cost, no matter what kind of peace; that the authority of the Government was equal to zero, the agitation against the Emperor in full swing, my abdication hardly to be avoided longer.

He added that the troops at home were unreliable and disagreeable surprises might come in case of a revolt; that the courier chests of the Russian Bolshevist ambassador, seized by the criminal police, had disclosed some very damaging evidence that the Russian Embassy, in conjunction with the Spartacus group, had long since thoroughly prepared, without being disturbed, a Bolshevist revolution on the Russian model. (This had gone on with the knowledge of the Foreign Office—which had received constant warning, but had either laughed at them all or dismissed them with the remark that the Bolsheviki must not be angered—likewise under the very eyes of the police, which was continually at loggerheads with the Foreign Office.) The men back from leave, he went on, infected by propaganda, had already carried the poison to the army, which was already partly affected and would, as soon as it had been made free by an armistice, refuse to fight against the rebels upon its return home.

Therefore, he declared, it was necessary to accept, immediately and unconditionally, any sort of armistice, no matter how hard its conditions might be; the army was no longer to be trusted and revolution was imminent behind the front.

PRINCE MAX INSISTENT

On the morning of the 9th of November,[1] the Imperial Chancellor, Prince Max of Baden, caused me to be informed again—as he had already done on the 7th—that the Social Democrats, and also the Social Democratic Secretaries of State, demanded my abdication; that the rest of the members of the Government, who had stood out so far against it, were now in favor of it, and that the same was true of the majority parties in the Reichstag. For these reasons, he continued, he requested me to abdicate immediately, since, otherwise, extensive street fighting attended by bloodshed would take place in Berlin; it had already started on a small scale.

I immediately summoned Field Marshal von Hindenburg and the Quartermaster General, General Gröner. General Gröner again announced that the army could fight no longer and wished rest above all else, and that, therefore, any sort of armistice must be unconditionally accepted; that the armistice must be concluded as soon as possible, since the army had supplies for only six

[1] Concerning the course of events up to the fateful 9th of November and this day itself there are authentic statements by an eyewitness in the book (well worth reading) of Major Niemann, who was sent by the Chief Army Command to me, entitled *War and Revolution* (*Krieg und Revolution*), Berlin, 1922.

to eight days more and was cut off from all further supplies by the rebels, who had occupied all the supply storehouses and Rhine bridges; that, for some unexplained reason, the armistice commission sent to France—consisting of Erzberger, Ambassador Count Oberndorff, and General von Winterfeldt—which had crossed the French lines two evenings before, had sent no report as to the nature of the conditions.

The Crown Prince also appeared, with his Chief of Staff, Count Schulenburg, and took part in the conference. During our conversation several telephone inquiries came from the Imperial Chancellor, which, pointing out that the Social Democrats had left the Government and that delay was dangerous, became most insistent. The Minister of War reported uncertainty among part of the troops in Berlin—4th Jägers, Second Company of Alexander Regiment, Second Battery, Jüterbog, gone over to the rebels—no street fighting.

I wished to spare my people civil war. If my abdication was indeed the only way to prevent bloodshed, I was willing to *renounce the Imperial throne, but not to abdicate as King of Prussia;* I would remain, as such, with my troops, since the military leaders had declared that the officers would leave in crowds if I abdicated entirely, and the army would then pour back, without leaders, into the fatherland, damage it, and place it in peril.

A reply had been sent to the Imperial Chancellor to the effect that my decision must first be carefully weighed and formulated, after which it would be transmitted to the Chancellor. When, a little later, this was done, there came the surprising answer that my decision had arrived late! The Imperial Chancellor, on his own initiative, had summarily announced my abdication—which had not occurred yet at all!—as well as renunciation of the throne by the Crown Prince, who had not even been questioned. He had turned over the Government to the Social Democrats and summoned Herr Ebert as Imperial Chancellor. All this had been spread simultaneously by wireless, so the entire army could read it.

### DENIES HE FORSOOK FOLLOWERS

Thus the decision as to my going or staying, as to my renunciation of the Imperial Crown and retention of the Royal Crown of Prussia, was summarily snatched from me. The army was shaken to the core by the erroneous belief that its King had abandoned it at the most critical moment of all.

If the conduct of the Imperial Chancellor, Prince Max of Baden, is considered as a whole, it appears as follows: first, solemn declaration that he will place himself, together with the new Government, before the Emperor's throne, to protect it; then, suppression of the address, which might have impressed public opinion favorably, elimination of the Emperor from all co-operation in the Government, sacrifice of the respect due the Emperor by suppression of the censorship, failure to come to the support of the monarchy in the matter of abdication; then, attempts to persuade the Emperor to abdicate voluntarily; and, finally, announcement of my abdication by wireless, in which the Chancellor went over my head.

This sequence of events shows the course—a perilous one to the nation—adopted by Scheidemann, who held the Chancellor in the hollow of his hand. Scheidemann left the Ministers, his colleagues, in the dark as to his real purposes, drove the Prince from one step to another, and finally summoned Ebert, declaring that the leaders no longer had the masses under control. Thus he caused the Prince to sacrifice the Emperor, the princes, and the Empire, and made him the destroyer of the Empire. After that, Scheidemann overthrew the weak princely "statesman."

Following the arrival of the wireless message, the situation was difficult. To be sure, troops were being transported to Spa for the purpose of going on undisturbed with the work at Great General Headquarters, but the Field Marshal now thought it no longer possible to reckon absolutely on their reliability in case rebellious forces should advance from Aix-le-Chapelle and Cologne and confront our troops with the dilemma of whether or not to fight against their own comrades. In view of this, he advised me to leave the army and go to some neutral country, for the purpose of avoiding such a "civil war."

I went through a fearful internal struggle. On the one hand, I, as a soldier, was outraged at the idea of abandoning my still faithful, brave troops. On the other hand, there was the declaration of our foes that they were unwilling to conclude with me any peace endurable to Germany, as well as the statement of my own Government that only by my departure for foreign parts was civil war to be prevented.

In this struggle I set aside all that was personal. I consciously sacrificed myself and my throne in the belief that, by so doing, I was best serving the interests of my beloved fatherland. The sacrifice was in vain. My departure brought us neither better armistice conditions nor better peace terms; nor did it prevent civil war—on the contrary, it hastened and intensified, in the most pernicious manner, the disintegration in the army and the nation.

### PROUD OF THE ARMY

For thirty years the army was my pride. For it I lived, upon it I labored. And now, after four and a half brilliant years of war with unprecedented victories, it was forced to collapse by the stab in the back from the dagger of the revolutionists, at the very moment when peace was within reach!

And the fact that it was in my proud navy, my creation, that there was first open rebellion, cut me most deeply to the heart.

There has been much talk about my having abandoned the army and gone to neutral foreign parts.

Some say the Emperor should have gone to some regiment at the front, hurled himself with it upon the enemy, and sought death in one last attack. That, however, would not only have rendered impossible the armistice, ardently desired by the nation, concerning which the commission sent from Berlin to General Foch was already negotiating, but would also have meant the useless sacrifice of the lives of many soldiers—of some of the very best and most faithful, in fact.

Others say the Emperor should have returned home at the head of the army. But a peaceful return was no longer possible; the rebels had already seized the Rhine bridges and other important points in the rear of the army. I could, to be sure, have forced my way back at the head of loyal troops taken from the fighting front; but, by so doing, I should have put the finishing touch to Germany's collapse, since, in addition to the struggle with the enemy, who would certainly have pressed forward in pursuit, civil war would also have ensued.

Still others say the Emperor should have killed himself. That was made impossible by my firm Christian beliefs. And would not people have exclaimed:

"How cowardly! Now he shirks all responsibility by committing suicide!" This alternative was also eliminated because I had to consider how to be of help and use to my people and my country in the evil time that was to be foreseen.

I knew also that I was particularly called upon

to champion the cause of my people in the clearing up of the question of war guilt—which was disclosing itself more and more as the pivotal point in our future destiny—since I better than anyone else could bear witness to Germany's desire for peace and to our clean conscience.

After unspeakably arduous soul struggles, and following the most urgent advice of my counselors of the highest rank who were present at the moment, I decided to leave the country, since, in view of the reports made to me, I must needs believe that, by so doing, I should most faithfully serve Germany, make possible better armistice and peace terms for her, and spare her further loss of human lives, distress, and misery.

## CHAPTER XIII

### The Enemy Tribunal and the Neutral Tribunal

WHEN the Entente's demand that I and the German army leaders should be surrendered for trial before Entente tribunals became known, I immediately asked myself whether I could be of use to my fatherland by giving myself up before the German people and the German Government had expressed themselves regarding this demand. It was clear to me that, in the opinion of the Entente, such a surrender would so seriously shake the prestige of Germany, as a state and people, for all time, that we could never again take our place, with equal rights, equal dignity, and equal title to alliances, in the first rank of nations, where we belonged.

I recognized it as my duty not to sacrifice the honor and dignity of Germany. The question resolved itself into deciding whether there was any way to give myself up which might benefit the German nation and not subject it to the above-mentioned disadvantages. Were there such a way I should have been ready without hesitation to add another sacrifice to those already made.

The question of my giving myself up has also been debated—as I know—in well-meaning and earnest German circles. Wherever this was due to psychological depression or failure to realize the impression which self-chastisement, self-debasement, and fruitless martyrdom in the face of the Entente must arouse, all that was needed was to recall the materially political origin of the Entente's demand, cursorily mentioned above, in order to arrive at a clean-cut decision—in other words, at an emphatic refusal.

It was otherwise with the considerations based upon the assumption that I might, by taking upon myself, before the eyes of the whole world, the responsibility for all important decisions and acts of my Government connected with the war, contribute toward making the fate of the German nation easier. Here was not an act of unpolitical sentimentality, but, on the contrary, a deed which, in my eyes, had much to commend it. The thought that, according to the Constitution of the Empire then in force, not I, but the Chancellor alone as was well known—bore the responsibility, would naturally not have bothered me with regard to this.

Had there been even the slightest prospect of bettering Germany's situation by taking such a step, there would have been no possible doubt for me personally as to what I should do. Already I had shown my personal willingness to sacrifice myself when I left the country and gave up the throne of my fathers, because I had been erroneously and deceivingly assured that I could, by so doing, make possible better peace terms for my people and prevent civil war. I should likewise have made this further attempt to help my people, despite the fact that, in the meantime, one of the considerations in favor of it which have been urged upon me—*viz.*, the prevention of civil war—had already turned out to be false.

### RECALLS PLIGHT OF VERCINGETORIX

There was, however, no possibility of helping the German people by such an act. Surrender of my person would have had no result beyond our obedience to the demand from the Entente that I be given up. For no tribunal in the world can pronounce a just sentence before the state archives of *all* the nations participating in the war are thrown open, as has been done, and is still being done, by Germany.

Who, after the unprecedented judgment of Versailles, could still summon up optimism enough to believe that the Entente nations would place their secret documents at the disposal of such a tribunal? Therefore, after careful reflection on my part, I gave the decisive importance that was their due to the above-mentioned weighty considerations of personal and national dignity and honor, and rejected the idea of giving myself up. It was not for me to play the rôle of Vercingetorix, who, as is well known, relying upon the magnanimity of his foes, surrendered himself to them in order to obtain a better fate for his people. In view of the conduct of our enemies during the war and in the peace negotiations, it was surely not to be assumed that the Entente would show any greater magnanimity than did Cæsar when he threw the noble Gaul into chains, subsequently had him executed, and, in spite of what Vercingetorix had done, enslaved his people just the same.

I wish to remark in a general way that it has always proved wrong to follow the suggestions of the enemy or to heed them to any extent. The well-meant suggestions regarding my giving myself up, emanating from Germans, also grew from the soil of the enemy demands, though perhaps partly unknown to those making them. For that very reason it was necessary to refuse to heed them.

Thus the only solution remaining is an international, nonpartisan court, which, instead of trying individuals, shall examine and pronounce judgment upon all the happenings leading to the World War, in all the countries taking part therein, after all the national archives, not merely those of Germany, have been opened up. Germany can well agree to this mode of procedure. Whosoever opposes it pronounces judgment upon himself!

My standpoint on the subject here discussed is expressed in the letter reproduced below, which I addressed, under date of April 5, 1921, to Field Marshal von Hindenburg, and which the latter has made public in the meantime. To make matters clearer, the letter which preceded it, from the Marshal, is also given.[1]

HINDENBURG'S LETTER

HANOVER, *March 30, 1921.*

YOUR IMPERIAL AND ROYAL MAJESTY:

I beg to thank Your Majesty most respectfully for his gracious interest in the illness of my wife. She is not yet out of danger.

I have little that is pleasant to report from our country. The troubles in Central Germany are more serious than they are represented to be by the Prussian Government. I hope that they will soon be suppressed.

The effects of the Versailles peace decree lie ever more crushingly upon the German people, and the object of this peace—the policy of annihilation of our enemies—comes more plainly to the fore every day. For the purpose of justifying this policy of force the fairy tale of German war guilt must be adhered to.

The spokesman of the enemy alliance, Mr. Lloyd George, is little disturbed by the fact that, on December 20th of last year, he declared that no statesman wished war in the summer of 1914, that all the nations had slipped or stumbled into it. In his speech at the London conference on March 3d he calmly remarked that Germany's responsibility for the war was fundamental, that it was the basis on which the Peace of Versailles was erected, and that, if the admission of this guilt should be refused or given up, the treaty would become untenable.

Now as before, the question of war guilt is the cardinal point in the future of the German nation. The admission of our alleged "guilt" regarding the war, forced from the German representatives at Versailles

[1] This letter and the letter from the Field Marshal which preceded it are reprinted herewith. The parts which are most important in relation to the matter in question are underscored in the text.

against their judgment, is wreaking frightful vengeance; equally so the untrue acknowledgment of Germany's "complicity" which Minister Simons gave at the London conference.

I agree with Your Majesty to the uttermost depths of my soul—in my long term of military service I have had the good fortune and honor to enter into close personal relations with Your Majesty. I know that all the efforts of Your Majesty throughout your reign were bent toward maintaining peace. I can realize how immeasurably hard it is for Your Majesty to be eliminated from positive co-operation for the fatherland.

The *Comparative Historical Tables* compiled by Your Majesty, a printed copy of which Your Majesty sent me recently, are a good contribution to the history of the origin of the war and are calculated to remove many an incorrect conception. I have regretted that Your Majesty did not make the tables public, but limited them instead to a small circle. Now that the tables, owing to indiscretions, have been published in the foreign press, partly in the form of incomplete excerpts, it seems to me advisable to have them published in full in the German press.

To my great joy I have heard that there has been an improvement recently in the health of Her Majesty. May God help further!

With the deepest respect, unlimited fidelity and gratitude, I am Your Imperial and Royal Majesty's most humble servant,

(Signed) VON HINDENBURG,
Field Marshal.

### THE KAISER'S LETTER

HOUSE DOORN, *April 5, 1921.*

MY DEAR FIELD MARSHAL:

Accept my warmest thanks for your letter of March 30th, ult. You are right. The hardest thing of all for me is to be obliged to live in foreign parts, to follow, with burning anguish in my soul, the awful fate of our dear fatherland, to which I have devoted the labors of my entire life, and to be barred from cooperation.

You stood beside me during the dark, fatal days of November, 1918. As you know, I forced myself to the difficult, terrible decision to leave the country only upon the urgent declaration of yourself and the rest of my counselors who had been summoned that only by my so doing would it be possible to obtain more favorable armistice terms for our people and spare it a bloody civil war.

The sacrifice was in vain. Now, as well as before, the enemy wishes to make the German people expiate the alleged guilt of "Imperial Germany."

### SILENT UNDER ATTACKS

In my endeavor to subordinate all personal considerations to the welfare of Germany, I keep myself completely in the background. I am silent in the face of all the lies and slanders which are spread abroad concerning me. I consider it beneath my dignity to defend myself against attacks and abuse.

In accordance with this policy of restraint I have also kept the *Historical Tables* mentioned by you strictly objective and made them accessible only to a narrow circle of acquaintances. I am utterly at a loss to understand how they have now become public through some sort of indiscretion or theft (?). The purpose inspiring me when I prepared the historical tables was this: To bring together strictly historical material by a systematic enumeration of sober facts, such as might enable the reader to form his own judgment of the historical happenings preceding the war. I found my most convincing sources, be it remarked, in the literature which has sprung up after the war, particularly in the works of natives of the enemy countries. Therefore I am glad that you find my modest contribution to history useful.

As to your suggestion to make the tables, which have been completed in the meantime, accessible to the German press, I thank you, and will follow it.[1]

Truth will hew a way for itself—mightily, irresistibly, like an avalanche. Whoever does not close his ears to it against his better judgment must admit that, during my twenty-six-year reign previous to the war, German's foreign policy was directed solely to the maintenance of peace. Its one and only aim was to protect our sacred native soil, threatened from the west and the east, and the peaceful development of our commerce and political economy.

Had we ever had warlike intentions we should have struck the blow in 1900, when England's hands were tied by the Boer War, Russia's by the Japanese War, at which time almost certain victory beckoned us. In any event, we assuredly would not have singled out the year 1914, when we were confronted by a compact, overwhelmingly superior foe. Also, every impartial man must acknowledge to himself that Germany could expect nothing from the war, whereas our enemies hoped to obtain from it the complete realization of the aims which they had based, long since, upon our annihilation.

The fact that my zealous efforts and those of my Government were concentrated, during the critical July and August days of 1914, upon maintaining world peace is being proved more and more conclusively by the most recent literary and documentary publications in Germany, and, most especially, in the enemy countries. The most effective proof thereof is Sazonoff's statement: "The German Emperor's love of peace is a guarantee to us that we ourselves can decide upon the

[1] This has meanwhile been done. The *Comparative Historical Tables from 1878 to the Outbreak of the War in 1914* were published in December, 1921, by K. F. Koehler, Leipsic.

moment of war." What further proof of our innocence is needed? The above means that the intention existed to make an attack upon one who was absolutely unsuspecting.

#### CALLS ACCUSATION FUTILE

God is my witness that I, in order to avoid war, went to the uttermost limit compatible with responsibility for the security and inviolability of my dear fatherland.

It is futile to accuse Germany of war guilt. To-day there is no longer any doubt that not Germany, but the alliance of her foes, prepared the war according to a definite plan, and intentionally caused it.

For the purpose of concealing this, the allied enemies extorted the false "admission of guilt" from Germany in the shameful Peace Treaty and demanded that I *be produced before a hostile tribunal.* You, my dear Field Marshal, know me too well not to be aware that no sacrifice for my beloved fatherland is too great for me. Nevertheless, a *tribunal in which the enemy alliance would be at once plaintiff and judge would be not an organ of justice, but an instrument of political arbitrariness, and would serve only, through the sentence which would inevitably be passed upon me, to justify subsequently the unprecedented peace conditions imposed upon us.* Therefore, the enemy's demand naturally had to be rejected by me.

But, in addition, the idea of *my being produced before a neutral tribunal,* no matter how constituted, cannot be entertained by me. *I do not recognize the validity of any sentence pronounced by any mortal judge whatsoever, be he never so exalted in rank, upon the measures taken by me most conscientiously as Emperor and King—in other words, as the constitutional, not responsible, representative of the German nation—* since, were I to do so, I should thereby be sacrificing the honor and dignity of the German nation represented by me.

## THE TRIBUNALS

*Legal proceedings having to do with guilt and punishment,* instituted solely *against the head* of one of the nations which took part in the war, *deprive that one nation of every vestige of equality of rights with the other nations,* and thereby of its prestige in the community of nations. Moreover, this would cause, as a consequence, *the impression desired by the enemy* that *the entire "question of guilt" concerns only this one head of a nation and the one nation represented by him.* It must be taken into consideration, moreover, that *a nonpartisan judgment of the "question of guilt" is impossible,* if the *legal proceedings are not made to include the heads and leading statesmen of the enemy powers,* and if their conduct is not subjected to the same investigation, since it goes without saying that the conduct of the aforesaid one nation at the outbreak of the war can be judged correctly only if there is simultaneous consideration of the actions of its opponents.

*A real clearing up of the "question of guilt,"* in which surely Germany would have no less interest than her foes, could be accomplished only if *an international, nonpartisan tribunal, instead of trying individuals as criminals, should establish all the events which led to the World War,* as well as all other offenses against international law, in order thereafter to measure correctly the guilt of individuals implicated in every one of the nations participating in the war.

Such an honest suggestion was officially made in Germany after the end of the war, but, so far as I know, it was partly refused, partly found unworthy of any answer at all. Furthermore, Germany, immediately after the war, unreservedly threw open her archives, whereas the enemy alliance has taken good care so far not to follow such an example. The secret documents from the Russian archives, now being made public in America, are but the beginning.

This method of procedure on the part of the enemy alliance in itself, combined with overwhelming damag ing evidence coming to hand, shows where the "war guilt" is really to be sought! This makes it all the more a solemn duty for Germany to collect, sift, and make public, by every possible means, every bit of material bearing on the "question of guilt," in order, by so doing, to unmask the real originators of the war.

Unfortunately, the condition of Her Majesty has become worse. My heart is filled with the most grievous worry.

God with us!

Your grateful

(Signed) WILHELM.

Ich kenne keine Parteien mehr,
kenne nur noch Deutsche.
Coblenz.
26/VIII. 1914.

# CHAPTER XIV

## The Question of Guilt

HISTORY can show nothing to compare with the World War of 1914-18. It also can show nothing like the perplexity which has arisen as to the causes leading up to the World War.

This is all the more astounding in that the Great War befell a highly cultivated, enlightened, politically trained race of men, and the causes leading up to it were plainly to be seen.

The apparent complicity in the crisis of July, 1914, should deceive nobody. The telegrams exchanged at that time between the Cabinets of the great powers and their rulers, the activities of the statesmen and leading private individuals in verbal negotiations with important personages of the Entente, were certainly of the greatest importance on account of the decisive significance assumed by almost every word when it came from responsible lips, by every line that was written or telegraphed. The essential basis of the causes of the war, however, is not altered by such things; it is firmly established, and people must never hesitate from freeing it, calmly and with an eye to realities, from the bewildering outcroppings from the events accompanying the outbreak of war.

The general situation of the German Empire in the period before the war had become continually more brilliant, and for that very reason continually more difficult from the point of view of foreign politics. Unprecedented progress in industry, commerce, and world traffic had made Germany prosperous. The curve of our development tended steadily upward.

The concomitant of this peaceful penetration of a considerable part of the world's markets, to which German diligence and our achievements justly entitled us, was bound to be disagreeable to older nations of the world, particularly to England. This is quite a natural phenomenon, having nothing remarkable about it. Nobody is pleased when a competitor suddenly appears and obliges one to look on while the old customers desert to him. For this reason I cannot reproach the British Empire because of English ill humor at Germany's progress in the world's markets.

Had England been able, by introducing better commercial methods, to overcome or restrict German competition, she would have been quite within her rights in doing so and no objections could have been made. It simply would have been a case of the better man winning. In the life of nations nobody can find it objectionable if two nations contend against each other peacefully by the same methods—*i. e.,* peaceful methods—yet with all their energy, daring, and organizing ability, each striving to benefit itself.

On the other hand, it is quite another matter if one of these nations sees its assets on the world's balance sheet threatened by the industry, achievements, and super business methods of the other, and hence, not being able to apply ability like that of its young competitor, resorts to force—*i. e.,* to methods that are not those of peace, but of war—in order to call a halt upon the other nation in its peaceful campaign of competition, or to annihilate it.

### NAVY MERELY PROTECTIVE

Our situation became more serious since we were obliged to build a navy for the protection of our welfare, which, in the last analysis, was not based on the nineteen billions yearly to which German exports and imports amounted. The supposition that we built this navy for the purpose of attacking and destroying the far stronger English fleet is absurd, since it would have been impossible for us to win a victory on the water, because of the discrepancy between the two navies. Moreover, we were striding forward in the world market in accordance with our desires and had no cause for complaint. Why, then, should we wish to jeopardize the results of our peaceful labors?

In France the idea of revenge had been sedulously cultivated ever since 1870-71; it was fostered, with every possible variation, in literary, political, and military writings, in the officer corps, in schools, associations, political circles.

I can well understand this spirit. Looked at from the healthy national standpoint, it is, after all, more honorable for a nation to desire revenge for a blow received than to endure it without complaint.

But Alsace-Lorraine had been German soil for many centuries; it was stolen by France and taken back by us in 1871 as our property. Hence, a war of revenge which had as its aim the conquest of thoroughly German territory was unjust and immoral. For us to have yielded on this point would have been a slap in the face to our sentiments of nationality and justice. Since Germany could never voluntarily return Alsace-Lorraine to France, the French dream could be realized only by means of a victorious war which should push forward the French boundary posts to the left bank of the Rhine.

Germany, on the contrary, had no reason for staking what she had won in 1870-71, so the course for her to pursue was to maintain peace with France, all the more so because of the fact that the combination of the powers against the German-Austrian Dual Alliance was continually becoming more apparent.

As to Russia, the mighty empire of the Tsars was clamoring for an outlet on the sea to the southward. This was a natural ambition and not to be harshly judged. In addition, there was the Russian-Austrian conflict of influence, especially in

Serbia, which also concerned Germany in so far as Germany and Austria-Hungary were allies.

The Russia of the Tsars, moreover, was in a state of continual internal ferment and every Tsaristic Government had to keep the possibility for a foreign conflict ever in readiness, in order always to be able to deflect attention from inner troubles to foreign difficulties; to have a safety valve as an outlet for the passions that might lead to trouble at home.

Another point was that Russia's enormous demand for loans was met almost exclusively by France; more than twenty billions of French gold francs found their way to Russia, and France had a voice, to some extent, in determining how they should be expended. As a result, it became entirely a matter of expenditure on strategic measures and preparations for war. The golden chain of the French billions not only bound Russia to France financially, but made Russia serve the French idea of revenge.

### PURPOSE OF "ENCIRCLEMENT"

Thus England, France, and Russia had, though for different reasons, an aim in common—*viz.,* to overthrow Germany. England wished to do so for commercial-political reasons, France on account of her policy of revenge, Russia because she was a satellite of France and also for reasons of internal politics and because she wished to reach the southern sea. These three great nations, therefore, were bound to act together. The union of these ambitions in a common course of action, duly planned, is what we call the "policy of encirclement."

Added to all this there was also the Gentlemen's Agreement which has only recently come to light and has already been thoroughly discussed in the "Hohenlohe" chapter; concerning this agreement I knew absolutely nothing during my reign, and the German Foreign Office was only superficially and unreliably informed.

When I learned of it, I immediately sought information about it from Herr von Bethmann. He wrote me a rather puzzling letter to the effect that there was surely something about it among the documents of the Foreign Office; that the German ambassador at that time in Washington, von Holleben, had made some confidential report on it, to be sure, but had not given his source of information, wherefore the Foreign Office had not attached any importance to the matter and had not reported further on it to me. Hence the said agreement had actually no influence upon Germany's policy, but it constitutes supplementary proof that the Anglo-Saxon world as far back as 1897 had combined against us, and thereby explains a number of obstacles encountered by Germany in her foreign policy. It also explains America's attitude in the war.

We were quite well acquainted, on the other hand, with the Entente Cordiale, its foundations and purposes, and it decisively influenced the course of our policy.

In view of the grouping of England, France, and Russia—three very strong powers—only one political course lay open to Germany, the threat of deciding Germany's future by force of arms must be avoided until we had secured for ourselves such an economic, military, naval, and national-political position in the world as to make it seem advisable to our opponents to refrain from risking a decision by arms and to yield us the share in the apportionment and management of the world to which our ability entitled us. We neither desired nor were we entitled to jeopardize our hard-won welfare.

*The aims of the Entente could be attained only through a war, those of Germany only without a war.* It is necessary to hold fast to this basic idea; it is of more decisive value than all accessory matters. Hence I shall not go into detail here, nor take up Belgian or other reports, nor the telegrams sent just before the outbreak of war. The thorough treatment of these details lies in the domain of research.

In Germany our situation was correctly understood, and we acted accordingly.

### SOUGHT ENGLAND'S FRIENDSHIP

Taking up once more our relations with England, we did everything in our power to bring about a rapprochement; we consented to the demand for limitation of naval construction, as I have shown in my report of Haldane's visit to Berlin. I went so far as to try to utilize my family connections. But in vain. The actions of King Edward VII are explained by the simple fact that he was an Englishman and was trying to bring to realization the plans of his Government. Maybe the political ambitions of the King, who did not begin to reign until well along in years, contributed to this.

We certainly did all that was possible to meet England halfway, but it was useless, because the German export figures showed an increase; naturally we could not limit our world commerce in order to satisfy England. That would have been asking too much.

As regards our policy toward England, we have been much blamed for having refused the offer of an alliance made us by Chamberlain, the English Colonial Minister, toward the close of the 'nineties. This matter, however, was far different in character, on closer inspection, from what it was represented as being.

First, Chamberlain brought a letter with him from the English Premier, Salisbury, to Bülow, in which the English Prime Minister declared that Chamberlain was dealing on his own account only, that the English Cabinet was not behind him. This, to be sure, might have meant the adoption of a course that was diplomatically permissible, giving the English Cabinet, which was responsible to Parliament, a free hand; but it turned out later, be it remarked, that the Liberal group in England was at that time hostile to a German-English alliance.

Nevertheless, in view of the fact that there was a possibility that the course adopted was a mere diplomatic formality—that Chamberlain might have been sent on ahead and complete freedom of action retained for the English Cabinet, which is a favorite method in London—Prince Bülow, with my consent, went thoroughly into the matter with Chamberlain.

It transpired then that the English-German alliance was aimed unquestionably against Russia. Chamberlain spoke directly about a war to be waged later by England and Germany against Russia. Prince Bülow, in full agreement with me, declined politely but emphatically thus to disturb the peace of Europe. In so doing he was but following the example of the great Chancellor, for Prince Bismarck coined the phrase—I myself have heard it repeatedly in the Bismarck family circle: "Germany must never become England's dagger on the European continent."

So we did nothing further at that time than to go straight ahead with our policy—*viz.,* we refused all agreements which might lead to a war which was not based directly on the defense of our native soil. The refusal of the Chamberlain offer is a proof of the German love of peace.

As to France, we sought to bring about an endurable state of affairs. This was difficult, for, in French eyes, we were the archenemy and it was impossible for us to acquiesce in the demands inspired by the policy of revenge. We settled the Morocco quarrel peacefully; no man of standing in Germany entertained the idea of war on account of Morocco. For the sake of peace we allowed France at that time to encroach upon the essentially legitimate interests of Germany in Morocco, strengthened as the French were by the agreement concluded secretly with England as to mutual compensation in Egypt and Morocco.

In the Algeciras Conference the outline of the Great War was already visible. It is assuredly not pleasant to be forced to retreat politically, as we did in the Morocco matter, but Germany's policy subordinated everything to the great cause of preserving the peace of the world.

We tried to attain this end by courtesy, which was partially resented. I recall the journey of my mother, the Empress Frederick, to Paris. We expected a tolerably good reception, since she was an English Princess and went, as an artist, to be the guest of French art. Twice I visited the Empress Eugénie—once from Aldershot at her castle of Fernborough, the other time aboard her yacht, in Norwegian waters, near Bergen. This was a piece of politeness that seemed to me perfectly natural, seeing that I happened to be very near her. When the French General Bonnal was in Berlin with several officers, these gentlemen dined with the Second Infantry Regiment. I was present and toasted the French army—something that was still out of the ordinary, but was done with the best intentions. I brought French female and male artists to Germany. All this sort of thing, of course, was a trifle in the great game of politics, but it at least showed our good will.

With regard to Russia, I went to the utmost trouble. My letters, published in the meantime, were naturally never sent without the knowledge of the Imperial Chancellors, but always in agreement with them and largely at their desire. Russia would doubtless never have got into a war with Germany under Alexander III, for he was reliable. Tsar Nicholas was weak and vacillating; whoever had last been with him was right; and, naturally, it was impossible for me always to be that individual.

I made every effort with this Tsar, also, to restore the traditional friendship between Germany and Russia. I was moved to do so not only by political reasons, but by the promise which I had made to my grandfather on his deathbed.

I most urgently advised Tsar Nicholas, repeatedly, to introduce liberal reforms within his country, to summon the so-called Great Duma, which existed and functioned even as far back as the reign of Ivan the Terrible. In doing so it was not my intention to interfere in Russian internal affairs; what I wanted was to eliminate, in the interests of Germany, the ferment going on in Russia, which had often enough been deflected before to foreign conflicts, as I have already described. I wished to help toward eliminating at least this one phase of the internal situation in Russia, which threatened to cause war, and I was all the more willing to make the effort since I might thereby serve both the Tsar and Russia.

The Tsar paid no heed to my advice, but created a new Duma instead, which was quite inadequate for coping with the situation. Had he summoned the old Duma he might have dealt and talked personally with all the representatives of his huge realm and won their confidence.

When the Tsar resolved upon war against Japan, I told him that I would assure him security in the rear and cause him no annoyances. Germany kept this promise.

### GRAND DUKE'S VISIT

When the course taken by the war did not fulfill the Tsar's expectations, and the Russian and Japanese armies finally lay before each other for weeks without serious fighting, the young brother of the Tsar, Grand Duke Michael, arrived at Berlin for a visit. We could not quite make out what he wanted. Prince Bülow, who was then Chancellor, requested me to ask the Grand Duke sometime how matters really stood with Russia; he said that he, the Prince, had received bad news and thought it was high time for Russia to bring the war to an end.

I undertook this mission. The Grand Duke was visibly relieved when I spoke to him frankly; he declared that things looked bad for Russia. I told him that it seemed to me that the Tsar ought to make peace soon, since what the Grand Duke had told me about the unreliability of troops and officers appeared to me quite as serious as the renewed internal agitation.

Grand Duke Michael was grateful for my having given him an opportunity to talk. He said that the Tsar was vascillating, as always, but he must make peace and would make it if I advised him to do so. He asked me to write a few lines to the Tsar to that effect, for him to deliver.

I drafted a letter in English to Tsar Nicholas, went to Bülow, told him what the Grand Duke had told me, and showed him the draft of my letter. The Prince thanked me and found the letter suitable. The Grand Duke informed the Russian ambassador in Berlin, Count Osten-Sacken, and, after he had repeatedly expressed his thanks, went direct to the Tsar, who then had peace negotiations begun.

Count Osten-Sacken told me, when next we met, that I had done Russia a great service. I was glad this was recognized, and felt justified in hoping, on account of this, that my conduct would contribute toward bringing about friendly relations with Russia. In acting as I did I also worked toward preventing the possible spread of a Russian revolution, during the Russo-Japanese War, across the frontiers of Germany. Germany earned no thanks thereby; however, our conduct during the Russo-Japanese War is another proof of our love of peace.

The same purpose underlay my suggestion which led to the Björkö agreement (July, 1905). It contemplated an alliance between Germany and

Russia, which both the Allies as well as other nations should be at liberty to join. Ratification of this agreement failed through the opposition of the Russian Government (Isvolsky).

It remains to say a few words about America. Aside from the Gentlemen's Agreement already mentioned, which assured America's standing beside England and France in a World War, America did not belong to the Entente Cordiale created by King Edward VII at the behest of his Government, and, most important of all, America, in so far as it is possible at present to judge events, did not contribute toward bringing on the World War. Perhaps the unfriendly answer given by President Wilson to the German Government at the beginning of the war may have had some connection with the Gentlemen's Agreement.

### AMERICAN FACTORS IN DEFEAT

But there can be no doubt that America's entry into the war, and the enormous supplies of ammunition, and especially of war materials, which preceded her entry, seriously hurt the chance of the Central Powers to bring the war to a successful termination by force of arms.

It is necessary, however, to avoid all emotional criticism of America also, since, in the great game of politics, real factors only can be considered. America was at liberty (despite the Gentlemen's Agreement) to remain neutral or to enter the war on the other side. One cannot reproach a nation for a decision as to war or peace made in accordance with its sovereign rights so long as the decision is not in violation of definite agreements. Such is not the case here.

Nevertheless, it must be noted that John Kenneth Turner, in his already mentioned book, *Shall It Be Again?* shows, on the basis of extensive proofs, that all Wilson's reasons for America's entry into the war were fictitious, that it was far more a case of acting solely in the interest of Wall Street high finance.

The great profit derived by America from the World War consists in the fact that the United States was able to attract to itself nearly fifty per cent of all the gold in the world, so that now the dollar, instead of the English pound, determines the world's exchange rate. But here also no reproach is at all justified, since any other nation in a position to do so would have rejoiced in attracting to itself this increase of gold and of prestige in the world's money market. It was certainly regrettable for us that America did not do this stroke of business on the side of the Central Powers.

But just as Germany objects with perfect justification to having had her peaceful labors combated by the Entente, not with peaceful, but with warlike means, so also she can and must enter constant protest—as she is already trying to do by means of published material—against America's violation of the right at the close of the World War.

Personally I do not believe that the American people would have consented to this; American women particularly would not have participated in the denial of President Wilson's Fourteen Points, if they could have been enlightened at that time as to the facts. America, more than other countries, had been misled by English propaganda, and therefore allowed President Wilson, who had been provided with unprecedented powers, to act on his own initiative at Paris—in other words, to be beaten down on his Fourteen Points. Just as Mr. Wilson omitted mention, later on, of the English blockade, against which he had protested previously, so also he acted with regard to his Fourteen Points.

The German Government had accepted Wilson's Fourteen Points, although they were severe enough. The Allies likewise had accepted the Fourteen Points, with the exception of those on reparations and the freedom of the seas. Wilson had guaranteed the Fourteen Points.

### FOURTEEN POINTS ABANDONED

I fail to find the most important of them in the Versailles instrument, but only those expressing the Entente's policy of violence, and even part of these in a greatly falsified form. Relying on Wilson's guaranty, Germany evacuated the enemy territory occupied by her and surrendered her weapons—in other words, made herself defenseless. In this blind confidence and the abandonment of the Fourteen Points on the one side, and in the outbreak of the German revolution on the other, lies the key to our present condition.

According to Turner, the Fourteen Points, as far back as the drawing up of the armistice terms, were, to Wilson, no more than a means of making Germany lay down her arms; as soon as this end was achieved he dropped them.

Already a very large part of the American people has arrayed itself against Mr. Wilson and is unwilling to be discredited along with him. I am not dreaming of spontaneous American help for Germany; all I count upon is the sober acknowledgment by the American people that it has to make good the gigantic wrong done Germany by its former President. For the atmosphere of a victory does not last forever, and later on, not only in Germany, but elsewhere, people will remember the unreliability of the American President and look upon it as American unreliability.

That is not a good thing, however, for the American people. To have the policy of a nation branded with the stigma of unreliability is not advantageous. When judgment is passed hereafter on American policy, people will forget that Mr. Wilson, unversed in the ways of the world, was trapped by Lloyd George and Clemenceau.

I have met—particularly at the Kiel regattas—many American men and women whose political judgment and caution would make it impossible for them to approve such a flagrant breach of faith as was committed by Mr. Wilson, because of its effect on America's political prestige. It is upon such considerations of national egotism, not upon any sort of sentimental considerations, that I base my hope that Germany's burden will be lightened from across the ocean.

Besides the injustice in the abandonment of the Fourteen Points, it must also be remembered that Mr. Wilson was the first to demand of the German reigning dynasty that it withdraw, in doing which he hinted that, were such action taken, the German people would be granted a better peace. Before the Government of Prince Max joined in the demand for my abdication of the throne, which it based on the same grounds as Mr. Wilson—that Germany would thereby get better terms—(prevention of civil war was used as a second means of bringing pressure on me)—it was in duty bound to get some sort of a binding guaranty from Mr. Wilson. In any event, the statements made, which became continually more urgent and pressing, contributed toward making me resolve to quit the country, since I was constrained to believe that I could render my country a great service by so doing.

#### ACCEPTED "SIGHT UNSEEN"

I subordinated my own interests and those of my dynasty, which certainly were not unimportant, and forced myself, after the severest inward struggles, to acquiesce in the wish of the German authorities. Later it transpired that the German Government had obtained no real guaranties. But, in the tumultuous sequence of events during those days, it was necessary for me to consider the unequivocal and definite announcement of the Imperial Chancellor as authoritative. For this reason I did not investigate it.

Why the Entente demanded, through Mr. Wilson, that I should abdicate is now obvious. It felt perfectly sure that, following my being dispossessed of the throne, military and political instability would necessarily ensue in Germany and enable it to force upon Germany not easier but harder terms. At that time the revolution had not yet appeared as an aid to the Entente.

For me to have remained on the throne would have seemed to the Entente more advantageous to Germany than my abdication. I myself agree with this view of the Entente, now that it has turned out that the Max of Baden Government had no substantial foundation for its declaration that my abdication would bring better terms to my fatherland.

I go even further and declare that the Entente would never have dared to offer such terms to an intact German Empire. It would not have dared to offer them to an imperial realm upon which the parliamentary system had not yet been forced, with the help of German Utopians, at the very moment of its final fight for existence; to a realm whose monarchical Government had not been deprived of the power to command its army and navy.

In view of all this, heavy guilt also lies on the shoulders of the American ex-President as a result of his having demanded my abdication under the pretense that it would bring Germany better terms. Here also we certainly have a point of support for the powerful lever which is destined to drag the Treaty of Versailles from where it lies behind lock and key. In Germany, however, Mr. Wilson should never be confused with the American people.

In setting forth my political principles in what follows I am actuated solely by a desire to contribute toward proving Germany's innocence of having brought on the World War.

From the outset of my reign German policy was based upon compromise of the differences which it found existing between nations. In its entirety, therefore, my policy was eminently peaceful. This policy of peaceful compromise became apparent in internal politics, at the very beginning of my reign, in the legislation desired by me for the protection of the workers. The development of social legislation, which placed Germany at the head of civilized nations in the domain of governmental protection, was based on a like foundation.

The fundamental idea of a policy of compromise went so far within Germany that the strength of the army would have remained far less than universal compulsory military service and the size of the population made possible. Here, as well as in the matter of naval construction, the curtailments demanded by the Reichstag were put up with by the Crown and the Government. Already at that time the question of Germany's capabilities of defense was left to the decision of the people's representatives. A nation that wished and prepared war would have adopted quite different tactics.

### INADEQUATE PREPAREDNESS

The more apparent the Entente's "policy of encirclement" and attack became, the more the means of protecting our welfare should have been strengthened for defensive reasons. This idea of natural and justified self-protection, by means of defensive measures against a possible hostile attack was carried out in a wretchedly inadequate manner.

Germany's desire for peace, in fact, was unable to develop this protection by land and sea in a manner compatible with her financial and national strength and with the risk which our welfare was bound to run in case of a war. Therefore, we are now suffering not from the consequences of the tendency toward aggression falsely imputed to us, but actually from the consequences of a well-nigh incredible love of peace and of blind confidence.

The entirely different political principles of the Entente have already been described by me, also our continuous efforts to get upon friendly terms with the individual Entente nations.

I do not wish to ignore completely the less important work done by Germany, also included within the framework of politics on a large scale, which was always inspired by the same purpose: to effect compromise of existing points of conflict. The Kiel regatta brought us guests from all the leading nations. We sought compromise with the same zeal on the neutral territory of sport as in the domain of science by means of exchange professors, and foreign officers were most willingly allowed to inspect our army system. This latter might be adjudged a mistake, now that we can look back, but, in any event, all these points are certain proofs of our honest desire to live at peace with all.

Moreover, Germany did not take advantage of a single one of the opportunities that arose for waging war with a sure prospect of success.

I have already pointed out the benevolent neutrality of Germany toward Russia at the time of the Russo-Japanese War.

At the time when England was deeply involved in the Boer War we might have fought against England or against France, which, at that time, would have been obliged to forego help from England. But we did not do so. Also, while the Russo-Japanese War was in progress, we might have fought not only against Russia, but also against France. But we did not do so.

In addition to the Morocco crisis already touched upon, in connection with which we set aside the idea of going to war, we also gave evidence of our desire for peace by overcoming the Bosnian crisis by diplomatic means.

When one considers these plainly visible political events as a whole and adduces the declarations of Entente statesmen such as Poincaré, Clemenceau, Isvolsky, Tardieu, and others, one is bound to ask one's self, in amazement, how a peace treaty, founded upon Germany's guilt in having brought on the World War, could have been drafted and put through. This miscarriage of justice will not stand before the bar of world history.

### BLAMES FRANCE FOR 1870

A Frenchman, Louis Guetant, delegate from Lyon to the Society for the Rights of Man, recently made this statement:

"If we once look upon events without prejudice, with complete independence and frankness, without bothering about which camp chance placed us in at birth, the following is forced upon our attention first of all: The War of 1914 is a consequence of the War of 1870. For, ever since that earlier date, the idea of revenge, more or less veiled, has never left us.

"The War of 1870, however, was prepared and declared by the French Government. The French Empire, indeed, needed it very badly in order to contend against interior troubles and its steadily growing unpopularity with the public. Even Gambetta, the wild tribune of the opposition, exclaimed: 'If the Empire brings us the left bank of the Rhine, I shall become reconciled with it!' Thus, it was a war of conquest; nobody bothered about what the conquered populations might have to say about it. 'We shall bend their will to ours!' Thus it is written in the law of the victor!

"And now, suddenly, the opportunity for doing this was to escape France. In view of the political difficulties and dangers of war caused by his candidacy, Prince Leopold declared himself ready to withdraw. That is bad! Without a pretext there can be no war!

"It was the same with France as with the milkmaid and the broken pitcher in the fable, only instead of, 'Farewell, calf, cow, pig, hens,' it was, 'Farewell, bloody profits, glory, victory, left bank of the Rhine, even Belgium!'—for the latter, too, lay on that left bank of the Rhine which France coveted. No, that would have been too hard, the disillusionment would have been too great, the opportunity must be created anew. The entire chauvinistic press, the entire clan of boasters, set to work and soon found a way. Gramont, Minister of Foreign Affairs, sent Ambassador Benedetti to visit Emperor William, who was taking the cure at Ems, and demand from him a written promise that, in case Prince Leopold should change his mind about his withdrawal, he, William, as head of the family, would take issue against this.

"The withdrawal of Prince Leopold was announced to France in a valid manner and officially accepted by the Spanish Government. There could be no doubt as to its genuineness. Nevertheless the Paris newspapers, almost without exception, clamored for war. Whoever, like Robert Michell in the *Constitutionel,* expressed his pleasure at the prospects for peace and declared himself satisfied, was insulted on the street. Gambetta shouted at him: 'You are satisfied! What a base expression!' Copies of his newspapers were stolen from the news stands, thrown into the river, hurled in his face! Emilie de Girandin wrote to him: 'The opportunity is unique, unhoped-for; if the Empire misses it the Empire is lost!' Then it was that preparation for the War of 1914 was begun."

Voices like this also, which are not unique either in France or England, must always be adduced as proof that the guilt is not ours.

### "MISTAKEN, BUT NOT GUILTY"

Our political and diplomatic operations in the course of decades were not, it must be admitted, faultlessly conceived or executed. But where we made mistakes they were caused invariably by the too great desire to maintain world peace. Such *mistakes do not constitute guilt.*

As I mentioned elsewhere, I even consider the Congress of Berlin a mistake, for it made our relations with Russia worse. The congress was a victory for Disraeli, an Anglo-Austrian victory over Russia, which turned Russian anger upon Germany. Yet—think of all that has been done since then to make up with Russia! I have partly enumerated these acts. And Bismarck's sole intention in bringing about the Congress of Berlin was, as I have pointed out, the prevention of a great general war.

Chancellor von Bethmann Hollweg also, who

had strict orders from me to maintain peace if it was at all possible, made mistakes in 1914; as a statesman he was not at all adequate to the world crisis. But the blame for the war cannot be put upon us simply because our opponents profited by our mistakes. Bethmann Hollweg wished to avoid the war, like all of us—sufficient proof of this is to be found in the one fact alone that he persisted, until the 4th of August, in his political inertia, negotiating with England in the erroneous belief that he could keep England out of the Entente.

While on this subject I wish also to call attention to the delusion under which Prince Lichnowsky, the German ambassador in London, was laboring. Soon after he had become ambassador, King George came to the Embassy to dinner. The King's example was followed automatically by the best society people in London.

The Prince and Princess were singled out for marked attentions and exceedingly well treated socially. From this the German ambassador drew the conclusion that our relations with England had improved, until, shortly before the war, Sir Edward Grey coolly informed him that he must draw no political conclusions from social favors and good treatment accorded to him personally.

Nothing could give a better insight into the difference between the English and German mentality than this. The German assumed social friendliness to be the expression of political friendliness, since the German is accustomed to express aversion and approval by means of social forms as well as otherwise. He is very outspoken about what he has on his mind.

### CHARGES ENGLISH INSINCERITY

The Englishman, however, makes a distinction; in fact, he is rather pleased if the man to whom he is speaking confuses form with substance, or, in other words, if he takes the form to be the expression of actual sentiments and political views. Judged from the English standpoint, the above-mentioned words of Sir Edward Grey were a perfectly frank statement.

The much-discussed nonrenewal of the reinsurance treaty with Russia, already touched upon by me, is not to be considered so decisive as to have influenced the question of whether there was to be war or peace. The reinsurance treaty, in my opinion, would not have prevented the Russia of Nicholas II from taking the road to the Entente; under Alexander III it would have been superfluous.

Prince Bismarck's view that the Russian ambassador, Prince Shuvaloff, would have renewed the reinsurance treaty with him but not with his successor, is naturally the honest, subjective way of looking at the matter—judged in the light of fact, however, it does not hold water, in view of what the two parties concerned had to consider at that time. For instance, the Under Secretary of State of the Prince, Count Berchem, stated officially in a report to the Prince that the treaty could not be renewed, which meant that it could not be renewed through Shuvaloff, either.

I thought that not the old treaty, but only a new and different kind of treaty, was possible, in the drawing up of which Austria must participate, as in the old Three-Emperor-Relationship.

But, as I said, treaties with Nicholas II would not have seemed absolutely durable to me, particularly after the sentiment of the very influential Russian general public had also turned against Germany.

Our acts were founded upon the clear perception that Germany could reach the important position in the world and obtain the influence in world affairs necessary to her solely by maintaining world peace. This attitude was strengthened, moreover, by personal considerations.

Never have I had warlike ambitions. In my youth my father had given me terrible descriptions of the battlefields of 1870 and 1871, and I felt no inclination to bring such misery, on a colossally larger scale, upon the German people and the whole of civilized mankind. Old Field Marshal Moltke, whom I respected greatly, had left behind him the prophetic warning: Woe to him who hurls the firebrand of war upon Europe! And I considered as a political legacy from the great Chancellor the fact that Prince Bismarck had said that Germany must never wage a preventive war; that German resistance would be neutralized if she did.

Thus the trend of the German policy of maintaining the peace was determined by political insight, personal inclination, the legacies of two great men, Bismarck and Moltke, and the desire of the German people to devote itself to peaceful labors and not to plunge into adventures.

Whatever has been said in malevolent circles about the existence of a German party favoring war is a conscious or unconscious untruth. In every land there are elements which, in serious situations, either from honest conviction or less lofty motives, favor the appeal to the sword, but never have such elements influenced the course of German policy.

The accusations, especially those which have been made against the General Staff to the effect that it worked for war, are pretty untenable. The Prussian General Staff served its King and fatherland by hard, faithful work, and maintained Germany's ability to defend herself by labors extending over many years of peace, as was its duty, but it exerted absolutely no political influence whatsoever. Interest in politics, as is well known, was never particularly strong in the Prussian-German army. Looking backward, one might almost say, in fact, that it would have been better for us if those in leading military circles had concerned themselves a bit more with foreign policy.

Therefore, how the Peace of Versailles, in view of this perfectly clear state of affairs, could have been founded upon Germany's guilt in having caused the World War, would seem an insoluble riddle if it were not possible to trace the tremendous effect of a new war weapon—*viz.,* the political propaganda of England against Germany—planned on a large scale and applied with audacity and unscrupulousness. I cannot bring myself to dismiss this propaganda by branding it with catchwords such as "a piece of rascality," etc., since it constitutes an achievement which, in spite of its repugnant nature, cannot be ignored; it did us more harm than the arms in the hands of our opponents.

To us Germans, such an instrument of insincerity, distortion, and hypocrisy is not pleasing; it is something that is incompatible with the German character; we try to convince our opponents with the weapon of truth as well as with other weapons. But war is a cruel thing and what matters in it is to win; after all, to fire heavy guns at civilized beings is not a pleasant matter, nor to bombard beautiful old towns, yet this had to be done by both sides in the war.

Moreover, we could not have developed a propaganda on a large scale like that of our enemies during the war for the very reason that they had no foes in their rear, whereas we were surrounded. In addition, most Germans have not the gift to fit a scheme of propaganda to the different nationalities of the nations upon which it is supposed to work. But, just as the English were more than our match with that terrible weapon of theirs, the tank, against which we could bring nothing of equal efficiency, so also were they superior to us with their very effective weapon of propaganda.

And this weapon still continues its work and we are compelled still to defend ourselves against it over and over again. For there can be no doubt that the unjust Peace of Versailles could not have been founded upon Germany's war guilt unless propaganda had previously accomplished its task and, partly with the support of German pacifists, instilled into the brains of 100,000,000 human beings the belief in Germany's guilt, so that the unjust Peace of Versailles seemed to many justified.

### HOPES FOR VERSAILLES REACTION

Meanwhile, things have changed, the barriers between nations have fallen, and gradually they are awakening to the realization of how their confidence was imposed upon. The reaction will be crushing to the makers of the Versailles Peace, but helpful to Germany. It goes without saying that, among the statesmen, politicians, and publicists of the Entente who really know, not a single one is really convinced of Germany's guilt in having caused the World War. Every one of them knows the real interrelation of events, and assuredly there never was a case where so many augurs smiled at each other over a secret held in common as the case of the responsibility for the World War. In fact, one may even speak of a chorus of such individuals, since twenty-eight nations took part in the war against Germany. But, in the long run, not even the shrewdest augurs will suffice to make world history. Truth will make its way forward and thus Germany will come into her rights.

The various stipulations of the Versailles Treaty are in themselves null and void, since they can be observed neither by the Entente nor by Germany. It has been possible for months to note what difficulties are arising in the path not only of Germany, but of the victors, as a result of such an extravagant instrument.

In many ways the treaty has been punctured by the Entente itself, and for this the reason is easily found. In the present highly developed state of the world, which rests upon free, systematic exchange of material and intellectual property, regulated solely by production itself, it is quite out of the question for three men—no matter how eminent they may be—to sit themselves down anywhere and dictate paragraphed laws to the world. Yet that is what the Versailles Treaty does, not only for Germany, but also, indirectly, for the Entente and America, since all economic questions can be solved by mutual, not one-sided, action.

The life of nations is regulated always—and most particularly in our day—not by paragraphs, but simply and solely by the needs of nations. It is possible, to be sure, to do violence to those national needs temporarily by the imposition of arbitrary decisions, but, in such cases, both parties concerned must suffer.

The world is in such a stage just now. Conditions like those at present cannot last; not guns, nor tanks, nor squadrons of airplanes, can perpetuate them. Therefore, their removal has already begun; for, if the peace of Versailles were really such a judicious, unimpeachable instrument, bringing blessings upon the world, there would not be constant need of new conferences, discussions, and meetings having to do with this "marvelous" document. The constant necessity for new interpretations is due, indeed, to the fact that the needs of highly cultivated and civilized nations were not taken into account when the peace was concluded.

One must not be pharisaical, however; up to a certain point the extravagance of the terms imposed by the victor after a life-and-death struggle is a natural consequence of the relief felt at having escaped alive from deadly danger.

Nevertheless, I know that Germany, if we had emerged victorious from the war, would have imposed quite different terms—*i. e.,* terms that would have been just and endurable. The peace treaties of Brest-Litovsk and Bucharest—which indeed are not at all comparable with the Treaty of Versailles—cannot be adduced against us. They were concluded in the very midst of the war and had to include conditions which would guarantee our safety until the end of the war. Had it come to a general peace, the treaty made by us in the East would have had a far different aspect; had we won the war, it would have been revised by ourselves. At the time it was made it was necessary to give preference to military requirements.

But enlightenment regarding the unjust Treaty of Versailles is on the way and the necessities of life among present-day nations will speak in imperious tones to victors and vanquished.

After years of the heaviest trial will come the liberation from a yoke imposed unjustly upon a great, strong, honest nation. Then every one of us will be glad and proud again that he is a German.

# CHAPTER XV

## The Revolution and Germany's Future

I DO not care what my foes say about me. I do not recognize them as my judges. When I see how the same people who exaggeratedly spread incense before me in other days are now vilifying me, the most that I can feel is pity. The bitter things that I hear about myself from home disappoint me. God is my witness that I have always wished what was best for my country and my people, and I believed that every German had recognized and appreciated this. I have always tried to keep my political acts, everything that I did as a ruler and a man, in harmony with God's commandments. Much turned out differently from what I desired, but my conscience is clean. *The welfare of my people and my Empire was the goal of my actions.*

I bear my personal fate with resignation, for the Lord knows what He does and what He wishes. He knows why He subjects me to this test. I shall bear everything with patience and await whatsoever God still holds in store for me.

The only thing that grieves me is the fate of my country and my people. I am pained at the hard period of trial which my children of the German land are undergoing, which I—obliged to live in foreign parts—cannot suffer with them. *That is the sword thrust which pierces through my soul;* that is what is bitter to me. Here in solitude I still feel and think solely for the German people, still wonder how I can better matters and help with enlightenment and counsel.

Nor can bitter criticism ever lessen my love for my land and people. I remain faithful to the Germans, no matter how each individual German may now stand with regard to me. To those who stand by me in misfortune as they stood in prosperity, I am grateful—they comfort me and relieve my gnawing homesickness for my beloved German home. And I can respect those who, impelled by honest convictions, array themselves against me; as for the rest, let them look to justifying themselves to God, their consciences, and history.

They will not succeed in separating me from the Germans. Always I can look upon country and people solely as one whole. They remain to me what they were when I said on the occasion of the opening of the Reichstag on the 1st of August, 1914, in the Imperial Palace: "I know no more of parties; I know only Germans."

The revolution broke the Empress's heart. She aged visibly from November, 1918, onward, and could not resist her bodily ills with the strength of before. Thus her decline soon began. The hardest of all for her to bear was her homesickness for the soil of Germany, for the German people. Notwithstanding this, she still tried to bring me consolation.

The revolution destroyed things of enormous value. It was brought about at the very moment when the German nation's fight for existence was to have been ended, and every effort should have been concentrated upon reconstruction. It was a crime against the nation.

### WIND AND WHIRLWIND

I am well aware that many who rally around the Social Democratic banner did not wish revolution; some of the individual Social Democratic leaders likewise did not wish it at that time, and more than one among them was ready to co-operate with me. Yet these Social Democrats were incapable of preventing the revolution, and therein lies their share of guilt for what is now going on, all the more so since the Socialist leaders stood closer to the revolutionary masses than the representatives of the monarchical Government and, therefore, could exert more influence upon them.

But the leaders, even in the days before the war, had brought the idea of revolution to the masses and fostered it, and the Social Democracy had been, from time immemorial, openly hostile to the earlier, monarchical form of government, and had worked systematically toward eliminating it. It sowed the wind and reaped the whirlwind.

The time and nature of the revolution were not to the liking of a number of the leaders, but it was exactly these men who, at the decisive moment, abandoned leadership to the most unbridled elements and failed to bring their influence to bear toward maintaining the Government.

It was the duty of the Government of Prince Max to protect the old form of government. It failed to fulfill its holy duty because it had become dependent on the Socialist leaders, the very men who had lost their influence on the masses to the radical elements.

Therefore, the greatest share of the guilt falls upon the leaders, and for that reason history will not brand the German working classes, but their leaders, with the curse of the revolution, in so far as these leaders participated in making the revolution or failed to prevent it—and it will also brand the Government of Prince Max of Baden with that curse.

The German workers fought brilliantly in battle under my leadership, and at home, as well, labored ceaselessly to provide munitions and war material. That is something which must not be forgotten. It was only later that some of them began to break away, but the responsibility for this lies at the door of the agitators and revolutionists, not at that of the decent, patriotic section of the working classes.

The conscienceless agitators are the men really responsible for Germany's total collapse. That will be recognized some day by the working classes themselves.

The present is a hard time for Germany. Of

the future of this healthy, strong nation I do not despair. A nation which can achieve such an unprecedented rise as that of Germany between 1871 and 1914, a nation which can maintain itself successfully for over four years in a defensive war against twenty-eight nations, cannot be driven from the earth. Economically, the world cannot do without us.

But in order that we may regain the position in the world which is Germany's due, we must not await or count upon help from outside. Such help will not come, in any event; were it to come, it would but mean at best our being mere Helots. Also, the help which the German Social Democratic party hoped for from abroad has not materialized, after all. The international part of the socialistic program has proved itself a frightful mistake.

The workers of the Entente lands took the field against the German people in order to destroy it; nowhere was there a trace of international solidarity among the masses.

### ANOTHER GERMAN MISTAKE

This mistake, too, is one of the reasons why the war turned out so badly for Germany. The English and French working classes were rightly directed—*i. e.,* nationalistically—by their leaders; the German working classes were wrongly directed —*i. e.,* internationally.

The German people must rely upon no other people, but solely upon themselves. When self-conscious, national sentiment returns to all the strata of our people our upward march will begin. All classes of the population must be united in national sentiment, no matter if their ways lie apart in other departments of the nation's life. Therein lies the strength of England, of France—even of the Poles.

If this comes to pass, the feeling of solidarity with all fellow members of the nation, the consciousness of the dignity of our noble land, the pride in being German, and the genuinely German conception of ethics, which was one of the secret sources of strength that have made Germany so great, will come back to us.

In the community of cultured nations Germany will again play, as she did before the war, the rôle of the nation with the greatest capacity for labor, and will once more march victoriously in the van in peaceful competition, offering not only to herself, but to all the nations of the earth, whatever is best in the domain of technical achievement, of science, of art.

I believe in the revocation of the unjust Peace of Versailles by the judgment of the sensible elements of foreign lands and by Germany herself. I believe in the German people and in the continuation of its peaceful mission in the world, which has been interrupted by a terrible war, for which Germany, since she did not will it, does not bear the guilt.

## More History from CGR Publishing
www.CGRpublishing.com

## Other books from CGR Publishing at Amazon.com

1939 New York World's Fair: The World of Tomorrow in Photographs

San Francisco 1915 World's Fair: The Panama-Pacific International Expo.

1904 St. Louis World's Fair: The Louisiana Purchase Exposition in Photographs

Chicago 1933 World's Fair: A Century of Progress in Photographs

19th Century New York: A Dramatic Collection of Images

The American Railway: The Trains, Railroads, and People Who Ran the Rails

The Story of the Ship

The World's Fair of 1893 Ultra Massive Photographic Adventure Vol. 1

The World's Fair of 1893 Ultra Massive Photographic Adventure Vol. 2

The World's Fair of 1893 Ultra Massive Photographic Adventure Vol. 3

World War 1: A Dramatic Collection of Images

The White City of Color: 1893 World's Fair

Ethel the Cyborg Ninja Book 1

Ethel they Cyborg Ninja 2

How To Draw Digital by Mark Bussler

How To Draw Pandas by Mark Bussler

## Other books from CGR Publishing at Amazon.com

Ultra Massive Video Game Console Guide Volume 1

Ultra Massive Video Game Console Guide Volume 2

Ultra Massive Video Game Console Guide Volume 3

Ultra Massive Sega Genesis Guide

The Art of World War 1

Chicago's White City Cookbook

Official Guide to the World's Columbian Exposition

How To Grow Mushrooms: A 19th Century Approach

The Great War Remastered WW1 Standard History Collection Vol. 1

Sinking of the Titanic: The Greatest Disaster at Sea

All Hail the Vectrex Ultimate Collector's Guide

Old Timey Pictures with Silly Captions Volume 1

The Aeroplane Speaks: Illustrated Historical Guide to Airplanes

Electricity at the World's Fair of 1893 Columbian Exposition

Captain William Kidd and the Pirates and Buccaneers Who Ravaged the Seas

Robot Kitten Factory Issue #1

**The Kaiser's Memoirs:**
**Illustrated Enlarged Special Edition**



**www.CGRpublishing.com**

Made in United States
North Haven, CT
02 June 2024

53227959R00198